The Journals of Grace Hartigan, 1951–1955

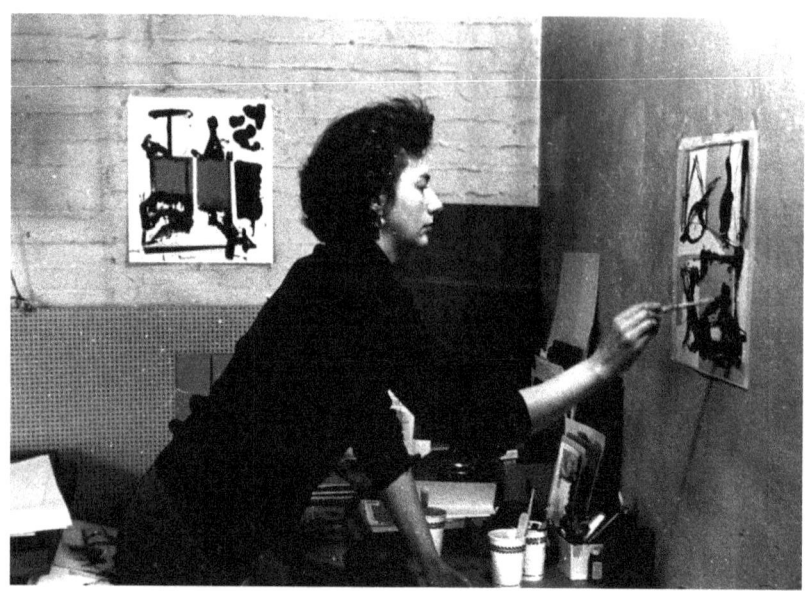

Photograph of Grace Hartigan applying the finishing touches to a silk-screen print in her *Salute* series. All three prints in this series were donated to the Special Collections Research Center at Syracuse University Library by Fay Chandler in 2007.

The Journals of Grace Hartigan

1951–1955

Edited by William T. La Moy and Joseph P. McCaffrey

Syracuse University Press

Special Collections Research Center
at Syracuse University Library

A copublication with the Special Collections Research Center,
Syracuse University Library, Syracuse, New York 13244-2010

The paper used in this publication meets the minimum requirements of the
American National Standard for Information Sciences—Permanence of Paper for
Printed Library Materials, ANSI Z39.48-1992.∞™

For a listing of books published and distributed by Syracuse University Press, visit
our Web site at SyracuseUniversityPress.syr.edu.
ISBN-13: 978-0-8156-0916-2
ISBN-10: 0-8156-0916-7

Library of Congress Cataloging-in-Publication Data

Hartigan, Grace.
    The journals of Grace Hartigan, 1951–1955 / edited by William T. La Moy and
Joseph P. McCaffrey.—1st ed.
        p. cm.
    Includes bibliographical references and index.
    ISBN 978-0-8156-0916-2 (pbk. : alk. paper)
    1. Hartigan, Grace—Diaries. 2. Painters—United States—Diaries. I. La Moy,
William T. II. McCaffrey, Joseph P. (Joseph Peter), 1949– III. Syracuse University.
Library. Special Collections Research Center. IV. Title.

    ND237.H3434A2 2009
    759.13—dc22
    [B]   2009006213

Manufactured in the United States of America

Contents

Gray-Scale Illustrations vii

Four-Color Illustrations ix

Acknowledgments xi

Editorial Note xiii

Introduction by Terence Diggory. xv

Recurring First Names. xxiii

Biographical Notes on Key Figures xxv

Journal for 1951 1

Journal for 1952. 21

Journal for 1953 66

Journal for 1954. 115

Journal for 1955 163

Index 191

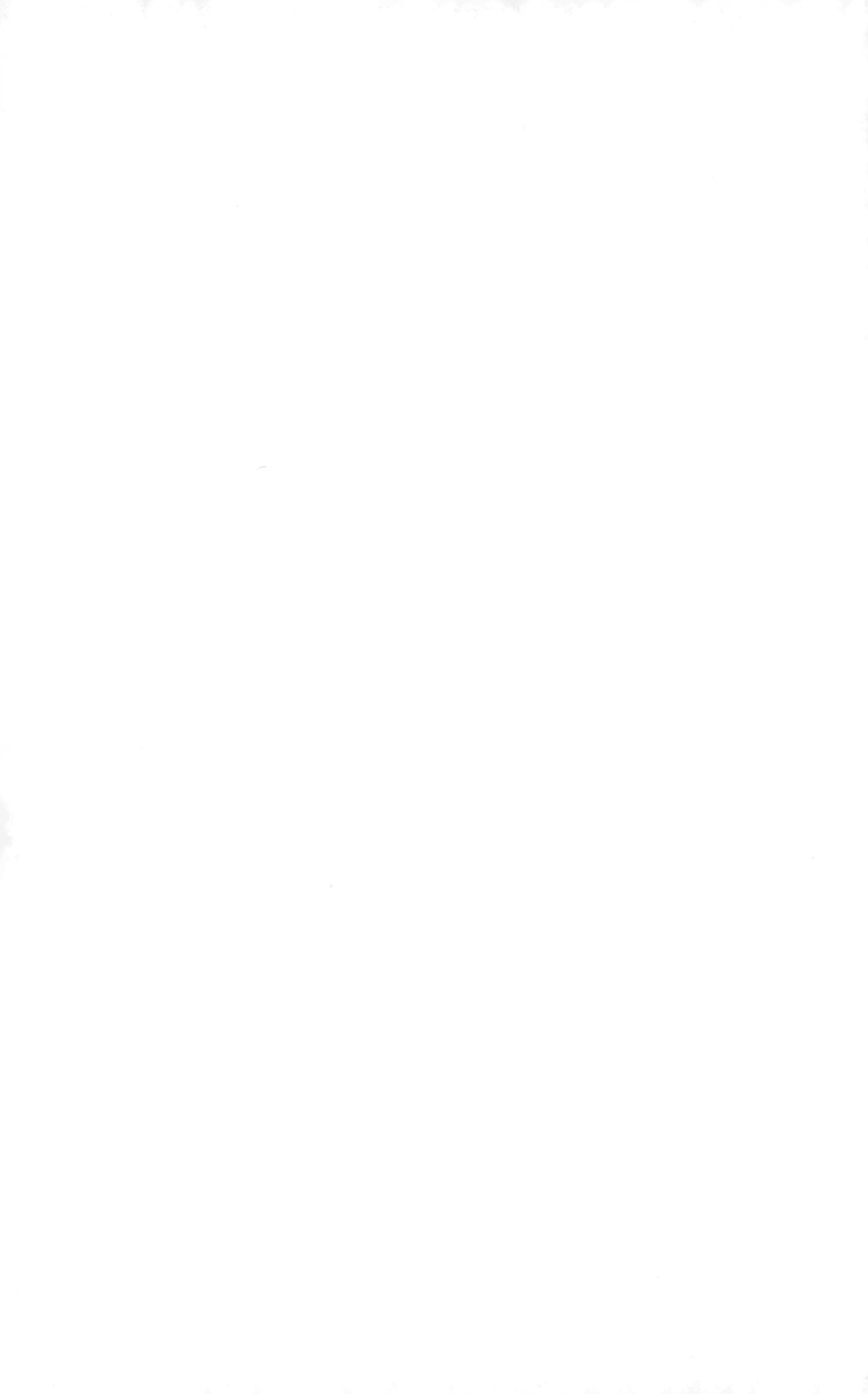

GRAY-SCALE ILLUSTRATIONS

Grace Hartigan applying the finishing touches to a silk-screen print in her
Salute series.   ii

The catalog from Hartigan's 1951 one-person show at the Tibor de
Nagy Gallery.   xxx

Hartigan and Alfred Leslie outside their studio in 1951.   3

John Bernard Myers and Hartigan making kites in Hartigan's studio for a
magazine feature that was never published.   6

Hartigan flying hand-made kites in Central Park. Strong winds destroyed
them.   7

John Bernard Myers, the artistic director of the Tibor de Nagy Gallery.   15

Frank O'Hara at his typewriter.   27

The cover of the catalog from Hartigan's one-person show at the Tibor de
Nagy Gallery in March of 1952.   29

Hartigan and Helen Frankenthaler mugging for the camera.   37

Note from Frank O'Hara to Hartigan, enclosed with a gift of Paterson
by William Carlos Williams.   40

Hartigan at sketching class.   48

The sketching class.   49

Sketch from Hartigan's journal of a lady on the subway.   53

Detail of the journal entry from 13 November 1952 concerning Hartigan's
views on expressionism.   58

A staged photograph taken at Coney Island with (left to right) Walter Silver,
Jane Freilicher, Grace Hartigan, and Larry Rivers.   59

Photograph of the painting Carousel.   64

The cover of the catalog from Hartigan's April 1953 show at the Tibor de Nagy
Gallery.   76

Richard Miller, Floriano Vecchi, and Grace Hartigan (left to right) working
on silk-screen prints for Folder 1.   87

Hartigan making silk-screen prints for Folder 1.   88

Hartigan hanging silk-screen prints for Folder 1 to dry.   90

Hartigan and Harry Jackson leaving for Mexico in 1949, soon after their
marriage.   93

Hartigan and Edi Franceschini in 1952.   102

Hartigan and Frank O'Hara hanging paintings.   112

Cover of the catalog for Hartigan's one-person exhibition at the Tibor de
Nagy Gallery in February of 1954.   120

Hartigan sketch that appeared in her February 1954 exhibition catalog for the Tibor de Nagy Gallery.   122

Hartigan dressed as a matador and posing in front of several works on the matador theme.   123

Hartigan's annotations on her February 1954 Tibor de Nagy Gallery catalog indicating the disposition of some of her paintings.   125

Marian Jim posing for *The Bride and the Owl.*   130

Bridal shop window on Grand Street in New York.   134

The second portion of Hartigan's journal entry for 11 April 1955 relating to the painting that would be renamed *Grand Street Brides.*   135

The manuscript journal entry for 14 April 1954 discussing "Bridal Store Mannequins" (it will be renamed *Grand Street Brides* in the entry for 26 April) and a review by James Fitzsimmons that Hartigan found most irritating.   136

Daisy Aldan and Olga Petroff (left to right) posing for *Two Women.*   139

Contact sheet with photographed poses for Hartigan's painting entitled *Masquerade.*   145

Hartigan in the dunes on Long Island.   147

Frank O'Hara posing for Hartigan's painting entitled *The Masker.*   150

Larry Rivers and Hartigan with her Italian straw hat on the beach at Southampton.   153

The cover of Hartigan's October 1954 one-artist exhibition at Vassar College in Poughkeepsie, New York.   155

The list of artwork in Hartigan's exhibition at Vassar College in October of 1954 with her annotations.   156

Cover of the catalog of Hartigan's March 1955 exhibition at the Tibor de Nagy Gallery.   168

List of the artwork in Hartigan's March 1955 exhibition at the Tibor de Nagy Gallery with her annotations.   169

Hartigan's ink sketch near her journal entry for 8 June 1955 while she was in Mexico.   181

Contact sheet with images taken during Hartigan's trip to Mexico.   182

FOUR-COLOR ILLUSTRATIONS

Plate 1. *Persian Jacket* (1952). Oil on canvas, 57½ x 48 in. (146 x 121.9 cm.). Gift of George Poindexter (413.1953). Digital image ©The Museum of Modern Art/Licensed by SCALA/Art Resource, New York (ART367504).

Plate 2. *Oranges #1 (Black Crows)* (1953). Oil on paper, 45 x 35 in. University at Buffalo Art Galleries: Gift of the David K. Anderson Family (2000-001-061).

Plate 3. The cover image of *Oranges: 12 Pastorals* by Frank O'Hara (New York: Tibor de Nagy Gallery, 1953). This publication consists of nine unnumbered mimeographed leaves that have been paperbound. The illustration pasted on the front cover is an original oil painting by Grace Hartigan. Courtesy of the State University of New York at Buffalo Libraries: The Poetry Collection.

Plate 4. *River Bathers* (1953). Oil on canvas, 69⅜ in. x 7 ft. 4¾ in. (176.2 x 225.5 cm.). Given anonymously (11.1954). Digital image ©The Museum of Modern Art/Licensed by SCALA/Art Resource, New York (ART340049).

Plate 5. Silk-screen print that appeared in *Folder 1* (New York: Tiber Press, 1953). It was based on the oil painting entitled *The Persian Jacket*. In her journal entry for 27 July 1953, Hartigan made this assessment of it: "I finished the second print Friday, 'The Persian Robe,' it is quite full and successful. It has an emotional intensity that I wasn't sure I could get in that medium, so I am really pleased."

Plate 6. *Grand Street Brides* (1954). Oil on canvas, 72 x 102 in. (182.88 x 260.35 cm.). Collection of the Whitney Museum of American Art, New York. Gift of an anonymous donor (55.27). Photograph by Geoffrey Clements.

Plate 7. *Masquerade* (1954). Oil on canvas, 207.7 x 219.1 cm. Anonymous gift (1955.493). Reproduction, The Art Institute of Chicago.

Plate 8. *Giftwares* (1955). Oil on canvas, 63 x 81 in. Collection of the Neuberger Museum of Art, Purchase College, State University of New York. Gift of Roy R. Neuberger. Photograph by Jim Frank.

ACKNOWLEDGMENTS

MANY PEOPLE have been of great assistance to this project. Robert Saltonstall Mattison, the Metzgar Professor of Art History at Lafayette College, whose monograph entitled *Grace Hartigan: A Painter's World* (New York: Hudson Hills Press, 1990) is the standard monographic work on the painter, served as a consultant for two exhibitions based on the Grace Hartigan Papers (one at Syracuse University Library and another at the university's Bernard and Louise Palitz Gallery at the Joseph I. Lubin House in Manhattan). He also contributed to an accompanying exhibition catalog that preceded the publication of the journals. His guidance and advice were greatly appreciated.

Of course, we were delighted with Terence Diggory's fine introduction to this volume. Diggory, the Ross Professor of Interdisciplinary Studies at Skidmore College, provides the context for the journals (and the art scene in New York during this period) and thereby makes them eminently more valuable and comprehensible.

We are obliged to Maureen O'Hara Granville-Smith, administratrix of the estate of Frank O'Hara, for permission to reprint five of Frank O'Hara's poems in their entirely in order to demonstrate the close collaboration and personal connections that existed between him and Grace Hartigan.

George Silver, the brother of Walter Silver, generously permitted us to incorporate into this publication the photographs by Walter Silver that are now part of the Grace Hartigan Papers.

Rex Stevens, the chair of the General Fine Arts and Drawing departments at the Maryland Institute College of Art and a long-time friend and associate of Grace Hartigan, assisted us with several inquiries.

Mary Beth Hinton and Lara Chmela labored tirelessly with the transcription of the text, and Michele Combs provided the excellent index for the volume.

We also need to acknowledge the encouragement provided by Suzanne E. Thorin, dean of libraries at Syracuse University; Sean M. Quimby, director of the Special Collections Research Center at Syracuse University Library; and Alice Randel Pfeiffer and Mary Selden Evans of Syracuse University Press. They empowered the staff of the Special Collections Research Center to develop and design a book entirely based upon the Grace Hartigan Papers held by that repository.

Most of all, we need to pay homage to Grace Hartigan for the unique window that she provided on this seminal period of American art. No one else directly involved in this movement succeeded in capturing such a documentary record of what became known as the New York School of painting and poetry (even though Hartigan generally disapproved of this designation). Moreover, her patience in reviewing the text and her generosity with her time made this project a rich and moving experience for all who were fortunate enough to share in it.

EDITORIAL NOTE

GRACE HARTIGAN did not write her journals for publication. She began them when she was twenty-nine, just after her birthday on 28 March 1951, and, as she notes in her first entry, "Who is as interested in the fine, minute aspects of oneself as oneself?" The journals served mostly as a means of grappling with problems relating to her painting; it is not a narrative of the events of her life (with the brief exception of her trip to Mexico in 1955). The journals functioned as a means of vocalizing the creative process. They also reveal that the New York art scene of the early 1950s was a difficult environment because the rivalries between critics, galleries, and artists made it hard to obtain dispassionate opinions. The journals, most importantly, provided Hartigan with an opportunity to establish an inner voice with which to examine her own artistic progress. The Special Collections Research Center at Syracuse University Library is in possession of them because they are a part of the Grace Hartigan Papers, which it solicited and began to receive from the artist in the 1960s.

In terms of the mechanics of reading this contemporary account of this critical era in American art, there are few simple concepts that should be borne in mind. The journals as published here are verbatim transcriptions; the spellings of words and names and the punctuation are exactly the way they were found in the original composition and spiral notebooks. There are very few revisions by Hartigan in the text, and when they occur, both versions are included. In addition, legible material that was simply (and sometimes heavily) crossed out has been retained. Any text that is within square brackets, however, is an added explanatory note, in some instances supplied by Grace Hartigan, or supplementary text from another source. Text that has been included from other sources (such as published reviews of exhibitions, poems of Frank O'Hara, or private correspondence) and interspersed within the journal entries has been set off by the use of a pair of ornaments ($\backsim$). Paragraph indentions have not been retained in quotations from reviews of exhibitions.

Any text that was underlined in the journals has been represented in italic type. If text was underlined twice or printed instead of written in script, it has been typeset in capital and small capital letters. In addition, the lists that appear in the text have been simulated typographically to look as much like the original as possible. Hartigan used the back pages of a few journals for some miscellaneous lists and jottings; this content has not been included.

With respect to the personalities that one encounters in the text of the journal, there is obviously a cluster of individuals who recur throughout the volumes. For these people, a list of first names and brief identifications were created. These are placed immediately before the first of the journals. The first time that an individual is mentioned in the text, there will be an identification of that person in square brackets. Thereafter, it may be necessary to refer to the lists for clarification. Of course, there are some names that do not appear with any regularity; for those references, we have supplied an identification in square brackets each time they occur.

This publication is based upon the journals kept by Grace Hartigan during the period between 1951 and 1955. These are part of the Grace Hartigan Papers that are housed in the Special Collections Research Center at Syracuse University Library. All of the photographs, unless otherwise specified, are from the Grace Hartigan Papers, and the vast majority of them were taken by Walter Silver.

Hartigan's journals consist of six separate volumes of various lengths. Volume one goes from 30 March to 31 December 1951. It is a composition book, and the writing in this volume is in pencil. The book is less than half full of writing. On the front is the notation "(copy)," which suggests that it is a re-transcribed version. Volume two covers the period between 2 January and 22 September 1952, and is also labeled "(copy)." It is a composition book that is virtually identical to volume one. It is written in pencil and is about half full of writing. Volume three covers 23 September 1952 to 5 March 1953 and is a spiral notebook. Written in pencil, the book is nearly full. Volume four extends from 6 March to 11 August 1953 and is a spiral notebook very similar to volume three. The entries were written with a fountain pen, and the book is full. There are several pages cut out between the entries for 2 April and 2 May, and Hartigan explains the reason for this in the entry for 2 May. Volume five is another spiral notebook documenting the time between 25 August and 30 December 1953. It is completely filled with entries written with a fountain pen. Volume six records Hartigan's thoughts over roughly a year and a half (2 January to 19 December 1954 and 1 January to 21 July 1955). This is another composition book that is two-thirds full of entries from a fountain pen and with nineteen pages excised at the end.

Most of the background research associated with this volume was conducted by Joseph McCaffrey while he was serving as the Dana Foundation fellow at Syracuse University Library. William La Moy, the curator of rare books and printed materials in the Special Collections Research Center at Syracuse University Library, designed the book in Adobe Minion Pro, an Open Type font, and oversaw the volume through production. The editorial operations were performed collaboratively by William La Moy and Joseph McCaffrey.

INTRODUCTION

by Terence Diggory

GRACE HARTIGAN emerged during the 1950s as a leading representative of the so-called "second generation" of New York School or abstract expressionist painters, the movement that won international standing for American art. In 1958, Hartigan and Sam Francis were the only two artists under forty chosen by the Museum of Modern Art to represent *The New American Painting* in a show that traveled to eight European countries. Older artists in the show included Willem de Kooning, Robert Motherwell, Barnett Newman, Jackson Pollock, and Mark Rothko. Hartigan was the only woman included.

The journals that Hartigan kept between March 1951 and July 1955, published here for the first time, provide a fascinating record of the production of the work that earned Hartigan a place in this movement, but it also provides a much more complicated record of one artist's relation to the movement than the retrospective and collective view that informed *The New American Painting* or subsequent accounts by art historians. The journal format reminds us that work proceeds day by day, and, while one day brings the satisfaction of achievement, the next day, it is "back to work, with fresh doubts" (31 March 1952). Moreover, the premise of the journal, that one is writing for and to oneself, emphasizes what Hartigan repeatedly calls the "aloneness" of the creative struggle (10 March 1952, 13 January 1953). Rather than describing an effort to join a movement, Hartigan's journals testify to her determination to be herself, even at the cost of separating herself from what she loves. "Pollock's new things are strange and powerful, but have little to do with what I'm working in," she reminds herself (27 November 1951). Starting one of her pivotal paintings of this period, *The Persian Jacket,* she admits to "hoping I don't remember De Kooning's seated women too well" (30 October 1952). After reading the great journal of the nineteenth-century French painter Eugène Delacroix, Hartigan draws this conclusion: "I must devote my energies toward finding my own expression, my best talent, what I must say, not what I like or admire or intellectualize about. This demands serious introspection, calm and time" (5 March 1953). Her journals are a product of that introspection and of time as it unfolded during the days she records.

Hartigan's life prior to the period of her journals is reflected in its pages in interesting ways. Born in 1922, she grew up in northern New Jersey, a region recalled for her in William Carlos Williams's publication entitled *Paterson,* which she received as a gift from her poet friend Frank O'Hara (8 August 1952).

In 1941, she married a hometown beau, Robert Jachens, but their marriage ended in divorce in 1947, having been disrupted by Jachens's military service during World War II and by emotional problems that Hartigan hints at when she compares Jachens with the art critic James Fitzsimmons, with whom she had a brief affair in 1953 (2 May 1953). Hartigan refers repeatedly to "guilts about Jeff" (21 December 1953), the child of her first marriage, who went to live with his father in California toward the end of the period covered in the journals. Despite the pain of separation, Hartigan was determined that no personal attachment would interfere with her devotion to painting. Tellingly, an early journal entry about Jeff crying himself to sleep because his parents are separated is soon followed by the report that "my children are scattered" (20 May 1951), referring to Hartigan's paintings.

To support herself during the war, Hartigan trained as a mechanical draftsman, but her education in painting and in the aesthetic problems of modern art was achieved largely through the means abundantly documented in her journals: through visits to museums and galleries, through reading, and through association with other artists. In 1948, she broke up with Isaac Lane Muse, her lover as well as sometime art teacher, to follow the lead of New York's most advanced abstract artists, Pollock and de Kooning, both of whom became friends and mentors. In 1949, Pollock and his wife, Lee Krasner, hosted the wedding of Hartigan and Harry Jackson; Jackson appears frequently in the journals as a fellow painter, although their marriage lasted barely a year. When the journals commence, Hartigan is sharing a studio on New York's Lower East Side with the painter Alfred Leslie. That relationship, too, shortly broke up, to be succeeded by a love affair with the photographer Walter Silver, which continued, off and on, for the remainder of the period of the journals. Besides providing emotional stability in her life, Silver placed the realism of his camera at the disposal of Hartigan's abstracting eye. For instance, his photographs of bridal shop windows near Hartigan's studio supplied crucial references for her culminating work of this period, *Grand Street Brides* (22 January 1954).

The tension between abstraction and realism is the chief complication in Hartigan's work of this period as well as in the relation more generally between the first and second "generations" of the New York School. Hartigan's early abstract work had attracted the attention of the critic Clement Greenberg, a leading advocate of Pollock. In 1950, Greenberg included Hartigan's *Secuda Esa Bruja* in a *New Talent* show that he and Meyer Schapiro organized at the Kootz Gallery on 57th Street. Even more important to Hartigan's career was her inclusion on a list of artists whom Greenberg recommended to John Bernard Myers for his new gallery, Tibor de Nagy, which became the headquarters for "second generation" painters. Hartigan's journals begin two months after her debut show at de Nagy, which introduced her as an abstract "purist," as Stuart Preston emphasized in his review in the *New York Times* (page xxx). After her second show at de Nagy the following year, Hartigan decided that she was "less and less interested in 'pure' painting" (31 March 1952). The problem of painting's content was looming larger in her mind, and she felt an urge to seek for content outside the self, the source of "expressionism" in the "abstract expressionism" of the first generation New York School. She undertook a series of studies based on old master paintings capped by a pair of "bather" compositions inspired by the modern masters Matisse and Cézanne, whose work she had seen in major museum exhibitions during the previous two years, but the chief revelation of this period—Hartigan refers to it as her "epiphany" (10 October 1952)—was Spanish painting. In Velázquez, Zurbarán, and Goya, she found a realism illuminated by an "inner light" (16 October 1952), a kind of poetic abstraction.

A number of factors supported Hartigan's turn away from pure abstraction at this time. There was, first of all, the spirit of the avant-garde itself, which rejects its previous embodiments in an endless quest for the new. Hartigan identifies "unceasing unrest" as "one of the essential qualities" of "the 'vanguard' artist," and she links her own possession of this quality to rebellion against parental authority: "I can hear my mother ever since I was a child, saying 'Grace you're so dissatisfied—so restless'" (8 October 1952). The same instinct led her to rebel against authority in the art world, whether institutional (the "new academy now, of the 'abstract'") or individual (the supposedly "objective judgement" of a critic like Greenberg) (15 October 1952). Her letter calling Greenberg to account is reproduced in the present volume (1 April 1954). At the same time, figurative elements were beginning to reemerge in the work of contemporary masters of abstraction, in the "strange and powerful" works by Pollock that Hartigan viewed at the Parsons Gallery in November 1951, and in "De Kooning's seated women" that Hartigan had the privilege of viewing in the artist's studio before they were first publicly shown at the Janis Gallery in March 1953. Although Hartigan maintained that Pollock's works "have little to do with what I'm working in," that was precisely what made them a powerful influence. In refusing to repeat their own successes, Pollock and de Kooning were encouraging younger artists to find their own way, as well, and not to assume that abstraction was the only way that led to the future. "No rules, I must be free to paint anything I feel," Hartigan resolved (31 March 1952).

"No rules" was the rule at the Tibor de Nagy Gallery. Although in her journal Hartigan occasionally expresses as much annoyance with gallery director John

Bernard Myers as she does with Clement Greenberg, it is for opposite reasons: far from being dogmatic, Myers was mercurial. It was hard to know where he stood at any given moment in the shifting pattern of allegiances among gallery artists, but at all times, he seemed open to variety. Some of the de Nagy artists, like Robert Goodnough, Alfred Leslie, and Helen Frankenthaler, remained committed to abstraction throughout the 1950s. Hartigan aligned herself more with the "new realists" Larry Rivers, Jane Freilicher, and Fairfield Porter (8 July 1955). She identified herself with neither group entirely, but as she turned away from pure abstraction, her subject matter developed in a direction that most closely paralleled that of Rivers. In January 1953, she wrote this in her journal: "I feel very attracted to a kind of painting where the 'subject-matter' is a cliché, there's something freeing about it. Rather than 'pure' painting, I now like the thought of as impure a picture as possible" (13 January 1953). In December 1953, Tibor de Nagy exhibited Rivers's scandalous appropriation of a national cliché, *Washington Crossing the Delaware*—scandalous, that is, to the avant-garde. With Rivers's painting in mind, Hartigan reported Harry Jackson's speculation that the de Nagy artists were moving in a direction that "will make painting more public, less art for artists and so revolutionize the whole 'special' ivory tower position of an artist in America" (4 December 1953). They were, in fact, moving in the direction that would become known in the following decade as Pop art. When the Whitney Museum in New York installed an exhibition entitled *Hand-Painted Pop* in 1993, they hung Rivers's *Washington Crossing the Delaware* and Hartigan's *Grand Street Brides* at the entrance.

An unusual feature of the de Nagy Gallery was the involvement of a group of young poets whom Myers eventually labeled, by analogy with the painters, the New York School: John Ashbery, Barbara Guest, Kenneth Koch, Frank O'Hara, and James Schuyler. To Myers, their presence was an essential component of a creative culture such as Paris enjoyed at the birth of modernism, when Apollinaire and Picasso were colleagues. The de Nagy Gallery published pamphlets of the poets' work, illustrated by gallery artists, and Myers promoted collaboration in Artists' Theatre productions under the direction of his partner, Herbert Machiz—whom Hartigan judged to be ill-suited to the task (5 November 1953). Hartigan counted the poets, especially O'Hara, among her closest friends. Seeing herself reflected in O'Hara's poems made her feel "as though I exist now" (11 August 1952). The extensive reading that she records in her journal often reflects the poets' guidance, as in the case of O'Hara's gift of Williams's *Paterson*. The poets' more direct influence on Hartigan's painting is evident in the way she interpreted her turn away from pure abstraction. The figures that appear in her newer work are "images" in the sense applicable to poetry, not photography. They are symbolic or metaphoric. An early "portrait" of O'Hara, *Frank O'Hara and the Demons,* gives rise to this comment in Hartigan's journal: "I could do the O'Hara picture because it isn't Frank, it's a symbol of something else for me, I don't know what" (9 July 1952). Ironically, painting the later *Oranges,* a series of twelve works on paper incorporating text from O'Hara's sequence of the same title, closed off "the possibility of looking at nature 'head on,'" as Hartigan understood it (10 February 1953). Then, in his essay entitled "Nature and New Painting" (1954), O'Hara reopened the door to nature by placing Hartigan's work, along with that of other new imagists, in the context of the poets' nature: "Modern life has expanded our conception of nature and along with it nature's role in our lives and our art—a woman stepping on a bus may afford a greater insight into nature than the hills outside Rome, for nature has not stood still since Shelley's day." The artist does not merely record the sight of nature—mere "realism"—but supplies "insight into nature," like the poetic "inner light" that Hartigan found in Spanish painting.

For Hartigan, as her journals make clear, insight into nature was intimately connected with insight into gender that was available to her as a woman who challenged male assumptions. As she began her turn away from pure abstraction in 1952, she made this entry in her journal: "I don't know what I'm after but whatever it is, if I must look conservative—reactionary—timid—or even (horrors) feminine—in the process then it must be. I think I know how really strong I am" (6 June 1952). The gendering of abstract painting as male was overdetermined, first, because nature, the basis of imagery in representational painting, was gendered as female; and second, because dependence on nature in representational painting was regarded as timid or weak, i.e., a "feminine" position. Hartigan's resolution that "I don't fear painting a bad picture or a weak one now" prepared her for the attacks she would face from male critics like Greenberg (6 June 1952), while at the same time, her claim that "I think I know how really strong I am" turned the tables on her attackers, implying that theirs was the position of weakness because they were merely following fashion, the new academy of the abstract. Hartigan had the strength to be herself.

Of course, what it meant to be oneself was highly problematic in an art world where expressionism had become as fashionable as abstraction. Paradoxically, while abstraction turned away from external nature, expressionism drew upon an internal nature, gendered male. Hence we have Pollock's macho assertion, "I am nature," in response to the suggestion that he work from nature. As noted above, in her reaction against expressionism, Hartigan sought for images outside the self, moving from the old masters to popular culture as her sources. However, her search seems to have led her to images of the self, complicated by the displacements of nature and gender just described. Consider the series of displacements at work in the full context of the 13 January 1953 journal entry quoted above, in which Hartigan states her fondness for cliché:

> I've just bought a chunky looking bunch of artificial flowers & leaves at the 5 & 10, also some apples. I feel very attracted to a kind of painting where the "subject-matter" is a cliché, there's something freeing about it. Rather than "pure" painting, I now like the thought of as impure a picture as possible—look at Courbet, he made his sentimentality his greatest strength.

Presumably, Hartigan had purchased those artificial flowers as the subject for a painting. They belong to popular imagery, purchased from "the 5 & 10," but unlike, say, the soup cans of Andy Warhol, they also belong to natural imagery. They are a version of nature gone dead, a cliché, as nature as a whole was viewed from the perspective of pure abstraction. Hartigan's intention, however, is to restore the flowers to life, so to speak, by making them into art. The risk of sentimentality involved in the attempt to transform the cliché is an expression of her strength as it was of Courbet's—doubly so, in her case, since the association between women and sentimentality was itself a cliché. In a sense, therefore, this painting of artificial flowers would be a symbol of self-transformation, or a symbolic self-portrait, like the "portrait of the poet wrapped in jungle leaves" in O'Hara's "Oranges No. 11." Interestingly, the image that Hartigan supplied to accompany that poem is an arrangement of flowers in a vase.

For Hartigan as a woman in the 1950s and for O'Hara as a gay man, seeking outside the self for images of the self was a condition of existence. Seeing herself as "the flowergirl" in O'Hara's "Poem for a Painter" (1952) made Hartigan feel "as though I exist now" (11 August 1952). Seeing himself variously reflected in Hartigan's *Ocean Bathers* and *Frank O'Hara and the Demons* inspired O'Hara to pray for "Grace / to be born and live as variously as possible." These lines appear in his central poem of the period, "In Memory of My Feelings" (1956), which is dedicated to Hartigan and echoes her name in the punning prayer for "Grace." The gay practice of assuming cross-gender "camp" names helps to explain the curious fact that Hartigan exhibited at the Tibor de Nagy Gallery under the name "George" until her fifth show in 1955, at the end of the period covered by the journals. She chose the name in homage to George Eliot and George Sand, women who adopted male pseudonyms to align themselves with the more advanced, "serious" trends in nineteenth-century literature, but within the inner circle at de Nagy the practice was self-consciously unserious, a theatrical reflection of straight society's construction of gay sexuality as un-natural. For example, James Schuyler's "camp" name was Dorabella, one of the two sisters at the center of Mozart's opera *Così fan tutte*. In a Hartigan journal entry, she refers to "my other self (George)" in the playful context of having her Tarot fortune read by Waldemar Hansen, John Bernard Myers's roommate (22 October 1952).

Filtering her experience as a woman through the lens of gay sensibility si-multaneously yielded new images of the self for Hartigan and new approaches to image-making. When she wrote in her journal that the image of O'Hara in *Frank O'Hara and the Demons* "isn't Frank, it's a symbol of something else" (9 July 1952), she was locating meaning where it has traditionally been located in literary interpretation: somewhere behind the image. In camp, and increas-ingly in literature that reflects its influence, like the poetry of the New York School, meaning resides entirely on the surface, in the moment of perfor-mance. Thus, in his poem "On Seeing Larry Rivers' *Washington Crossing the Delaware* at the Museum of Modern Art" (1955), O'Hara exclaims, "our hero has come back to us / in his white pants." Along the same lines, Hartigan's re-sponse to Rivers's painting leads her to a discovery that excites her as much as her discovery of Spanish painting, and for related reasons: "I admire Velasquez & Goya, the portrayals of kings, queens and court life, costumes, etc. with the *irony* they use in these interpretations" (4 December 1953). The irony is that there is nothing behind the costumes (like Washington's "white pants") but that the costumes give life to the figures who inhabit them. Scarcely more than a month later, in January 1954, the motif for *Grand Street Brides,* "a store win-dow jammed full of mannequins in cheap white lace bridal gowns," stimulated Hartigan's imagination as the occasion for a "modern court scene" (22 January 1954). When O'Hara approached the finished work to write about it in "Nature and New Painting," he was prepared to accept its irony: the fact that Hartigan's brides "face without bitterness the glassy shallowness of American life which is their showcase."

If Hartigan stands among these brides, boldly daring "to look conserva-tive—reactionary—timid—or even (horrors) feminine" (6 June 1952), O'Hara stands, quite literally, in a complementary group in the painting *Masquerade* (1954). As models for this painting, Hartigan gathered together some of her de Nagy friends, including O'Hara, Ashbery, and Jane Freilicher, along with people involved in the short-lived magazine *Folder* (1953–54), an enterprise, like de Nagy, in which collaborations across the arts flourished and sexual identities crossed conventional boundaries freely. Daisy Aldan, the editor of *Folder,* was in a marriage of convenience with Richard Miller, whose gay partner, Floriano Vecchi, introduced Hartigan to printmaking. Hartigan was certainly aware of the significance of masking as a homosexual theme, but as a theme for her painting, it interested her within a wider range of associations. While working on a double-portrait of Daisy Aldan and her lesbian partner, Olga Petroff, Hartigan reflected in her journal, "Perhaps my sphere of interest or 'subject material' could be called 'façade,' the empty gesture, the dead ritual, the costume, the mask" (4 May 1954). In this light, her contemporary portrait of O'Hara as *The Masker*, employing the same costume that O'Hara wears in *Masquerade*, appears to revise the earlier *Frank O'Hara and the Demons*. Rather than suggesting meaning behind the figure, symbolically, *The Masker* concentrates meaning in "the empty gesture" of the figure itself, theatrically. Although it is a single figure, it is hardly identical to itself, but rather contains the potential for multiplying into many guises, some of which Hartigan captured in *Masquerade*. As O'Hara writes in "In Memory of My Feelings," "The conception / of the masque barely suggests the sordid identifications."

With her discovery of this theme and its related approach to image-making, Hartigan was set for a lifetime of invention. Many of the motifs to which she returned throughout her career appear in the list of "Ideas" that we sense her scribbling with excitement into her journal on 4 December 1953, the date of her second great "discovery" after Spanish painting. Her predictions were inaccurate only in their exclusions. Both still life and landscape continued to furnish her with subject matter from time to time, along with the more "exotic" or "romantic" interests she acknowledges: "Opera, ballet, theater" (*The Divine Sarah*, 2006); "Restaurants—diners in evening clothes. Elegant homosexuals" (*Manhattan*, 1986); "High fashion world" (*Riviera*, 1966); "Movie world" (*Hollywood Interior*, 1993); and Judith Malina's "Egyptian jewel-look" (*Coloring Book of Ancient Egypt*, 1973). The consistency with which Hartigan pursued these themes over a career spanning six decades proves that she remained faithful to her early resolution to "obey my instincts, they are the only things I can trust" (5 November 1953). That trust gave her the courage to challenge "'Pure' painting à la New York School" (23 January 1952) as early as 1952, and it sustained her when she left New York in 1960 to join her new husband, Winston Price, in Baltimore, where he was a medical researcher. She maintained affiliations with New York galleries, although her personal presence in the art world necessarily lessened as a result of her move. She further extended her influence through teaching at the Maryland Institute College of Art. Now, with the publication of Hartigan's journals, we all become Hartigan's students as we follow her education day by day in one of the richest painting cultures the world has known.

Recurring First Names

Al	Al Leslie
Barney	Barnett Newman
Bob	Bob Jachens
Clem	Clement Greenberg
Daisy	Daisy Aldan
Dwight	Dwight Ripley
Edi	Edi Franceschini
Esta	Esta Leslie
Fairfield	Fairfield Porter
Floriano	Floriano Vecchi
Frank	Frank O'Hara
Harold	Harold Rosenberg
Harry	Harry Jackson
Helen	Helen Frankenthaler
Jackson	Jackson Pollock
Jane	Jane Freilicher
Jeff	Jeff Jachens
Jim or Jimmy	James Schuyler
Joan	Joan Mitchell
Joe	Joe Hazen
John	John Bernard Myers
Kenneth	Kenneth Koch
Larry	Larry Rivers
May or May Natalie	May Natalie Tabak
Nell or Nellie	Nell Blaine
Richard	Richard Miller
Tibor	Tibor de Nagy
Waldemar	Waldemar Hansen
Walt	Walt Silver

Biographical Notes on Key Figures

DAISY ALDAN (1923–2001) was born in New York City, received a B.A. degree from Hunter College and an M.A. degree from Brooklyn College in 1948, and did further graduate study at New York University. She was primarily known as a poet, editor, and translator.

JOHN ASHBERY (b. 1927) was born in Rochester, New York, and was educated at Harvard and Columbia. He has published more than twenty collections of poetry, written extensively on art, and received numerous prizes and awards. He left New York City for France in 1955 on a Fulbright grant and lived in Europe until the mid-1960s, when he returned to the United States.

WILLEM DE KOONING (1904–97) was educated in Rotterdam (his birthplace), came to the United States in 1927, and settled in New York City the next year. In the late 1930s and 1940s, his abstract paintings helped define the New York School and the abstract expressionist movement in American art.

TIBOR DE NAGY (1909–94) was born in Debrecen, Hungary, and educated in England, Germany, and Switzerland. He was a banker in Hungary before immigrating to America at the end of World War II. He opened the Tibor de Nagy Gallery with John Bernard Myers in 1950; de Nagy served as business manager. The gallery showed the work of many of the New York School artists in the 1950s, as well as publishing poetry, prints, and plays.

HELEN FRANKENTHALER (b. 1928) was born in New York City. She was educated at Bennington College and studied with Hans Hoffmann. Like Jackson Pollock, she worked on raw canvas that was then stained with color ("stained painting" or the "color-field style").

CLEMENT GREENBERG was a Syracuse University graduate and a prominent art critic in New York during the period when the journals were being kept by Grace Hartigan.

BARBARA GUEST (1920–2006) was born in North Carolina and educated at the University of California at Berkeley. She published many volumes of poetry and was a critic and biographer. She was awarded the Frost Medal for Lifetime Achievement in 1999 by the Poetry Society of America.

GRACE HARTIGAN (1922–2008) was born in Newark, New Jersey, and moved to New York City in 1947. She spent most of 1949 painting in Mexico and returned to New York in 1950. At her third show at the Tibor de Nagy Gallery, she sold *The Persian Jacket* to the Museum of Modern Art, and her career was firmly established. She moved to Baltimore in 1960, and began directing the graduate program in painting at the Hoffberger School of the Maryland Institute College of Art in 1965.

HARRY JACKSON (b. 1924) is a painter and sculptor and Grace Hartigan's second husband. He was born with the name of Harry Shapiro on the South Side of Chicago.

KENNETH KOCH (1925–2002) was born in Cincinnati, Ohio, and attended Harvard at the same time that Frank O'Hara and John Ashbery did. He completed a doctorate at Columbia, where he taught for many years. He began publishing poetry in the early 1950s and won many prizes, including Guggenheim and Fulbright awards.

ALFRED LESLIE (b. 1927) was born in New York and attended New York University. He shared a studio with Grace Hartigan in 1951. As a painter, he was a member of the second generation of abstract expressionists but returned to a more realistic style in the 1960s.

JOAN MITCHELL (1926–92) was born in Chicago and attended Smith College and the Art Institute of Chicago. She moved to New York City in 1947 and was included in the "second generation" of abstract expressionists, along with Grace Hartigan, Larry Rivers, and others. She moved permanently to France in 1959.

JOHN BERNARD MYERS (1919 or 1920–87) was born in Buffalo, New York, and moved to New York City in 1944 to become managing editor of *View* magazine. After *View* ceased publication, Myers opened the Tibor de Nagy Gallery in 1950 in partnership with Tibor de Nagy; Myers served as gallery director. The gallery was home to many artists of the New York School and published books of poetry and prints, as well as literary magazines. Myers wrote many articles of criticism as well as a book on the New York School poets. He and de Nagy dissolved their partnership in 1970.

FRANK O'HARA (1926–66) was born in Baltimore, Maryland, and grew up in Grafton, Massachusetts. He served in the navy during World War II and earned degrees from Harvard and the University of Michigan. He moved to New York City in 1951. His curatorial work at the Museum of Modern Art, as well as his poetry and art criticism, made him central to the New York School. He died after being struck by a motor vehicle in 1966.

LARRY RIVERS (1925–2002) was born Yitzoch Loiza Grossberg in Bronx, New York, and changed his name in 1940 when he began work as a jazz saxophonist. After service in World War II, he studied at the Julliard School and New York University, earning a B.A. degree in art education in 1951. His first one-man show was in 1949, and he exhibited annually at the Tibor de Nagy Gallery from 1951 to 1962. He worked in video, film, and sculpture, as well as in painting and lithography.

BARNET LEE ROSSET (b. 1922) was the publisher of Grove Press from 1951 to 1985. Grove published many of the New York School poets, as well as Henry Miller, Samuel Beckett, the French avant-garde, and the American "Beat" writers.

JAMES SCHUYLER (1923–91) was born in Chicago and served in the navy in World War II. After the war, he lived in Italy and was W. H. Auden's secretary. Moving to New York City, he roomed with John Ashbery and Frank O'Hara for a time. He worked at the Museum of Modern Art and as an art critic and editor. He published many volumes of poetry for which he received numerous prizes, but he also wrote novels and plays.

FLORIANO VECCHI (1921–2005) was born near Bologna, Italy, and came to New York City in 1952. He and Richard Miller opened the Tiber Press in 1953, with Miller as the business manager and Vecchi in charge of design and printing. Vecchi was a pioneer in silk-screen printing and taught the technique to many artists, including Grace Hartigan and Andy Warhol.

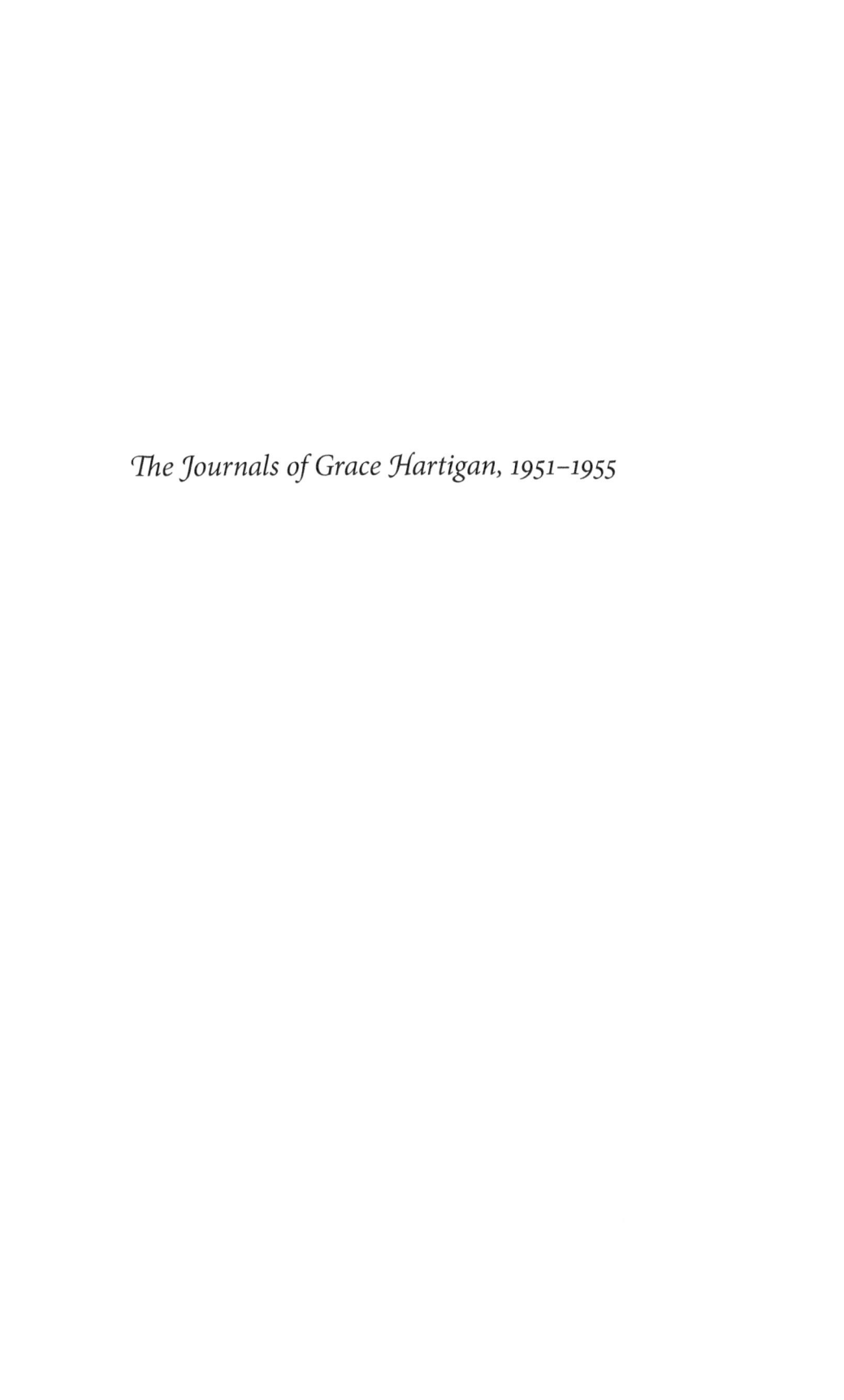

The Journals of Grace Hartigan, 1951–1955

The catalog from Hartigan's 1951 one-person show at the Tibor de Nagy Gallery. It identifies her as "George" Hartigan, an homage to the nineteenth-century literary figures George Sand and George Eliot. The handwritten notes are those of Grace Hartigan. The painting entitled *King of the Hill* went to the Worcester Art Museum according to these annotations.

∼

The following text is a portion of Stuart Preston's review of Hartigan's first one-person show on page eighty-nine of the *New York Times* for 21 January 1951: "[George Hartigan] is a purist, isolating eloquent color relationships from any attempt at representation. Stabs and swirls of pigment, beating a tempo, now slower, now faster, revolve and interweave from one edge of the canvas to the other. It is an enlivening formal exercise, raised from the elementary level of vitality which any nervous brushwork can produce by its inventive and frequently beautiful harmonies of pungent color."

∼

JOURNAL FOR 1951

March 30, 1951
A journal can be the only real expression of an egotist, far more than a letter—who is as interested in the fine, minute aspects of oneself as oneself?

I'm just twenty-nine. In another year I shall be thirty, time to begin to fulfill the "promise," and since my show in January I have finished only one picture. This thing of finish for a picture is very strange, hard to determine that final point. "Baroque Square" is aborative in many ways, taller than I and wide as my arm's stretch and I feel that I couldn't add another thing to it without changing the idea completely. There have been two small things too, but they aren't much. I think I've honestly faced the problem of drawing for the first time. Something may come there.

Even at this stage both "Aries" and "Six Square" have identities of their own. Had them from the very beginning. Wonder if this has been true before. Certainly so with "King of the Hill." I worked for months on a feeling of red, pink and yellow. And when it resolved it was without intellectualization, it was like a trance state.

Odd experience walking up Rivington St. yesterday. Suddenly I couldn't read. I looked at signs, ads, and the words were as though it was a language I couldn't understand. It has happened once before. Wonder what it means? The whiteness (and weakness) of "Silver Nutmeg" was there from the start. But "King is Dead" began with everything in the palette, so did "Months and Moons."

No it isnt easy if you're honest.

I have recently been glad that I am not facile. What comes is from the guts.

March 31
No one asks me how my painting is going. Because I'd be too eager to tell, even before the question? What is it about a social gathering that gives me the frenzied desire to make my strength felt? It only alienates, but I persist. Clem [Clement Greenberg, a prominent art critic] and Jackson [Jackson Pollock, artist] act very strange, as though they didn't know what role to play. What would you say to Jeanne d'Arc at a cocktail party?

Try taking the yellow deep out of "Aries".

Easy for Helen [Helen Frankenthaler, artist] to be the fairy princess, she hasnt seen the dragon yet.

April 10
Went with John [John Bernard Myers, artistic director of the Tibor de Nagy Gallery] and Al [Alfred Leslie, artist] to see Goodnough's [Robert Goodnough, artist] pictures. Last night. They are strong and serious, and each one has a feeling of entity, you see it at one time, as a whole. Keying is partly the answer, and I've been reworking "Aries" this morning to get more oneness there. As I look at "Baroque Square" now it seems to fight with itself, to pull apart. Same with the small inscape I just brought to the gallery, think I'll take it home and work on it more.

A predominant color seems also necessary to this "all-overness" making cool and warm color contrasts very difficult to achieve.

If I rework "Baroque Square" I will first replace all reds and oranges with a grey or light blue.

"Aries" finished.

Re-working "Baroque Square".

April 14
Working again after a few days mulling over the last two canvases.

Trying now to put a lot of vigour into a small canvas. A problem.

Out of all colors but earths, reds, white and black. A little cobalt. It will be interesting to see if I can work with these limitations.

Someone said that Rubens painted himself into his canvases more than any other artist has done. I think that's true now—it certainly can be said of Pollock.

April 17
"Six Square" looks singularly uninspired so far. Musn't let that frighten

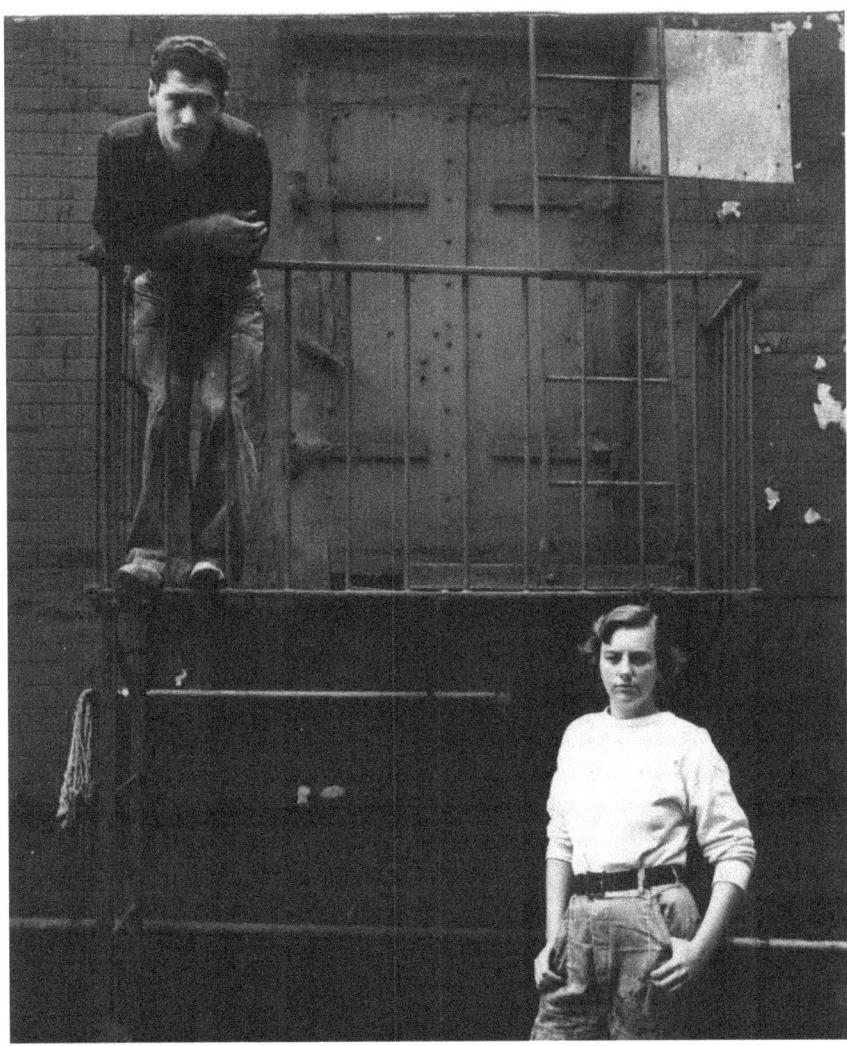

Hartigan and Alfred Leslie outside the studio that they shared in 1951.

me—Paraphrasing [Henry] James, "the highest creative act is to go into the studio." Al has an 8 ft x 12 ft canvas (unstretched, unsized) tacked up on his wall—next to it 6^2 looks like a midget.

Something dull about using Dutch Boy white lead. It's cheap, and I use white by the pounds. Shiva has an underbody white, fast drying that I think I'll try.

Getting enough money for materials is a constant worry. John is trying to get us a few hundred dollars to last us through the summer so we needn't take any jobs. It would be a good breather—I resent leaving the studio.

In order to find my own way I must reject all these ideas of tensions, diagonal construction etc that I've been playing with.

We could live on so little, if only a small income came from painting sales.

Little Nick [a janitor for the local tenements, who according to Grace Hartigan, "used to have a monkey on his back—I mean a real one"] came to clean the roof—he loves the studio, says it's like living in Coney Island.

The coming group show [at the Tibor de Nagy Gallery] is on my mind a great deal. I'm thinking of course of how my painting will stand up, also of the impact of us hung as a group. So far I think Al and Goodnough are the most powerful. Helen is too thin, Harry [Harry Jackson, artist and Hartigan's second husband] has dropped the ball—he may recover.

It seems that I must first make complete chaos on a canvas before I can find any order.

"One must have chaos within one to give birth to a dancing star."

A picture must reach out to its edges and gather itself in.

Your color is getting too sweet!

April 19
Spent yesterday with Al seeing shows—Rothko, Matta, de Kooning, Hare, Roszak and came home with the usual "57th St headache."

I liked the Rothkos—they seemed more all-over this time, and the color exciting and intense. Not my direction by any means nor is de Kooning for that matter. His show was disappointing—a tremendous "odds and ends" feel to it, without the dynamism and search that I sensed in the large canvas at the Mus. Mod Art Abstract Show. [A note in the margin reads "Excavation."] Greenberg said the other night he's trying to talk himself into a position that he can only paint himself in.

April 24
After Six Square is finished I think I should experiment with bolder color, taking more chances than I have in the last few canvases. It takes many more years of painting experience than I have to really create new color—Rothko is doing it now to some extent.

April 25
I think sometimes that what keeps me painting is the complete feeling of repulsion I experience on looking at my "finished" pictures.

Aries and 6^2 seem tremendously feminine in their color—which of course I detest.

I'd like to achieve something like the quality of somber richness that Miro had in the great maroon and black pictures.

April 26
Just finished seaming Baroque Square with Patch last and a strip of canvas. A successful operation, makes me breathe easier.

No more canvas and I am obsessed with the idea of Black Spring (?) a very violent, dark painting in blacks, grays, brick reds and purples.

April 27
Perhaps I can work blacks and reds into 6^2 to strengthen it. It fades away next to Baroque Square.

April 28
Won't have to paint a black April—the blacks and reds are working well into 6^2. I like it as I haven't liked anything in a long time. It's all about what's going on in me now—I didn't know if I could get it down in paint.

April 30
Six Square is finished, and now looking at the three newest things to-gether I feel that they are complete for what they are, but they're not big enough yet, not nearly big enough.

∾

John Bernard Myers captured the kite-flying party of the Tibor de Nagy gallery artists in his book *Tracking the Marvelous* (New York: Random House,

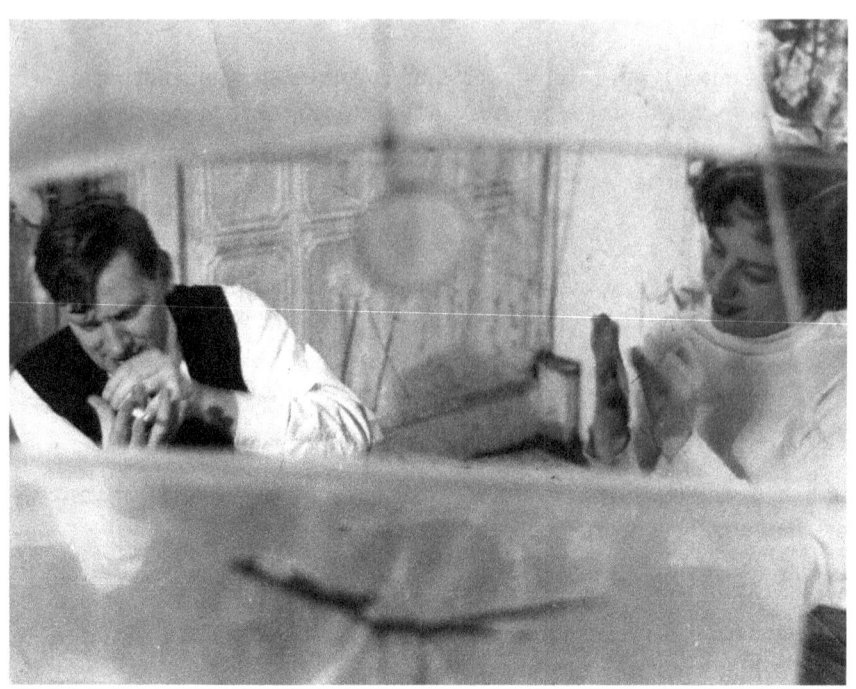

John Bernard Myers and Hartigan making kites in Hartigan's studio for a magazine feature that was never published.

1983) on pages 139 and 140: "The weather was improving [end of March 1952] and Grace [Hartigan] invited about twenty people, all [Tibor de Nagy] gallery artists and her friends, to a kite-making party. The kites were constructed in her Essex Street loft, but the following day they were carried up to Sheep Meadow in Central Park to be sent aloft. The kites, some big and lengthy, others small, were colorful, goofy and beautiful. But when we got to the park the wind began to blow at what seemed hurricane speed. Simply hanging onto the kites became difficult. Still determined to get them in the air, we did our best, only to have them dashed to the ground or blown to bits. All of the kites were ruined. 'A real fiasco is what we've got!' yelled Grace. 'Let's get out of here.' How I wish someone had taken pictures of the mess."

Jeff [Jeff Jachens, Hartigan's son] cried himself to sleep after I brought him home because Bob [Robert Jachens, Hartigan's first husband and Jeff's father] and I aren't together with him. It was heart-breaking to hear him, there was

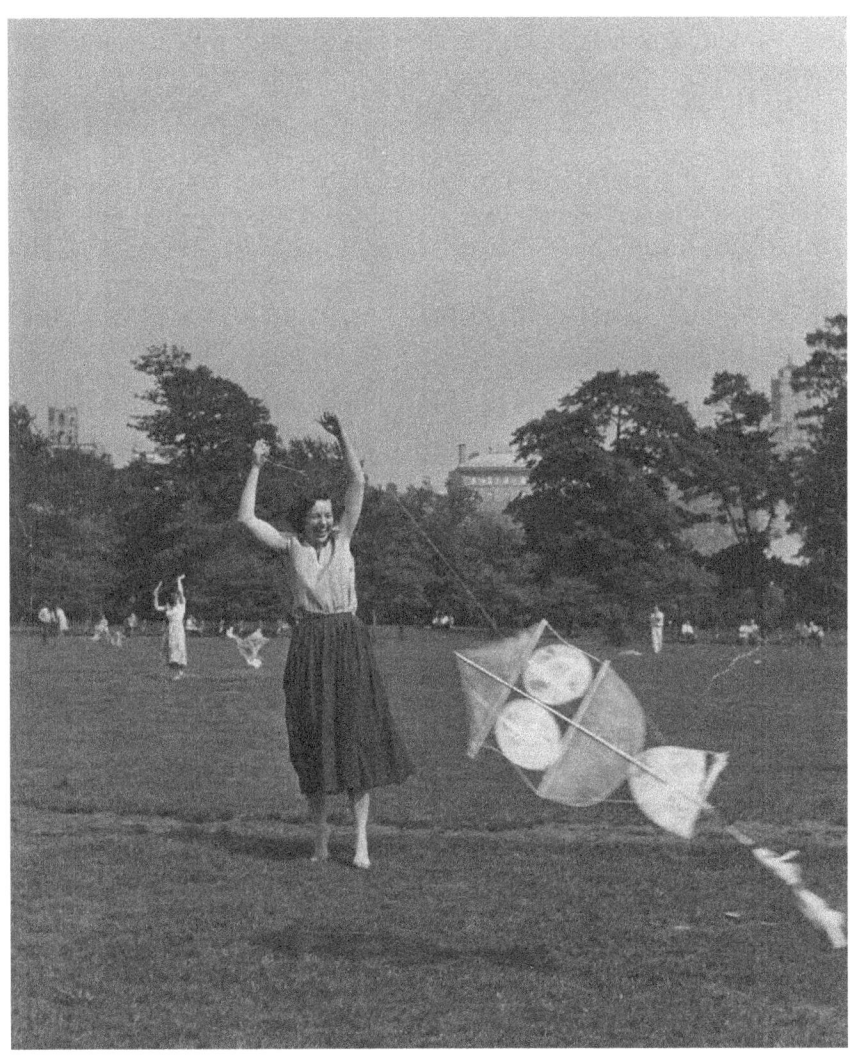
Hartigan flying hand-made kites in Central Park. Strong winds destroyed them.

nothing to be said that could soothe him—he has his tragedies defined for him at an early age.

May 16
Haven't painted much to speak of for two weeks. The group show, thinking

about working at something to get money, Life magazine with the kite project plus this 9th St. show have drained us both.

May 20
My children are scattered—Baroque Square at the gallery, now Six Square at 9th St. It stands up well enough in such company, but its not what I want yet, not nearly. Al's picture makes the most powerful gesture. Harry is getting the bulk of the critical attention from the New Generation show—strange, for his stand is the most cowardly of us all—even Helen reaches higher, hence more seeming failures.

May 23
For the last three days I've been working as a file clerk all day and painting each evening. All of which must prove that when the fire is burning, nothing else matters.

The paintings are strange, very light in key and I'm most confused about space and the surface. In what way must the surface be explored?

June 1
Very warm—just bought a lot of canvas duck. I'm so impatient to begin that I've tacked an unsized piece on the wall. There's a lot of ideas in "King is Dead" that I haven't fully explored. Pollock I hear is painting the figure-image. Strange.

June 6
This is the first picture in a long time that's made me feel sick and furious at it. Maybe that's good. I'm fed up with everything I've been doing. None of it has any meaning.

June 11
"Thalo" is finished as far as I want to go with it. It's powerful I think and ambitious—the whites don't quite work—but I want to leave it. I think I can learn from it later on. I worked on a four square canvas to-day, started it yesterday. It may be overly explosive, but I kind of like it. I needed to work with enamel again, it seems to have freed a lot of things.

Glad the season is ending, this summer should be productive. 9th St. is down—I learned from that show. This is the last week of the New Generation show. Tibor [Tibor de Nagy, financial director of the Tibor de Nagy Gallery] may sell the yellow picture [*Lemons*] to John Ritter, if so we won't have to work at jobs much this summer. Have a lovely piece of 7 foot x 9 foot #10 canvas that I'm aching to start on. Must fix my wall first, then tack it up and size it. I feel strong—if it keeps up some good paintings may come.

June 18
Have three new pictures from the last month—"Thalo," "White," and "Four Square" which if not satisfy at least interest me. Today I started on the 7´ x 9´. It's taut as a drum on the wall nailed onto planks. It's the largest one I've attempted, and it's exciting.

June 19
Quite a day of painting. Al has finished a large picture that bowled me over. It's his most articulate and powerful work to date—It's so fine that I can't even envy it. I've finished (but for a few final touches) my large canvas too, but I haven't any perspective on it with that painting in the other room on my mind.

June 20
I look at my canvas with fresh eyes this morning and I see it's not finished at all.

June 21
Letting the big canvas rest for a while, and I'm re-working "Aries"—it seemed terribly confined compared to the newer things. Better re-name "Aries"—I've come to dislike zodiacal or mythological titles. "With Red" perhaps.

I have a feeling of how the big one must be—the yellow isn't right. Hard for me to use a lot of yellow right now.

I like the idea of oranges and greys, whites and blacks.

"Thalo" needs re-working too, what an endless process!

June 26
A very pleasant evening with John at Peggy Osborn's [wealthy backer of the Tibor de Nagy Gallery and its artists] yesterday. She has become along

with John an ardent and loud "Al" worshipper which gets annoying—what a tremendous ego I must have!

I haven't brought in any money for over a month now—my painting has benefited, but not the budget—I'm becoming concerned and guilty. But I loathe the idea of hunting for something.

Maybe now I've finished my big picture—"The Cue". I think I reached way into cubism for the solution—but I'm sure no one will see it that way but me.

This has been the most fruitful month of work I have ever had.

June 29
I continue to be enchanted with "Cue"—the rain is pouring down, and in the muted light it looks especially powerful. I'm trying to quiet my frenzy about money and a job through the weekend, and work more on "Thalo"—I'd like it to be harsh and grating in color—say purple and greens.

July 5
I'm working three days a week, 3:00 PM to 11:00 PM at a travel bureau in the Savoy Plaza. It may or may not last through the Summer.

Al is studio-hunting, Nana [Hartigan's grandmother, "a great influence in my life"] died yesterday, and if one draws upon personal agony for pictures then I'll be a great artist.

"Thalo" needs more identity still. Perhaps I can paint for a while to-day before I go to the funeral parlor.

July?
[Hartigan remarked that she did not know what date it was.]

My life has become calmer than when I last wrote, and I'm working hard in spite of the fool three day a week job.

Paul [Paul Brach, art collector] and Harry have seen "The Cue" and feel it is ambitious but unrealized. They may be right, but I couldn't do anything to it without destroying things in it that seem important. I'm very happy with "Thalo" now—it needs a new name—I've done things with some of the blues that are very good. "White" looks better all the time—I must thank Clem for seeing it for me. 4^2 (Cicada?) is still good but the red one pulled at itself and I'm working on it some more. I've finished three small things—one of which "Portrait of A." I think is very good. A real problem to make a small picture big and important, but it's coming.

I'll need more canvas soon, and with Al having his own studio August 1st the problem of money is worse than ever. I must admit it feels good to have 25 Essex my studio alone. The place looks fine and open now that it is divided only in half instead of in three.

It's very hot and humid but I'm content to be here at work, I feel good things coming now.

July 19
It seems that every period of productivity fools me into believing that it will last forever. It never does, and I'm on three canvases that are strange, strained and don't want to work at all within themselves. The only thing that keeps me calm is the memory of times like this and the feeling that out of these struggles come truer pictures.

July 30
After a week and a half of insanities, ills and heart breaks [separating from Leslie] I feel so strongly again that my only real peace with myself comes with work. Not that I'm painting well to-day, but the search itself means so much. It is in this way and with this knowledge that I'll be able to face the emotional tensions of being alone again

Aug. 3
Hitting the depths.

Aug 9
Painting went well to-day. No longer desperate—just deeply sad.

Aug 10
Summing up:
Two large canvases "The Cue" and "Blue Inscape." Then—"The Blue G.", "Portrait of A." "White", "Mid-August," "Cicada" and the small red canvas that

John took home with him. I feel reasonably satisfied with them—disregarding the perpetual feeling that nothing is quite enough, yet.

I have only small canvases left now and God knows where the money for more will come from. Maybe I'll miraculously sell a picture when the season starts. Barr's [Alfred Barr, official of the Museum of Modern Art] interest in the picture that was at 9th St. should mean something—and the newest pictures are much better I think.

Aug 21.
Trying to come to grips with myself on canvas again after some time at the shore with Jeff and my family.

As far as working is concerned, I feel more changes coming. It's good to get away from it for a while. Helen's back and says the same—gives some kind of concentrated perspective.

Can't wait to smell Fall.

Aug. 31
Found Walt [Walter Silver, photographer] and peace and freedom to begin working intensely. Finished two pictures in the last couple of weeks which aren't much—too easily arrived at.

Have started to-day on a 6 ft x 7½ ft canvas—"The Hero" tentatively. Don't know what I want with it yet, but I'd like it to be rich and somber both—grays, browns, blacks maybe.

Sept 1
Working on "The Hero" with a gray end of summer wind banging the studio windows and doors.

Too much white—want to work some deep umber in.

Been painting my guts into this picture. Don't know if it's finished, but it has something good so far.

Sept 7
Been sitting and looking at "The Hero" for the last two hours and I still can't

make up my mind about it. I think the color is what bothers me—its too dead and arbitrary. But then I think color must come dynamically, as part of the painting process itself and not as an isolated aim.

The weather is wonderful, full and cool and golden. And I'm undeniably depressed by the thought of the next two weeks, working six days a week. This business of working seems so endless—wonder if I'll ever sell any of the damn pictures.

Sept. 12
"Hero" stinks, let's face it.

6 hours later. Not so bad now, but still needs work.

Sept 13
Waldemar [Waldemar Hansen, writer and friend of John Myers] for lunch, and to see the new work. He found it exciting and changed. Likes best (and I must agree) "Portrait of A." "The Blue G." and "The Cue." He also liked "Lemons" and found the deep roots of cubism somewhere under.

Working more on "The Hero" and it is coming well now I think.

Sept. 18
Still tremendous struggle to make Hero resolve. Haven't had enough time in the studio, to much working at job and honeymooning with Walt. As a result I become furious inside, and lash at the canvas as though it were to blame. I must come to know myself better.

Sept. 24
Back to painting again—what a strange picture this one is! I've been on it and nothing else for about a month now and it sure shows stress of some sort. I feel a picture must have a look of coming all at once, with ease—no matter how much struggle was involved. "Hero" certainly doesn't look "easy" at this stage!

Sept. 25
Worked all day yesterday and part of to-day on "The Hero," and now I think it is nearly there. It is harsh and strong. Not at all lyrical.

Oct 3

The last month and a half has been almost artistically sterile. I've been emotionally very happy with Walt, but I have worked at the Savoy too much, and I feel terribly pent-up and unrealized. I can't work on much to-day, I've been away so long it makes it difficult to walk in the studio cold and paint well. If the financial arrangement with Walt works out it will be the most ideal situation I've ever had.

I feel charged with all kinds of things. Seeing Goodnough's pictures was exciting—he is starting to construct with color and I am deeply interested. I find my own work lacking—"The Hero" is forced, I think. Maybe I can get on it again after this last week of the travel bureau is over. Bless Walt, he is doing more than even he knows.

Larry's [Larry Rivers, artist] show just opened and it is good, but still too eclectic. He has the stuff though—he'll paint wonderfully some time. He is of course the genius with John—wish J. wouldn't play us off one against the other as he does.

Oct 15

This is the beginning of something I guess—no more job "work"—as long as it's all right for Walt—I'll know if it's too much.

I just rubbed out the whole of "The Hero" which means I have *nothing* from the last two months. It makes me feel miserable, but I must hold on to myself, I know things will come now with all this time to work.

Oct 16

Working on some things which interest me—eliminating black and working with pure brilliant colors and a lot of white.

Oct 17

More work with blue, orange, yellow and white.

John Reed [photographer who had the studio underneath Hartigan's at 25 Essex Street] finds the new things "pleasant and charming enough but decorative." Sends chills of self-doubt through me, the more fool I.

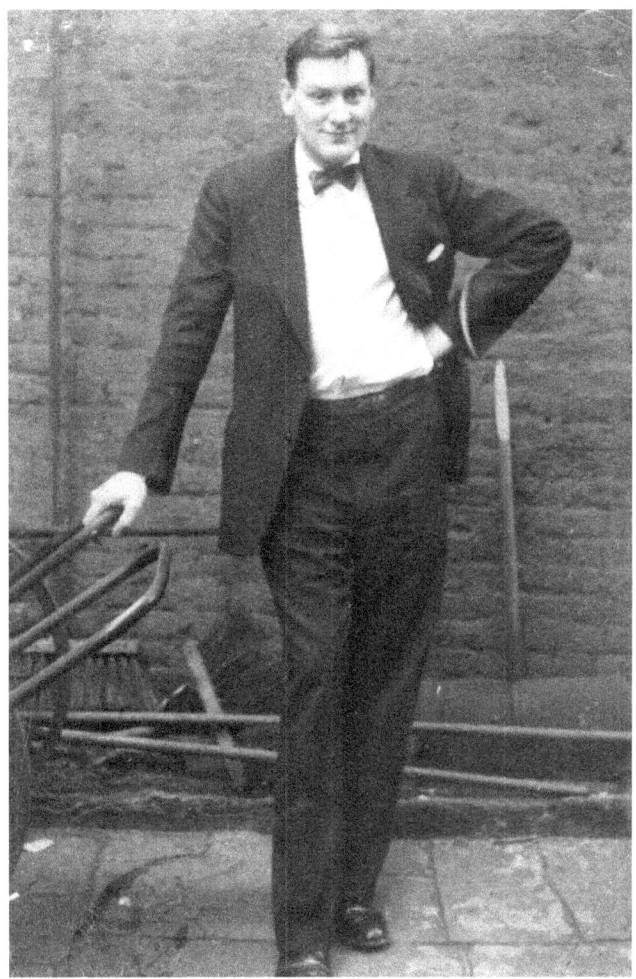

John Bernard Myers, the artistic director of the Tibor de
Nagy Gallery.

John [John Myers] just called to say Helen and I will be in the University of
Illinois annual.

Oct 23
I work every day now at painting, but everything is very very painful, so
painful its really impossible to write about it. I wonder if it has always been
such agony to paint searchingly. Helen, Al and I are all going through a crisis

at the same time—Helen to such an extent that she wants to give up painting entirely.

Oct 29
This last week of painting has been revolutionary for me. How I have changed specifically I can't tell, but I know for me the "all-over" picture is finished. It had become a formula and it took Clem to open my eyes. It isn't only a joke to say my "lyrical period" has ended—these new pictures have a different feel to them entirely, and I'm going to need all my strength to stand by them—I know their faults.

There are three new things, "Studio Landscape," "The Hero" and "Cat" of which I am most interested in "The Hero." I've learned from Picasso in it, and there's more to learn there.

Oct 30
The all over picture has died.

Repainting "The Cue."

Nov 1
"The Cue" is massive and monstrous now, and I'm absorbed in a "sculpture," if it can be called that.

Nov 6
These new things are still too knowing. I must reach somehow into the complete unknown for my search.

It is all very difficult.

The only way to discover oneself is to paint from the areas of blind, inspired feeling. How to reach into there is the problem. These new pictures are what I should have been doing months ago, now I must find what I should be doing now.

I must not paint pictures which are comforting to my eyes.

To shock the bourgeouis is easy—to shock the "avant-garde," that's the thing. To shock oneself is the most important of all.

I am nauseated with the expressionistic, the baroque, the active surface, the rhythmic. We must be massive and ugly to find something new.

Nov 9
Reworking and reworking over and over again. Of the whole time since spring I have only "The Blue G." and some small things left. Nothing is enough, nothing satisfies me. I think my show should best be called "Work in Progress".

Maybe "The Cue," "Pumpkin's World" "Cat" and "Iceland" are finished. Maybe.

Also "The Hero"? "Studio Landscape"?

Nov 14
"The Confidence Man"? "Paris, 1920"?

Have been stretching and sizing new canvas, and I'm going to try to leave these recent pictures alone until I get more perspective on them.

Nov 19
John believes that my "theme" is terror, which to me is provocative as an idea, but has nothing to do with painting.

Made more changes on "The Cue," I think it has a certain power now.

Saw Al's new pictures last week—he's working with religious themes—the new work is very strong and searching.

I think I've learned from the big Matisse retrospective, just what specifically I can't articulate as yet

Nov 21
"Pumpkin's World" now "The Horseman"

Nov 26
Back to facing white canvas, wondering what to impose on it, how to violate it.

Leaving alone the pictures that interest me—

"The Hero," "The Cue," "The Horseman" and "Paris, 1920."

"The Cue" doesn't come off as powerfully as its size demands, but I can't touch it again for a few days.

Pollock opens to-day, his work is in a new direction.

I must work and work on a canvas until the "subject" reveals itself. Then the picture resolves. Filled to-day with doubt.

Nov. 27
Pollock's new things are strange and powerful, but have little to do with what I'm working in.

Drawing to-day.

Nov. 28
My God how hard it is to paint.

Nov 30
Feel positive to-day, so painting is going well.

Pollock's pictures were scribbled on with ink—some mad artist-vandal wrote filth all over them and the walls. Powerful work brings violent reactions.

This 5½ ft x 6 ft canvas is in a good juicy stage. Hope I can bring it off with these maroons, pinks and blacks.

Dec 3.
At Helen's Saturday with the Pollock's, Clem, Barney Newman [artist] and Dzubas [Friedel Dzubas, artist]. Clem got on his kick of "women painters." Same thing—too easily satisfied, "finish" pictures, polish, "candy"; said Al, Larry and Goodnough all struggle. Makes me realize how alone I am. Am I to scream at him "I struggle too, I do! I do!" He said he wants to be the contemporary of the first great woman painter. What shit—he'd be the first to attack.

The issues are beginning to define themselves.

More changes on "The Cue".

Have three very strange "portraits" which interest me—and well along on the 5½ ft x 6 ft canvas.

Dec 4
The 5½ x 6—"Woman" is coming very strangely with a heavy-handed stylization.

Dec 6
"Woman" is finished except for a few more touches after it dries. It interests me very much.

Dec 11
"Cue," "Horseman," Hero, Paris 1920 and now Woman seem to hold up strongly. Still fondest of Horseman but is it because of the direction or just love as I loved "Months and Moons"?

Small things are as hard as ever for me. I do have a small "Red Sun" on wood which I like, also 3 or 4 drawings, but when I see Al's prolific and excellent mass of work, hundreds of collages and drawings I feel very strange and thwarted.

Dec 17
Very good day to-day, in spite of the bitter cold.

I'm working in ski clothes. Finished "Woman," also a nice smaller picture which I think I'll strip along with "Red Sun" and take up to the gallery. *Maybe John can sell one.* Also am pleased with one or two of the recent drawings.

Dec 27
Back to work again after Xmas, which for some reason (except for Walt) seemed especially dismal this year.

Now that I see it with fresh eyes I don't feel satisfied with "Woman".

The Paris show [show selected by gallery owner Leo Castelli that included Hartigan's *Paris, 1920*] is on at Janis [the Janis Gallery] before leaving for France. John is in a dither because Goodnough's picture is hung way in the office—just another indication of the increased jealousy and hatred and pettiness we must be prepared for.

Dec 31
May now have finished "Woman"—also small picture "Black Widow." Tomorrow, 1952.

Journal for 1952

Jan 2, 1952
A deadening day in the country yesterday at the West-Herma's [Penny West, a painter, and her husband] with John, Tibor, Larry, Jane [Jane Freilicher, artist], Al and Walt and the dull bunch out there. Could have been fun, but the atmosphere is so heavy and almost anti-art, real alive art, that everyone was depressed beyond hope.

For the new year, the resolution must be harder work, and more and more search and courage.

I think what I need now is a huge canvas to involve and lose myself in. I'd like to do a "massacre" and I'm making a few sketches from Delacroix—then lots of drawings of my own.

May do sets for the Living Theater, would be fun if I could have my own way.

Jan 5
Pen and gouache drawings for "Massacre" in between nursing Al at his studio through a siege of flu.

Jan 7
Bought from Al yesterday a 7 ft x 12 ft canvas for the Massacre. Will tack it up and glue it to-day. I intend to make many drawings along the way. Al was very excited by the recent ones.

"Woman" too facile, going to mess it up now. "Black Widow" doesn't make it yet.

Later:
Did some things with Woman which are awkward but quite interesting—will look at it a while now.

Filled with the excitement which comes before beginning a new, big canvas.

Jan 9
The big canvas is gleaming white and formidable.

Did another study this morning—Death. Had thought of beginning the painting with line drawing—but think setting the color idea would be more freeing as a beginning. I think of pea greens, yellow greens, pink greys, black, a lot of white and some blues.

I think this will be a very important painting for me—a real change in direction. I find the things of mine which interest me most now are those dealing in some sense with the "subject" or "object." A very difficult thing to pursue after the painting of the last 25 years.

Later:
Work went well to-day, the sketch is there, stated in big simple terms.

Jan 11
Everything coming with the greatest amount of difficulty and confusion.

Later—
I musn't be too impatient—it's really going as well as I could expect this soon.

Jan 15
Massacre in a state of juicy chaos.

Joan Mitchell's [artist] show yesterday—a fantastic display of youthful talent and virtuosity, without the real thing.

Jan 16
M. coming well to-day, but still too baroque and active—Must feel through to Simplicity. It might help if I could turn it upside down, but it's impossible to do alone.

Jan 17
Been working on M. all day in a white heat, really blind, and now that I see what's there I'm stunned. Could this be I? It seems all the things I hate—the activity, the brushing, impressionistic borrowings—like Rivers and De Niro [Robert De Niro Sr., artist], but with more horror. This is now in this stage like "Woman"—I don't know what to think.

As I look more, there is one thing I like—the massive weights in some of the movements.

Jan 23

Ill again, strangely unlike my usual healthy self. We're all so self-conscious about neuroses these days—I look for the roots there, with no results.

Goodnough opened yesterday in the rain, a strange quiet opening with only a few artists, writers and Leo [Leo Castelli]. I realize now how far apart our work is, and although I know his is strong and may be plastically sounder than mine I can't get excited as before.

"Pure" painting à la New York School just doesn't excite me these days, and in a way I feel alone in my direction except for about three of Al's new pictures. But then he too goes off on a pure kick like Barney Newman—this all black business—What in hell I'm driving at I dont know.

Massacre looks horrifyingly bad, I'm drinking coffee for strength to take it off the wall and turn it around, what madness.

Jan. 24

Much work yesterday and this morning on M. Now I see Matisse in it, but if I must go to him for my need for Simplicity, so be it. I was weaned on him anyhow. We must use what we must, and not be afraid. Strange new picture "Portrait of W." on top of "Studio Landscape."

Jan. 29

Walt here re-wiring studio. Likes "Portrait of W." and "Massacre". M. holds up well, except for upper left hand corner. Into it with some black, when that dries will try white drawing. Starting plans for show—maybe will show after group show in March if Bouché [René Bouché, illustrator for *Vogue* magazine] is smart enough to withdraw this year.

Working on base of sculpture to show in group. Sculpture I think I'll call "The House."

Dwight [Dwight Ripley, financial backer of the Tibor de Nagy Gallery] is withdrawing help at the end of the season—lean days ahead for the gallery. Still, Newman, Rothko, Pollock all leaving Parsons [the Parsons Gallery]. The Club [both a loose association of New York School artists and the place at which they gathered for discussions and programs] split in bickering factions—all those middle-aged, bitter, tired painters. I feel wonderfully alive and strong in spite of it all.

Feb. 4
Painting incredibly bad to-day, feel emptied since I've finished Massacre and Portrait of W.

Most of to-day on odds and ends, destroyed all the small pictures and one larger as well as half of the recent drawings. Don't want to settle for less than what I have in the big ones. Al over Sunday. Walt photographed us talking. He liked Massacre very much.

Good talk with Waldemar last night about technique versus concept, conscious control versus automatic creation.

Walt is looking for a job. I may have to work for a month to raise show expenses. The thought depresses me terribly.

Destroyed "Woman." It was awful.

Feb. 7
Much showing of work yesterday to C. Coggeshall [Calvert Coggeshall, art collector], who was a bit put off by them at first (except for Portrait of W.), but then showed a restrained enthusiasm for Massacre.

Helen, Al and Walt later—Helen very enthusiastic. Trying to-day for a good ink drawing from M. to use on my catalogue. Concerned with the problem of the scale of small pictures.

March 5
A whole month gone and I haven't even lifted a brush. Worked three weeks at a clerical job that was a miracle of stupidity, all the time low, really despairing. And now we're more broke than ever, but both agree it's impossible to live with me when I'm not painting.

Helped Al hang the group show of drawings and sculpture—that plaster thing of mine "The House" is in it. I must without modesty say it is the most daring piece there. Al's big figure is strong and emotional, but traditional in the direction of Giacometti. All of Larry's are unbearably lyric. No one is doing enough, daring enough, *including me!*

I am appalled when I look at these pictures how far they are from what I feel I must do—and I'm showing in less than three weeks! Massacre has something I must admit, but it's far, far from enough.

March 10

Consumed all last week with doubts and horrors. Constant deadening sense of dissatisfaction with my work, but I musn't let it inhibit me so completely. Al, Larry, Jane, Frank [Frank O'Hara, poet], Joan Mitchell and I spoke at the Club Friday night with John as moderator. It was rather violent and after Al made some of his typically brazen gestures as "I invented painting", Charlie Egan [gallery owner] almost had apoplexy and rushed up to hit him. I was overwhelmed with the bitter aloneness of all of us, which I may have expressed in some of my remarks. And I am just now recovering from the nervous tensions of opening yourself before so many people.

Frank wrote me a tender and moving poem—I feel like the flower-girl to-day a little, the air has a hint of that March ice thaw.

Poem for a Painter

The ice of your imagination lends
an anchor to the endless sea of pain,
a harsh cry to the dumb smack who's again
caught in the pitiless tide of hot ends.

Such a trough as I'm in! blind in the rain
the minotaur, hero, struggles. Embrace
engulfs him, and no Muse but the whore. Grace,
you are the flowergirl on the candled plain
with fingers smelled of turpentine. New Year
be shouted, but not by serious you.
Sea and engine crash on the hapless ear

but your ice holds fast, willed art in a nest
of worlds. Hold fast this vessel as your guest,
for fiery spindrift tears me into view.

The text of this poem is taken from page eighty of *The Collected Poems of Frank O'Hara* (Berkeley and Los Angeles: University of California Press, 1995, by arrangement with Alfred A. Knopf, Inc.) edited by Donald Allen. It is used with the permission of Maureen Granville-Smith, administratrix of the estate of Frank O'Hara.

∼

Could something be done with the theme of sudden death?

I'm terribly concerned with scale of all size pictures now.

Stretching and stripping pictures for my show. I feel as though I'm dressing corpses to be laid out.

It is wonderful to be free once more, even if it is freedom to suffer.

March 12
Can't seem to get to work. Took photos of pictures last night. To-morrow Goodnough coming to review show for Art News. Also Helen, Clem and Waldemar to look.

March 14
My back is breaking from working on strips all day. Saw Picasso's "Desire" last night which was a real sex circus, a lot of fun.

Goodnough here yesterday an hour late, which made for general chaos, also annoyed by Harry's presence—that phoniness that he wears like a cloud around him. Pseudo-masculinity, pseudo-directness, pseudo-seriousness— he's a mess! Clem liked Massacre and Portrait of W. very much—but there is a way in which the most powerful painters are the ones he feels the least for (me, Al, Bob [Bob Goodnough]). He seems to get most "sent" by Rivers, Harry, and that master of mediocrity, Dzubas. Sometimes I think he recognizes in Pollock only his most surface qualities. Pollock is set against us now, guess he feels threatened. We're all against each other in some sad way.

Helen mad about picture which I formerly called "Woman" that I've worked on again. Going to look at it a while, I don't know about it.

Still have drawings to frame and catalogues to send out. Also stretchers for the two big pictures.

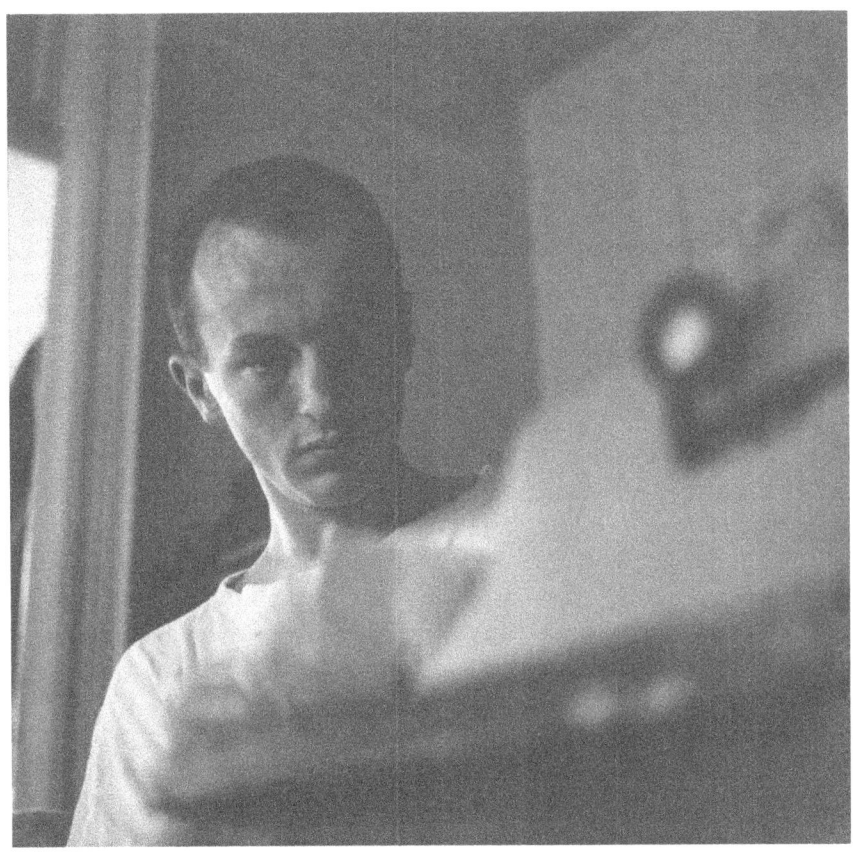
Frank O'Hara at his typewriter. Photograph by Walter Silver.

March 21
Only a few days to the show, and I do have many namable and un-namable anxieties.

The catalog is good-looking, the drawing worked out especially well.

Helen has just backed out of helping me hang the show—she and Clem want to see the Vienna pictures in Philadelphia. Makes me a little bitter when I remember all the help I gave her at her show.

Yesterday Frank was here to see the pictures and have lunch. He's writing something on Al, Bob [Goodnough], Larry, Jane and me. The day was spring magic in a way, and we had a real rapport on some rare levels.

Then Waldemar and I went to the flower show in the evening which was un-excelled mad bourgeois vulgarity. All those obscene forced flowers. We had a close sad talk over coffee later.

March 29

In a way this is the end of a year. I am thirty and my show is hanging. Any kind of "success" as far especially as sales are concerned seems farther away than ever. At least I'm not completely dependent on sales, Walt doesn't quite make enough to keep the studio going but it's a terrific relief that he does so much. As far as the show is concerned, I have done it and now I'm anxious to get back to painting. If nothing sells I'll have to go to work for a while again to pay Gonzalo [art photographer] and Berkeley [art movers].

One thing I feel is a concentration of a nucleus—Al, Bob [Goodnough] and me—Larry, Jane, Waldemar, Frank and John Ashbery [poet]. I am upset about Helen for in the rejection of Clem I feel that she will go too. Clem dealt the death blow after my opening with his proclamation that Harry is the greatest American painter since Pollock. What's this greatest and less great business anyhow? A horrifying way to judge at any time but especially now when everything is so difficult and painful. The idea of some kind of com-petition is terribly destructive. I think Clem has proved himself completely irresponsible. This is the worst thing that could ever happen to Harry—he overestimates his talent as it is.

≈

Stuart Preston had this commentary on the show in the *New York Times* on 30 March 1952: "George Hartigan, showing ebullient canvases, large and small, at the de Nagy Gallery finds artistic salvation in generous swabs of handsomely harmonized color which loop and frolic in and out of each other. She is a good hand with the brush but the pen-and-ink drawings are rather niggling."

≈

March 31

Back to work, with fresh doubts. The show is going very slowly so far, no sales, poor attendance. It's hard to realize that I must face all the old strug-gles all over again—ignorance, animosity and worse of all apathy from the

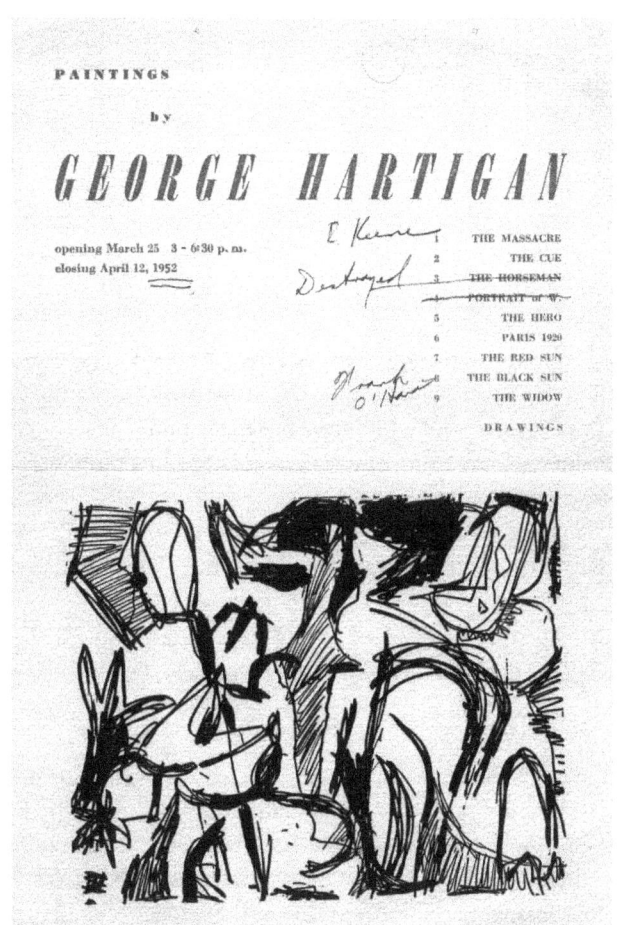

The cover of the catalog from Hartigan's one-person
show at the Tibor de Nagy Gallery in March of 1952.

public—bitterness and jealousy from the artists. Even among ourselves petti-
nesses and bickerings. On top of all this one's own torments and weaknesses,
what a horror it is.

I wonder what I learned from the show? Something about color—use of yellow and red, don't know what. A lot about content, less and less interested
in "pure" painting. I am a bit pleased with the small drawings. "The Massacre"
holds up well, but in some ways it sprawls too much. "The Cue" still looks all

right, but as Barney [Barnett Newman] said it's too expressionistic. "Portrait of W" is a blind alley.

I really loathe expressionist painting down to the last splashy brush stroke. There is something about Matisse—In the end though all these ideas mean nothing—you have to paint your way through it. No rules, I must be free to paint anything I feel.

April 1
Maybe what I want aside from more "content" or meaning is more architecture in painting. Something like art for the museums as Cezanne said. I do want a certain stillness about a picture—but emotionally meaningfull. All very difficult since when strong emotion begins to show obviously then the work becomes expressionism.

Looking at Seurat reproductions, enchanted by the vibrant "stillness" of the form.

Destroyed all yesterday's work and to-days. Intensely dissatisfied.

April 2
Working now with a theme, as I did with "Massacre," hoping something will come that way. Doing drawings on [Randall] Jarrell's poem "The Knight, Death and the Devil" which in turn was based on Durer's engraving. No reason why painting shouldn't be premeditated and sustained in this particular way, with every license to change and leave the sketches of course.

A great difference between the "expressionistic" and the "baroque."

April 3
Drawing more to-day, not too well. Most interested in "The Knight" which I did yesterday.

Strange how old hat the extreme can look when the basis isn't firm enough. Thinking of Josés [de Rivera] sculpture—he sent me a catalog. How he loathes the "humanistic" in art. All that Bauhaus business is so dead. It's a mistake to try to be new, "up-to-date."

Goodnough's review of my show came out in Art News with a reproduction of "Portrait of W." Looks good. The review is serious with a good point made about the brushing. I do feel most of these pictures are history for me. I'm facing the unknown again, the pain of it all.

⁓

Robert Goodnough made these remarks in the April 1952 issue of *Art News* after seeing Grace Hartigan's second Tibor de Nagy show: "*The Cue* curves and twists paint over the surface of a 12-foot canvas, opening into swelling movements that lead the eye from one side to the other and back, giving one a sense of strength and considered mood. Similar in treatment, but even more decided and better in color is the flamboyant *The Hero,* rough and sturdy and carrying the feeling of a strong image-in-the-making directly to the edges of the canvas. Characteristic of these paintings is the feeling that each area is given equal consideration and importance. *Portrait of W.* is more quiet, the brushwork is not so evident, having disappeared in a further search for mass relationships which resolve into reserved fullness that continues to be refreshing."

⁓

April 8
Spent most of yesterday at the Met seeing the Cezanne show. I am filled with it, and the overwhelming need to make my own work more solid. They all talk of Cezanne these days—the Club—but in a way that's so dry. I am most interested in the bather pictures, the large one and all the small ones. He was doing something there—the way he opened up a back for instance. I want to use this in some way. I want to draw from him as well as from Rubens, Delacroix, Breughel and of course Titian and Tintoretto. I tried to see some of my favorites yesterday but they are all put away while the Met is being re-done. I must go again Monday and look at that Delacroix—also the small Seurat study. I have a book of Rembrandt drawings which are wonderful though I must admit of all the things at the Met only the little Bathsheba really excites me.

I'd like to try painting cool blues, greens, greys, black and white for a while.

April 9
I am feeling a little bitter right now. Not one sale, and again the problem of working at a job to pay debts—we [Hartigan and Silver] owe to-gether about $400 or $500—my disillusionment with Helen and Clem, my disgust with all my paintings. And that seductive monster Spring wanting me to hope all

over again. It takes more than a lifetime to paint, and then all these added anxieties!

I've been making some small drawings from Cezanne—what a genius! But I must put him aside when I face the canvas or I'm completely inhibited.

April 10
Making nothing but muddy, awkward messes, what agony. It's as though I'd forgotten how to paint. Anxieties, doubts, unrest.

Two drawings—"The Knight" and "Death" One painting study—"The Devil."

April 11
Painting on "Death, The Knight and The Devil." I hate what comes out of me but there it is—a nightmare of messy brushwork.

Good Friday—I feel myself crucified to-day.

April 14
All morning at the Met, seeing Cezanne again.

The big pictures are back from the gallery this afternoon—what a farce.

D, The K & the D doesn't look too bad to me.

April 18
Tuesday I begin work at a drafting job for about two months. It means giving up painting entirely for that period, but I hope to save enough money to paint without interruption thru the whole summer. One thing it will do which is good at this time—cut off daily phone conversations with John, hence all gossip and petty arguments, involvements in politics of the stinking art world. I'll see a few people in the evening from time to time and generally try to mull over what I feel about my working direction. Feel a need to cut myself off from everything.

The "Fifteen Americans" show [exhibition at the Museum of Modern Art] is mediocre—I must have been blind all along about Pollock. There is no doubt that all that business has watered down, it seems empty to me.

June 2
The nightmare is over for a while and I'm back to work. I feel strange in the studio, the host turned somehow into guest.

It's good to be with myself again, terrifying but at least the terrors are my own, and not those of the outer world. I'm in complete chaos about painting, what to do, where to begin again? Al and I were saying this last night—he hasn't painted since his marriage. He intends to start on an 11 ft x 11 ft canvas, but I feel that wouldn't help me any longer. I do need a prop in some way, perhaps it will be "nature."

June 3
Sketched from the model last night at Larry's. I think it's good for me again and I'm interested in what is coming out. My approach is far different from the others—Nell [Nell Blaine, artist], Larry, de Niro, Jane, Leatrice [Leatrice Rose, painter]—the remnants of the European impressionist and expressionist tradition. I may be subjective, but if this is all the exploring that the younger artists are going to do then I haven't much hope for painting. I feel alone.

Oil study from Titian.

June 4
Bought paint—still the canned crap, can't afford better. Also chicken wire, plaster and wire cutters Going to work on a "sculpture."

June 5
Sculpture yesterday, painting to-day.

The usual difficulties.

June 6
Painting small oil from Tiepolo's "Trojan Horse."

I don't know what I'm after but whatever it is, if I must look conservative—reactionary—timid—or even (horrors) feminine—in the process then it must be. I think I know how really strong I am, and if a great painter like Matisse could paint weakly and timidly to clear his eyes for what was to come then I can too. I don't fear painting a bad picture or a weak one now. Oh, the mystery of the image. Nature, you monster you. I was on the edge of sucumbing to the need of looking "modern"—abstract—contemporary.

All of which is fashion, not painting, and is most dangerous.

The Tiepolo didn't come off yet but St Serapion (after Zurburan) has something I think.

June 9
St Serapion still looks interesting this morning, terribly awkward.

Worked more on The Knight, Death, and the Devil. I must say it's a peculiar picture. In spite of my ideas and dreams of a calm painting I am far from it. I suppose it takes years to achieve a real calm—look what Cezanne went through.

I feel the tremendous need for self-discipline and I'm painting from reproductions. Not with deep space, but certainly not flat or even as up to the surface as my own work has been. I'm filled with enthusiasm, this has been a good day. I feel I've learned a great deal.

June 10
Worked more on oil study from Rubens. Now reworking The K, D, & D with more fidelity to the engraving.

June 12
Finished The Knight, Death and the Devil. I like it but fear I couldn't exhibit it. Very puzzled as to my motives, but feel I must trust my instincts. Want to attempt something from nature directly, will try the little park and trees with passersby from the front window.

June 13
D, K & D bothers me—I think it's still too "all-over," an idea which I must discard while still maintaining a picture up to the surface.

That's why St Serapion is good, also the drawings I've been doing from the model. They keep an image but strongly hold the surface at the same time. Will work more on D K & D with this in mind.

The idea of painting from the window is definitely out for me—at least now anyhow. It's too confusing.

The way D K & D is in this stage I may as well ask Larry and Jane over and we three can sign it. I think I should work from more architectural repro-ductions at this time. My romanticism is so strong I needn't encourage it. Boticelli might be good—Poussin also.

June 16
Worked more this morning on K D & D—it still doesn't have that coming to-gether that would make it live. Must leave it alone for a while now. Working on a Boticelli "Venus."

June 17
Been staring at K D & D. It seems tight and "closed" compared with the free-dom, boldness and openness of "The Massacre." But it has a tenseness which interests me. I have felt that Massacre sprawls too much.

June 20
I feel to-day like Conrad after he finished "Nostromo"—after it he could think of nothing more to write. I can't go on and on painting after the masters—but as long as I'm feeling the pictures I guess it will run its own course.

Jane, Larry, John Myers, John Ashbery, Jimmy Schuyler [poet] and Frank were over Wednesday and were very enthusiastic, particularly over K D & D. Larry and I had quite an argument over the spatial solution of the bottom part of St Serapion—but I think he was arguing falsely from his own timidity. I'm not interested in pat spacial solutions. I'd rather have something which interests me even if it doesn't work well.

I'm in a dilemma over the Rubens Tribute Money which I'm working on now. I don't know quite how to treat the heads—there is a tremendous implication in painting a face, I can't deny it.

It was in April 1948 that I left Ike [Ike Muse, Hartigan's first art teacher]. Ever since then—four years—I've been painting away from "nature," non-objectively almost. So I am now faced with an overwhelming strangeness and difficulty. Guilt too, I suppose. The "am I modern" fear, worry that I'm sucumbing to outside influences (Larry, Jane, de Kooning), these worries are ego difficulties of course, but there are more plastic worries.

I'm making a small oil now from the photo of Helen and me laughing. The great problem is how to keep the heads away from caricature and expression-ism, and in the realm of true moving painting. Al solved that so well in his "Christ Dead" and the numerous self-portraits. Paint, not line, is one of the clues. I may visit the Frick and Met later to-day and study some paintings.

June 23
Just ordered 5 yards of 5′ duck Have several plans for paintings but have reached the end of my canvas. Like to do a "Carousel" picture about as large as "Months and Moons" with some of the horror I feel about "fun." Also want to do a large male nude based on the O'Hara drawings, a painting of the Terrible Angel from Rilke, and a dancer something maybe on the ballet "The Cage."

June 24
Started the O'Hara painting to-day. I was lying awake thinking of it last night and became eager to get at it. Didn't have any canvas the right size so I turned "Sacuda" from Mexico over and am painting this on the reverse side.

June 30
Haven't painted since Barbara Guest [poet] was over. Walt and I have been sick with food poisoning of some sort. I've become unbearably restless and it feels good now to be in the studio.

Saw the "Demoiselles d'Avignon" again at the Mod. Museum and something clicked, who knows what.

Must work a lot more on the O'Hara figure.

The Molyneux collection has some breath taking tiny Renoirs. It's unbeliev-able that he could get so much on so small a surface. I think it takes great maturity and control. The 15 Americans upstairs looked terribly sprawling and empty.

Must get more architecture in my painting.

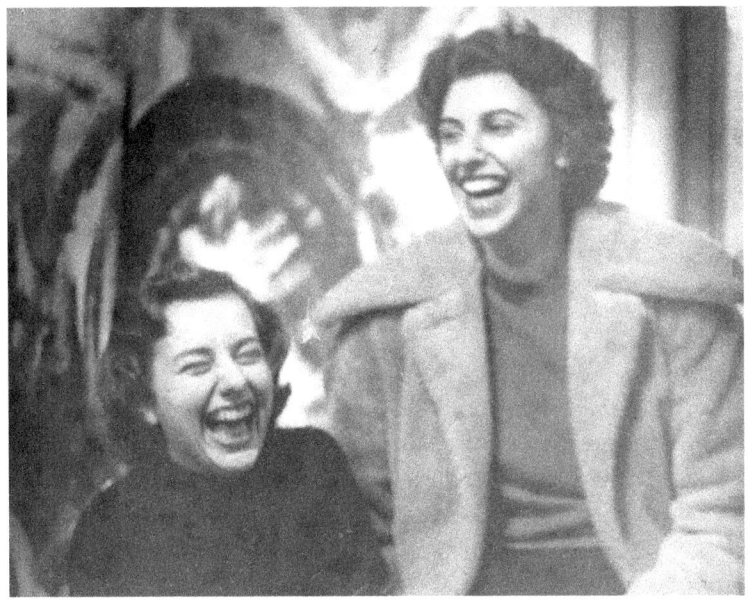
Hartigan and Helen Frankenthaler mugging for the camera.
Photograph by Walter Silver.

Another thing I found through a talk with de Kooning is that what I'm looking for in my painting is my "world," my content. It's a very serious thing, and
I must have time to be quiet with myself in order to find it. In a way I understand why Al and Esta [Esta Leslie, Al Leslie's wife] have retreated so. It is
impossible to keep one's stability in the midst of other people's chaotic lives.

July 9
Working on a drawing—"Terrible Angel." I think it is the only theme of
those I listed previously of which I could make something. The others are
too specific to allow play. The carousel theme might work out because I feel
a possibility of strangeness involved. But I believe now that I can't work
directly with nature, that all the clues are indirect and finding them will be
the process of a lifetime. I could do the O'Hara picture because it isn't Frank,
it's a symbol of something else for me, I don't know what. Such things as demons, gods, death, heroes, devils, saints—the 'themes' that were used before
"genre" painting came in are more my "world." This is one thing Al and I have
in common, although I think it is absolutely unconcious with him. This way
we're different from Jane, Larry, Helen, Harry, and also from de Kooning,

Twarkov [Jack Twarkov, painter]. This is apart from plastic considerations of course—these are impossible to discuss truly, and any attempt to do so ends up in the dryest kind of classroom jargon.

I don't mean by this that I'm interested in "lofty" themes, but that when I try to paint a specific person, incident or place I feel too restricted, too bound to *it* (the idea) and not to the painting. This is all very well but now where to begin?

Beethoven once said "I dread the beginning of these large works. Once into the work and it goes." I feel the same about the start of a painting. I'm attempting a "Hunt" on the Rubens' wolf-hunt. The thing for me now is to know from the start of a painting what each thing "is"—ie a wolf hunter, horse, dog, etc. Then from there I can go deeper and deeper into myself.

July 11
"Who, if I cried out, would hear me among the angelic orders?

Beauty is nothing but the beginning of Terror we're still just able to bear." [from "The First Elegy" of the *Duino Elegies* of Rainer Maria Rilke]

July 14
I have a pornographic photograph in which two men are wearing masks. It gives the most peculiar aura, like an Ensor painting. Too bad his show isn't on now, I think I could get much more from it. In a way his horror sense was his limitation rather than his release, he became more involved with his source than he was with the painting itself.

The heat is oppressive to-day, but I have a feeling I want to open up the "figures" in this "hunt" painting so I intend to work in spite of it.

PM
I feel like a mother who has given birth to an idiot—I know it lives so I can't destroy it—but I hate it.

July 17
Been much too self-conciously analytical about painting and subject material lately. What interests me at this time is finding my "subject." It's important to keep working, the problems will resolve better that way.

Its been so hot I've felt lethargic, but now I'm working on a painting of John Ashbery, hoping to get away from the violence and "expressionism" of "The Hunt."

July 21
Walt came down to the studio with me for lunch, and was struck by the "ugliness" of the newest pictures. Also by their complete "unsaleability." He makes it so fortunate for me that I don't have to worry about sales—it would ease the pressure of course if I sold from time to time. But he said it would only mean "little luxuries"—which I certainly am only too willing to do without as long as I have all my time free.

God knows how long it will be before I sell anything. Even after Walt so carefully built up the sale of "Rough Ain't It" (such an easy picture to like!), the girl's husband couldnt stand the sight of it in the house.

Aug. 8
Back from a week at the shore with Jeff and my family. It was sweet to be with Jeff, but my parents are impossible. I had forgotten just how impossible. I was in a strangely withdrawn trance-like state the whole time, without a single intense thought or feeling. A kind of protective shell, so that I could bear it. Amazing in the American middle-class the worship of the "extrovert" personality. Mother tries to force this on Jeff when he is a naturally shy and gentle child.

Frank came for lunch last week before I left, and we spent a wonderful few hours to-gether. He liked his picture, and it must have liked him, it looks so solid to-day.

I am at a bit of a loss again, but may do a large blue bather thinking of the Cezanne and Matisse paintings. Also a carnival, or carousel or something of the sort. I looked a lot for this theme last week.

Beginning to feel tremendous money pressures again. The apartment rent isn't paid, we owe $30.00 to the gas company and they're turning off service next week—$15.00 to the phone co. and I haven't paid Berkeley yet. If something doesn't happen with Walt I will have to go to work again. If I could be more house-wify and practical it might be better—we're down to our last ten dollars and last night I made broiled sweet breads and had a French

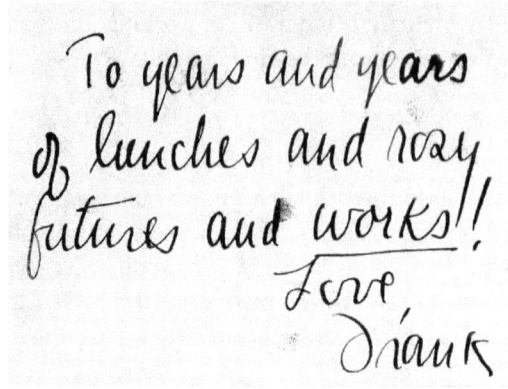

Note from Frank O'Hara to Hartigan,
enclosed with a gift of *Paterson* by William
Carlos Williams. The note and the book were
cherished by Hartigan.

red bordeaux for dinner. May as well go broke with a flourish—remember Fitzgerald!

Frank sent me Paterson of William Carlos Williams with a charming note. It strikes home terrifically and I feel very close to it.

Starting a bather on half of the blue painting I had in the New Generation show. I feel that the sacrifice is well worth it. It was a very beautiful picture but not interesting enough to keep.

Aug. 11
Painting on the blue bather and writing a prose poem. The bather is my most eclectic picture to date, but it's good and sturdy.

Overwhelmed by Frank's poems. The one of me ["Portrait of Grace"] makes me feel as though I exist now. I get so confused about myself, as though only the paintings are real. This poem makes me have an existence.

A thousand happy mirrors are fighting to be seen.

PORTRAIT OF GRACE

Her spinning hair webbed lengthening through
amber silk, where the colored plaster and laughter
find division.
                    Silently, the presence spills
its inviolable distances into the studio. Blue.
Most remote white of a mountain range in hours
of weeping. The trees are felled,
they fed that silken mesh. And now to ocean,
the roses grow. The plated ordure that sings
its dust into the feet, it shall be snow; she bears
no memory like a mast, nowhere becalmed, enraged,
no spear.
                    If each thing become crystal,
"I'll not construct that flaw," to be beauty itself,
then must she take forests in her arms of water
and disappear behind us, while we greet that clarity
of sunrise which is woman's praise, so ripe
in its begrudging. She does not falter, she has gone.

She will darken, decisive as a light bulb, when
the building crumbles. She had thought herself tough,
but now each day, trembling and cloudy she sighs,
feathered, for that virginity which seeks her out.
The harp would flee her pale fingernails,
but the sea may flatten into a smile before she's done
with those bruisings.
                    She has not a natural voice.
She's not a star.
                    She has ridden sidesaddle to churches,
is no frequenter of palace or barn. Now
celebrate her, for that light which is anguish will
again and again illumine her our shores, coming to her
as a downy bird, but she will not forget the eagle.
Her eyes are not glass children. Let not that firebrand
stolen from the summits mark her brow.

The text of this poem is taken from pages eighty-seven and eighty-eight of *The Collected Poems of Frank O'Hara* (Berkeley and Los Angeles: University of California Press, 1995, by arrangement with Alfred A. Knopf, Inc.) edited by Donald Allen. It is used with the permission of Maureen Granville-Smith, administratrix of the estate of Frank O'Hara.

∾

Aug. 15
"After all, the nature of truth is this—one's life work might end up called "A Trip to the Zoo".—James Schuyler

Aug. 18
For some reason I feel completely dry and empty. I don't know whether to force myself to work or not in these periods. If I do, what comes out seems to lack the "magic."

The blue bather seems finished—it is an oddity compared with the other pictures. Whatever these pictures are there is one thing they are not—"genre" painting. How I dislike intimate pictures. Matisse in his best pictures is never cozy, he always puts you off.

The weather is singing to-day, while I drink iced coffee and stew and fret over money and painting.

Aug. 19
I feel it might be good if I involved myself in a large painting project, the amusement park or fun idea I've had. I may work it on top of the Horseman, which never really did come off for its size. I'd like to work on this a long time, making many drawings and studies as it evolves—I want it to have a lot in it, yet not be too active. I think of yellows and greys.

Aug. 22
Stopped after beginning "Carousel" to work for temporary employment service for three or so weeks as a receptionist. It's ironic, but in a way it finishes off this dying summer and when I emerge from the trance it will be my weather, fall. Walt has a good job now so this may mean the last I work for a good while.

Sept. 22
This period of outside work wasn't so bad or else I was much calmer. It will

take so long to paint what I must paint that a month away doesn't seem to matter. And now another season has begun.

I've been spending a half reflective, half bustling day around the studio. I have a half-formed feel for where I'm going—some things remain to be revealed, I still need to "tense up" my work in some way it's hard to describe what I mean. I want to paint smaller pictures and to draw a lot, some from Bosch—he is very important to me now. But I *don't* see him the way the surrealists did.

In the last letter from Waldemar he says "the sooner I regard my writing not as suicide or shutting a final door, but the only world I have in which I can bring some sort of order and meaning—so much the sooner will I have chosen my destiny instead of waiting for it to choose me."

Such true words. I think I've eliminated all other motives from my work other than that of painting itself, my world in which I must bring my kind of order. From now on I must find what *my* order is.

The last time Larry was here he asked me while looking at the Ashbery painting, whether the figure was sitting down. I said I didnt know—and he told Frank later that he found it incredible that I didn't, that I had after all made the figure so I must know if it sat or not. I could only say that I'm making paintings, not humans, but what's the use—it points up the abyss between that kind of thinking (or seeing) and mine.

Many things are different this year. I feel really connected with my direction, and close to only three people, none of them painters—Walt, Waldemar and Frank. The gallery has some serious problems but I can't actively involve myself any more. It looks like a withdrawn, work-filled winter ahead for me.

Sept. 23—1952
I have temporarily abandoned the large Carousel ptg. that I started last month. I want for a while to see if I can paint smaller pictures—when they are *all* large, the true significance of a big canvas is lost—ie the "big" picture, a "work," a "masterpiece" I'm far from ready for a summing up—I scarcely know what I'm about yet.

Sept 29
Suffering lately from such overwhelming doubts that I find it difficult to write. In a constant state of depression.

Sept 30
I am suspicious of the paintings from the last several days. (Six O'Clock, Maharaja #2, & Dido) They came so quickly and easily, with so little struggle that it seems they couldn't possibly be any good. They must sit for a while before I know what I feel about them. Even then what will I know?

Oct. 1
Interested in using extreme contrasts, jet black to white white—but the problem of transitions is difficult, the white tends always to jump or to surface itself. It's the greatest fault in the O'Hara picture. These two recent small pics are getting at it—through agitation of the paint surface things stay of one piece—this however is an impressionist solution, and one I'm not satisfied with. I may find some help in the Spanish painters—Velasquez, Zurburan, Goya when I visit the Rembrandt show Friday.

I have criticized de Kooning for overworking a painting, but oversimplifying is just as great a crime—look at Avery [Milton Avery, painter] for a horrible example.

I used to feel that the only authentic creative emotion was a kind of blind, inspired rapture—I still believe that this is sublime but there can also exist a much cooler working condition, a kind of calm knowing that I've experienced lately as never before.

Oct. 2.
Waldemar here, particularly excited by the O'Hara picture. Every thing looked terrible to me in spite of his enthusiasm. Feel as though I must take another start. Working on two "academic" portraits—one of myself & one of Jeff. I don't know why, just have to do them.

Dido needs much more work—in fact I may destroy it entirely, 6:00 & Maharaja #2 stand, but they aren't much.

Oct. 6.
During the forum for WNYC on Saturday, I became filled with the sense of

alienation—all the gallery artists were there but Goodnough, and any sense of rapport I may have had with anyone has vanished. Oddly enough a few notes of sympathy were struck with Fairfield [Fairfield Porter, artist]—and a few, very few with Al. But I find his childish "attitudizing" too much to take right now. At one point they all paid the most disgusting homage to some of the older painters—de Kooning, Pollock, Newman, Rothko etc. It seemed so servile that I had to strike a note for Edward Hopper—who really does interest me at the moment. But I am in such a state of change that I feel anything I might say could have no lasting value.

Harry said a few good things about "felt" painting, but so pompously! I felt strangely that the only people there who hadn't "sold out" part of themselves to other interests were, beside myself, Al, Jane, Fairfield—and oddly enough, Larry! He does try to be corrupt, but there is something so real in spite of it all.

This is a strange and difficult time for me. I feel as though I'm getting the first pieces of a jigsaw puzzle about myself, but I don't know where to put them yet.

To add irony to irony, I've been elected a member of the painters club!

Not displeased with the start of the seated male & female figures over "Dido"—I'd like it lower in key, with strong greys, yellows & browns.

Oct 8.
Rather than doubt those time when painting goes well I should probably be deeply grateful—for all too soon afterwards comes terrible uncertainty, and a kind of fumbling agony.

Thinking of the "vanguard" artist, I believe one of the essential qualities is an unceasing unrest. I can hear my mother, ever since I was a child, saying "Grace you're so dissatisfied—so restless!" My greatest curse and greatest *potential* asset, all in one.

I have many pitfalls, one of them being the desire to *force* the resolution of a picture rather than letting it come at its own pace. I was making that mistake with this version of "6:00"

Oct 9.

Been fretting up and down the studio trying to decide whether this "six o'clock" is good and all the other pictures are terrible—or vice versa. In some way it's entirely different from everything else I've done—altho I have the feeling I've seen it before, so obviously it's not *that* original. It's active and baroque, and I'm completely disgusted and discouraged. I'm going up to the Met to see the Rembrandts.

Oct 10—

Yesterday was what Joyce calls an epiphany—or revelation. When I saw the new Velasquez of the horse & rider—and then rushed to the Spanish room to see Goya, Zurburan, more Velasquez—and even Murillo & El Greco, I was overcome with excitement—And then the Manet funeral procession and the Manet's and Goyas at the Frick really overwhelmed me. I feel as though I am seeing for the first time, this is all terribly important to me. I just returned from the library with books on Spanish art & Goya and I'm filled with new feelings for the last few pictures I've worked on—the Hell with France, viva Spain! Going to spend an intensive day studying & painting.

This has been coming on for a long time—even those murals, terrible as they are, in the El Faro café meant something to me—and now the time in Mexico takes on meaning. My "heavy hand" in painting is really just not a "French" hand. I must now find some way in my work of bringing in these new feelings and discoveries.

Struggling all day with the two versions of "Six-o'clock." Very painful, I don't know yet just what it is I want to do.

Oct 13—

Here early to-day, still filled with enthusiasm but quieted a little by the realization that new "tastes" are only the first step into a maze of darkness—I have so far to go, and its all unknown, all still to be revealed. I think I will keep the small version of "six o'clock"—call it "The Sitters"—do a larger one later as things become just a bit clearer. I intend to do a ptg of John Myers from a very stylish photograph I have—I think of a lot of black, with a very white face & shirt. Want also to do a few things after Velasquez & Goya.

There is a man coming to the gallery to-morrow from the University of Ill. to select things for their annual. John wants me to bring up more "important" pictures, and I'm terribly confused about my work now. Of the three large pics—Hunt, D K & the D, & Frank OH I think I am most interested in D K & D—but I can't carry any of these to the gallery, & I still haven't paid Berkeley. And of the smaller pictures, the only two possibilities are "the sitters" and "Maharaja 2"—and I've no idea if either of them are any "good." This is a most confusing time for me.

Heard last night at Cooper Union the John Cage concerto for prepared piano, percussion etc. It was a lovely thing, full and rounded, with great delicacy—like an exquisite Klee. He doesn't seem to be a "big" composer—perhaps Feldman [Morton Feldman] or Edi F. [Edi Franceschini] will be, that must be seen. Had quite a talk at the Cedar [the Cedar Tavern at University Place and Tenth Street in Greenwich Village was a hangout for artists and poets] later on, Fairfields pictures, which have been criticized by the "vanguard" (cultists) as old hat, and by the conservatives as inept. A good position to be in, shows that something is stirring

Oct. 14
Brought the other self portrait—"Venetian Self-Portrait" & Maharaja #2 to the gallery—John & Fairfield were terribly enthusiastic over the self port—oddly enough it looked not at all academic up there—I was afraid it might—No one likes the small Maharaja paintings (except Frank)—John objected to the faces in this version. Nevertheless I intend to work more on the theme. I have destroyed both seated figure pictures, may go back to the idea later on.

Working more on portrait of John—I feel free now to make it as "realistic" as I must.

Reading about Goya with intense interest.

Oct 15
Had the first session of the sketch group here last night. It was a good group—Larry, Miles [Miles Forst], Jane, Fairfield, Nell B [Blaine], Allan K [Allan Kaprow, painter], Wolfe K [Wolfe Kahn, painter] & his girl, Al Kresch and Frank and Kenneth K [Kenneth Koch, poet]. I painted directly from the model, a pleasant little study which looks quite agreeable this morning.

Allan K. annoyed me with his criticism of the painting from John's photo—"The Impressario" which he thought was all caricature & very little painting

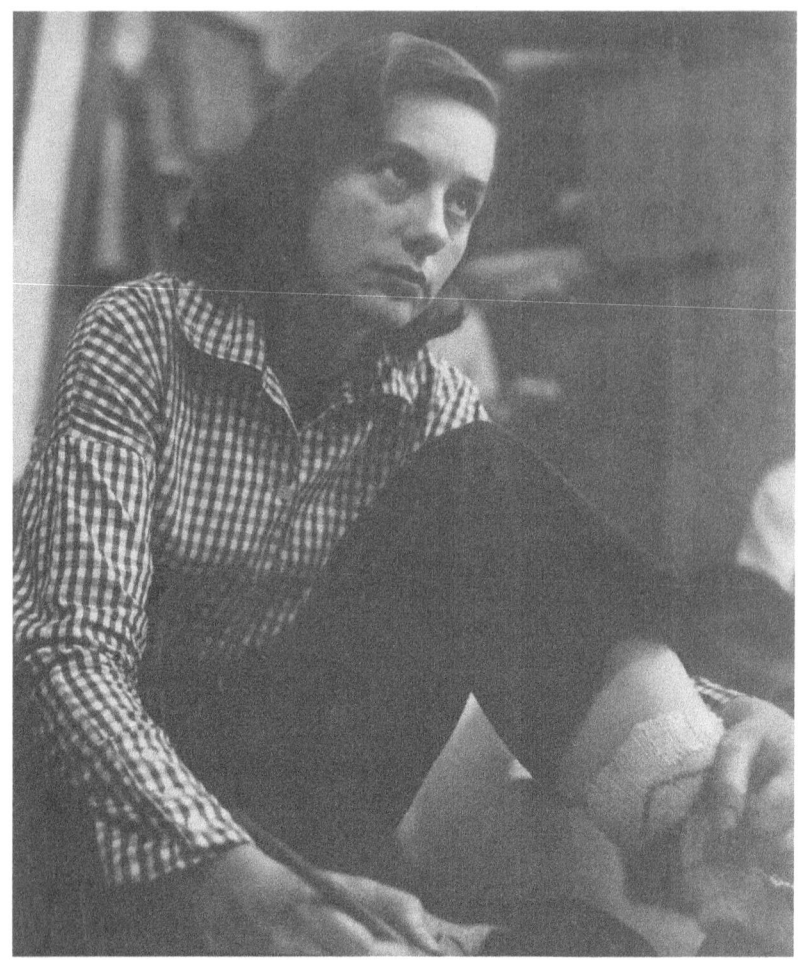

Hartigan at sketching class. On the reverse of this photograph is written "I love this —." The handwriting appears to be that of Grace Hartigan. Photograph by Walter Silver.

quality. I suddenly realized that most of the unpleasant criticism I've received lately has been from him—*loaded* criticism, as though much more were at stake than the merit of the pictures involved—I seem to get this kind of thing from men (Clem for instance) I think it's sexual in implication in some peculiar way. Fortunately for the ptg—for I'm so unsure at times I may have impulsively destroyed it—Larry, Jane, Frank and Fairfield were enthusiastic in their praise, so it must have some merit.

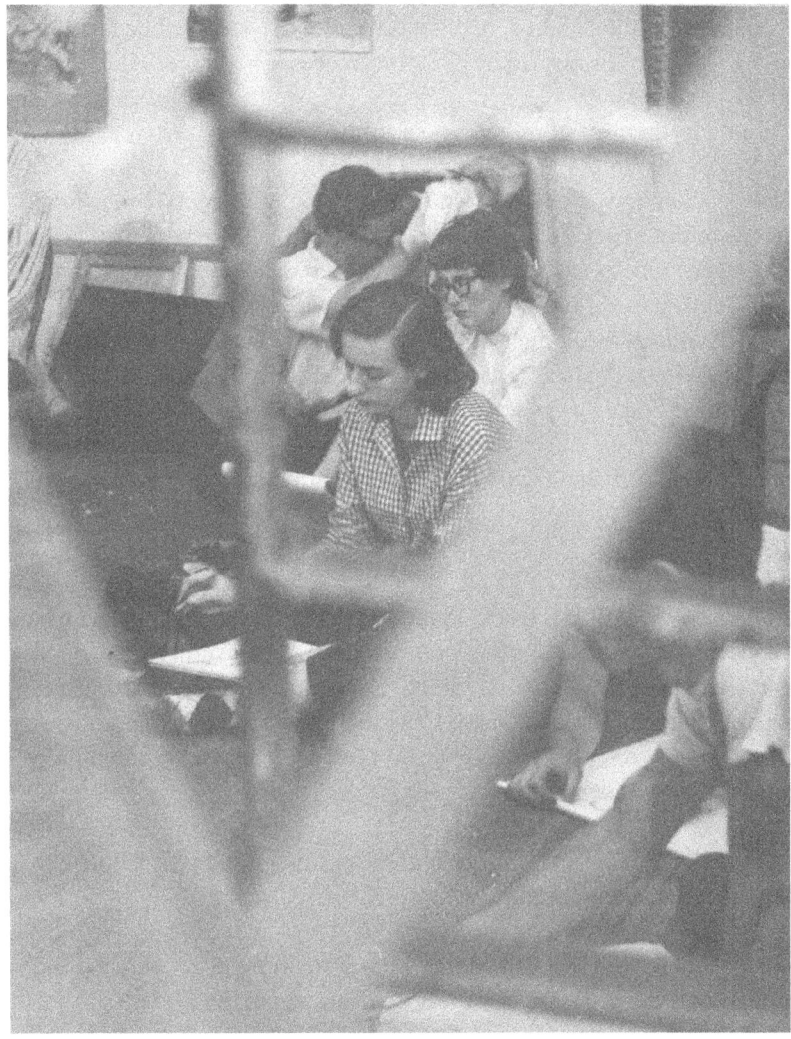

The sketching class. Hartigan is in the center of the composition.
Photograph by Walter Silver.

I find very often that people who make a "thing" out of their cool detach-
ment and "objective judgement" are often the most vicious & involved critics
(Motherwell [Robert Motherwell, artist], Clem, Allan). Whereas a terribly
subjective viewer, such as Larry, *can often be quite* rewarding.

Just talked with John, and I sometimes think he has as difficult a time as the painters—without the joy of the work involved.

The men selecting work for the Illinois annual were there yesterday, and were completely unimpressed. They had seen the "vanguard" show in San Francisco, liked my painting very much, and no doubt hoped to see more of the same in different colors. They hated what John showed them, only said "It will be interesting to see what happens in a year or so". Maybe they are right, perhaps museums shouldn't concern themselves with pictures from "in-between" periods. But somehow I feel that these new things have as much—more—than the old. There is a new academy now, of the "abstract," and this new Tanniger [Tanager] gallery is showing young academic painters, really.

John does have courage in going on with something that contains so few material rewards.

Oct 16.
Reading over my journals trying to recapture my old depression as Jim S. [Schuyler] says in a poem. What I'm trying to do is get some articulate ideas about where I'm going, what I'm doing. But am faced with the obvious fact that I am an instinctive painter, and that this "reaction," this "naturalism" has been storing up for almost two years. So I just must see it through blindly and trust in my own instincts

The painting of the Velasquez "Infanta" looks strange and stiff, a little like American colonial painting.

My involvement with Spanish painting has something to do with learning about tonal values, massing of volumes. Also some of the "inner light" of painting.

Note—Oct. 14, 1954
Reading this over to-day, I took out the Velasquez Infanta copy, and find my reasons for liking it so well these last two years—in spite of the fact that nobody else has ever cared for it. It seems to have clumsily anticipated every thing I'm doing now in the "Masquerade" and "The Masquer".

Oct 22
I'm confident of my ability to handle a head now, the ptg of John Ashbery &

the Velasquez Infanta pictures seem well done to me. I'm beset with problems though. So far all these things have been without reference to a front "plane" except for the Impressario. I must work with feet, full figures & feet that is, in order to find out about placing them in space.

I'm going to attempt something from a photograph of the Pope walking in his garden.

Did a lousy dwg from the model last night. I wanted to do something understated and subtle, and it ended up weak & delicate. I was terribly tired, having gotten up early to go to Aunt Kates funeral with Dad. Most peculiar feeling of bewilderment at seeing all my relatives and kneeling through a Catholic mass. Some of the ritual was fascinating, it's all so dead and empty and everyone is so bored and unfeeling. I wonder why they pay lip service even? There may be source material for future work there, I don't know.

Waldemar read Walt's & my Tarot fortune Mon. night—all obstacles for the Queen of Swords this coming year, obstacles & change. The Hangman on my right, the Fool on my left, and my other self (George) standing behind me. [For her early exhibitions, Hartigan identified herself as George Hartigan in homage to George Sand and George Eliot.]

Made a brief visit after the funeral to the Hispanic Museum—must return, they have at least one terrific Zurburan—a seated monk—the Goya Duchess of Alba, and a wonderful Velasquez head of a child.

Then foolishly went to the Brooklyn Museum in the afternoon. They have almost no Spanish art—a mediocre Goya and a terrible dramatic Ribera. I was delighted again with the early American formal portraits though, they have great charm. Also a few good Courbet landscapes.

Oct 23.
Eating warm, fresh from the oven chaleh and drinking black coffee, looking at my most recent pictures. Compared with the "Old Musician" of Manet on the table, they look sick.

Edi Francesceni & Don Monacco [musician] were over late yesterday afternoon. They seemed quite sympathetic—I said what I felt I was doing was rediscovering my sources, my roots—that I don't want to take anything for granted. Why must I go on from Picasso—or even the impressionists? I'll go to Goya, the first of the moderns, and see what happens from there.

I've been very upset the last few days over my working methods—ie using reproductions or photographs. I feel I must work from life or memory—a photograph is too stated, too much *there*.

I'm going to attempt something from Aunt Kates funeral.

Oct. 24

Took out Art Treas. of the Louvre from the library, and there's a magnificent Zurburan I'd like to use as a basis for a "Last Respects" painting of Aunt Kate—lying in the coffin, flowers banked on a diagonal, that old Irish nurse kissing her brow, and me, Dad, perhaps Jack & his wife & Uncle John in the group around the coffin.

Went to the Met Mus yesterday afternoon and looked a long time at the Manet Funeral Procession. Going to work on my Fun. Proc. now.

Oct 27.

Al & Esta came over yesterday, and we went with them to Hoboken for dinner (lovely brook-trout) Al & I had a fierce talk, the first in a long, long time. He spoke of my paintings he saw at the gallery, and felt that they were so unoriginal that I shouldn't show them. I argued that if I was an artist of merit and distinction, then anything I did had quality & was worth seeing. He said he thought this might be true from the historical point of view—in the long range viewing, but not now that it was important to keep ones reputation as a "forerunner," that what I would do eventually in painting will be so different from what I'm doing now that these pictures should *only* be interesting to me since I obviously feel it necessary to do them.

He may be right—I've been giving it a lot of thought. Certainly the paintings don't look any too brave to me this morning. He had only two new things, which are in a similar direction as his former work, but with increased power and energy.

But they have the "New York School" look which I told him I was anxious to avoid. He accused my things of having the "German expressionist" look, which chilled my heart, since I want to avoid that even more!

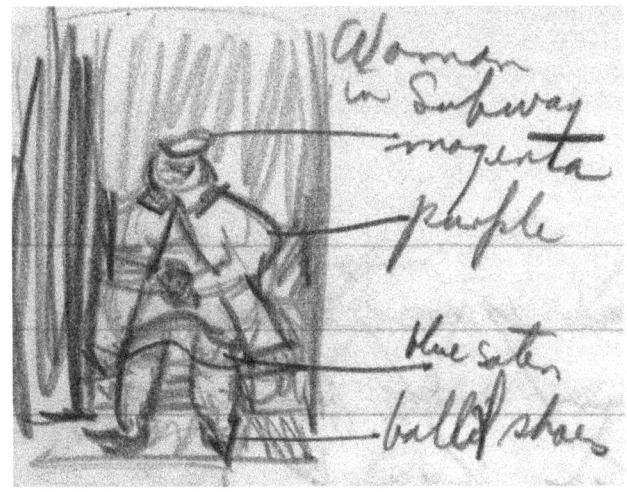

Sketch from Hartigan's journal of a lady on the subway.
The composition is reminiscent of that of *The Persian Jacket*.

He said that I should have gone through long ago what I'm involved with now, but since I didn't, and since this in many ways is an anachronism, I should keep it in the studio.

Oct 29
I feel the grey breath of winter on my neck to-day, and I'm making a brew of water, paper & flour to stuff into the window cracks. Must fix the stove too, it needs a new belly.

I'm discontinuing the sketch group Last night only Nellie [Blaine] & Leonard showed up, and it's much too expensive for so few people. If I could afford it I'd love to have the model alone, but I can't, so it's out of the question.

Al's remarks must have upset me very much because I got terribly drunk Mon. evening at the Castelli dinner. Alfred Barr came—I think we were all sufficiently charming to him. And I was more than sufficiently charming in my drunken state—to of all people, Harry and Dzubas! It must be that I feel so superior to them it makes me quite secure. Frank was drunk too, and he got quite incensed over Als remarks—he kept offering to give me a good slap if I paid any attention to what he'd said.

I realize of course that Al is terribly bitter and personal—and not only a little mad. And I'm so insecure that anyone could give me a jolt temporarily. I went deep into myself, re-questioned everything I've been doing, and can only feel I'm right. My show won't be for about six months anyhow, and Lord knows what I'll have painted by then.

Oct 30.
In many ways these drawings I've been working on interest me more & present more possibilities than anything I've done so far. I intend to do a seated woman oil from two of the dwgs using them as a starting point and hoping I don't remember De Kooning's seated women too well.

Nov. 3.
John just called with his uptown voice and the presentation of three possible picture sales—the small white self portrait head for $50.00, an early gouache from the first show for 50, and King of the Hill from the first show for $100.00. Terribly low prices, especially for K of the H, which is one of the best pictures from that time, but it does mean I wouldn't have to go to work for Xmas money so I guess I'll sell them. God, at least it's something—I haven't sold anything for almost two years.

I must be suffering from late autumn ennui to-day, I feel so melancholy. There's so much I want to do with my painting, and I haven't begun to even touch it yet. I went Friday to see a show at the little Tannager gallery—six painters, all "advanced"—and most of them influenced by the Tibor de Nagy gallery. I felt this, but Paul Brach said it so I knew it wasn't only *my* ego. Jim Benton has a new painting which is quite like my work early last year. Strange to see this happen when I haven't begun to "sell" yet.

This seated woman is coming well. I'm trying to get the architecture to work well, and learning as never before the value of subtle adjustments—first big massing and blocking, then small relationships.

Nov 4
Just voted for Stevenson on my way to the studio. I have never been so involved in an election before—I'm almost superstitious, in that I feel if he wins, then the next four years will be positive & good for me and all artists. If not, they will be dark & discouraging years. He is potentially a great man, a rare thing indeed in American politics.

The seated woman may be finished—"The Persian Jacket." I like some of it quite well, I think the tonalities are handled strongly in some places. But it is still too loose & not architectural enough. Of course, this can't all be solved in one painting—I must make more drawings and small pictures.

Nov. 5.
Been spending the morning trying to overcome the deep depression Eisenhower's victory has given me. Part of my personal involvement stems from some kind of strong identification with Stevenson I'm sure. I'm going to paint intensely, as never before, and to live an inner, restricted life as never before. The next four years should be black indeed.

I've finished "The Persian Jacket"—In many ways I believe it's the best painting I've ever done. It's a little forced and stylized in some places, but it has all I've learned so far from the masters in it, especially the Spanish masters. It is close in handling to the O'Hara picture & D K & the D but more tense and disciplined. All these things really came from the Massacre, which I'm looking at now with amazement that I could have done it last January. Frank has written an essay on me which pleases me no end, I'd like to use it as my catalogue for the coming Spring show if it isn't too long.

Nov. 11
I've been feeling very good and stimulated for the last few days. For one thing, I have a much clearer sense of what I want to do ever since finishing "The Persian Jacket." I feel about ready to start doing studies and drawings for the large "Carousel" painting which I've had in mind for some time.

Then too I can't underestimate the great lift that selling three pictures has given me. Not necessarily the money, because $200 less ⅓ on time payments amounts to very little—but the sense of being wanted and appreciated is so satisfying at this time.

Also Barbara Guests nice remarks & request that I illustrate her book of poems, and above all reading Franks essay "Hartigan on Sunday"—which is a tremendous work & I'm not sure I deserve it.

Sunday evening at the Cedar, sitting after hearing the Feldman work with Waldemar, Sandy, Edi, Don [Monacco]—then Alan & Ben, I was madly exhilerated & stimulated, with a strong sense of my own destiny. These people are all more "mine" than they are any other painter's.

"Do you remember in far December how the spokes glittered and wheeled and promised? I fainted near the door, knowing I was you and you disappeared in charge of the currency which had risen, had fallen, on your own sable brow. Could you have meant less, could you have trapped me and forgiven me, could you have relented and freed me? Is that the meaning of these faces in your eyes, the same faces though infinitely varied and colored and hung?"—From "Hartigan on Sunday, 1952" by F. O'Hara

Nov. 12—
So much stimulation (lately) can be overpowering. I hope that phone is silent all day, I have so much work to get into.

Frank was here most of yesterday afternoon. We went over the essay together, & he decided to change some things in the more "analytical" section, specifically in "period 5" after this painting from the masters & the portrait period. It's so wonderful to have that written—I never knew how to think about my past work before, and now its all clear & stated & I can forget about it. We must get the money to have it printed for my show.

Even more than the essay I am excited by the plans we formed for me to illustrate "Oranges, 12 Pastorals." I intend to start to-day, making each pastoral on 1 sheet of large paper, oil on paper, printing the poems myself as an integral part of the illustration. This is a huge undertaking that will take several months, and I'm very excited by it. I think that this, the drawings for Carousel & the huge painting, plus other drawings and 2 portraits—one of Waldemar and one of Frank will be my whole winters work & will be very rewarding for me. I have worked all day on the first poem, with the black crows & Ophelia theme. I am pleased with it, because it has set a mood for the other eleven that I want to sustain. It is perhaps a little "Munch"-ish, but maybe I can get away from that in the others while still keeping an emotional intensity.

Nov 13
Ran into Al late yesterday afternoon on 8th St. We had coffee and a brief honest talk. The same old thing—subject material, expressionism, the "look," etc. We are both really tempted & attracted by the same things in painting, and

both want to get over it & into something lasting & new. But our approaches are different. If it is expressionism that I'm to fear (Al said he could envision my show with horror, walking around seeing one tormented painting after another), if it is

EXPRESSIONISM

that is the pitfall then I'm going to grapple with the monster, use it, drain it, eat it, and eventually I KNOW I'll throw it away.

Fundamentally I believe in a calm, architectural art. If I must go through the fire to reach it, so be it.

Nov 17.
John, Jerry Goodman & Sandy were over yesterday afternoon to see pictures. General atmosphere of approval & enthusiasm, John wild about "The Impressario" & the poem paintings. My show date is to be March 31. It will probably work out like this—

Paintings—   The Carousel (to be done)
                       The Knight, Death & the Devil
                       Frank O'Hara
                       The Persian Jacket
                       The Impressario
                       The Hunt
                       St Serapion
Some portraits (heads) John Ashbery Venetian Self-Port.
    " drawings—(mostly the charcoal ones)
Poem-paintings for "Oranges,"
    12 pastorals by Frank O'Hara

Nov. 19
Jane and I spent a pleasant lunch and afternoon yesterday at each other's studios. Her new place is on East 11th St, a nice walk away, and we strolled along Orchard St gossiping & window shopping, & we each bought a little painted saucer.

Some of her new things are lovely, but they lack the fire of last years pictures and they often are timid and almost sentimental. I think she, Larry & I are all feeling our lack of a solid, academic background as a basis to go on. Her desire to "draw" well makes her timid & fearful. I have learned that "technique" must be approached with the same hand & courage, the same directness as

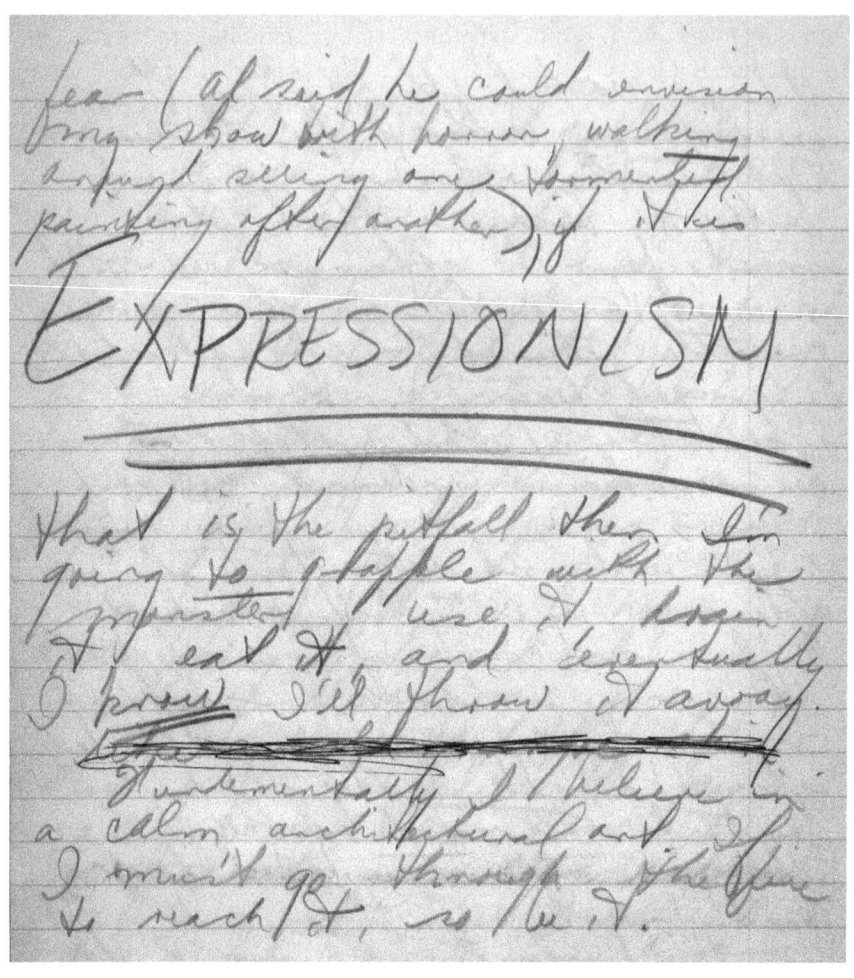

Detail of the journal entry from 13 November 1952 concerning Hartigan's views on expressionism.

"expression". Of course I do have a great deal more competence than I had ever realized, and it seems to be growing all the time. This anxiety of Jane's flavors all her criticism & appreciation of other people's work, and makes her overlook inspiration in favor of virtuosity. I hope this is only a temporary condition, for her sake.

I've been in a real slump so far this week. The show of masterpieces at the Met was terribly exciting, but it hasn't helped me into working. The Courbet

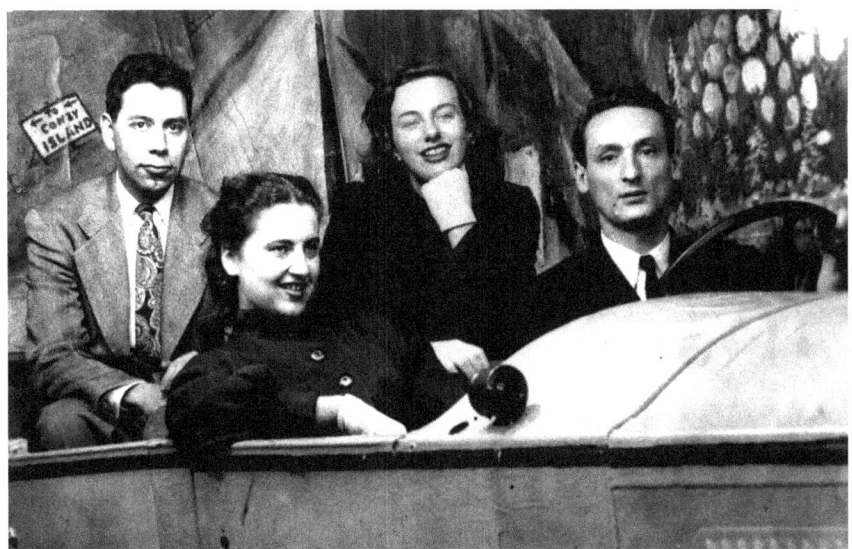

A staged photograph taken at Coney Island with Walter Silver, Jane Freilicher, Grace Hartigan, and Larry Rivers arrayed from left to right.

reclining nude with parrot looks terrific—also the Goya Maja's & the Manet female bullfighter. The Titian Venus is so stupendous I can't even think about it, it's too discouraging. I have discovered new things in Ingres that I never appreciated before.

Nov 21

A whole week of dampness and rain, complete self-doubt & despair. This is odd considering all the encouragement I've had lately, but that doesn't seem to touch my inner turmoil. The approaching holidays fill me with dread. I must get money for presents, especially for Jeff, and it may mean working unless I sell St. Serapion.

Sandy is coming to-day to pose for the main figure in the Carousel. I've made some drawings in pen & ink, and it's beginning to take shape in my mind. I think of it in grays, golds & greens, the main figure a horse & boy, escaping from the merry-go-round, the other children riding, a large back view of a mother waving. I want it quite "realistic," and so I'm doing research on horses, pigs, giraffes, tigers etc for the Carousel itself.

I've put "Oranges" aside for a while, I want to get involved in a "big" work.

Al was over yesterday, filled with enthusiasm & praise for the new things, much to my delight & surprise. He made some good suggestions for small changes in the Persian Jacket, which I effected. I also destroyed the large head of Jim & John A. as a monk after he left, they looked so bad.

Waldemar & I last night were discussing J. G's [Jerry Goodman] work, and I said he tended to think that horror was art. I said that the artist works not from despair but from hope, from order not chaos. W. agreed that personal suffering had very little to do with art. It may conceivably be used, but only as a remote source, not as substance.

Nov. 25
Feeling very depressed and alone to-day. I'd like to go to my contemporaries to feel challenged and inspired, but every one I know seems not ambitious enough. Perhaps not Al, but he's difficult to get hold of and I suspect his "career" has gotten hold of him right now a little too much. Walt & I saw the Whitney show Sun, and it was so DEAD, everything looked alike, the non-obj. ptgs were as academic as the social realism. Went yesterday to the open-ing of the new Hansa gallery, run by Wolf Kahn, Alan Kaprow, Jan Muller & some other artists, a kind of co-op idea. It's a nice space, a good size loft, but the paintings weren't much. Wolf had a few nice things, very earnest, kind of post-Soutine landscapes & still-lives. Jan Muller is good, one of the best of the post-Mondrian shuffling small squares group, like Grillo [John Grillo]. But they're all so *safe*, no one takes any chances.

I've stretched new canvas for the Carousel on the stretcher that held the old "Horseman" from the last show. Now I need money for glue and white lead. I'm all out of paint, and I'm eager to paint this in good color, Bellini anyhow, which I can get at a 40% discount. I don't know whether to get a job for a few weeks or wait and see if John sells St. Serapion.

Intend to go up to Central Pk this afternoon and sketch from the carousel there.

Dec. 2
The first snowfall is filling the studio with a soft grey light, and I'm feeling very content—Walt & I fixed the stove with a new belly, and he bullied me

into finally getting coal. I banked the fire yesterday on leaving, and it was still going this morning at 10:30. So the studio is quite comfortable. The big canvas is sized with good French rabbit glue, and the first coat of lead white (thinned with real gum spirits of turp.) is drying on it now. I still want to work it with good paint, but we talked money last evening & decided the hell with Xmas presents, I'm not going to get a job unless something for only a week turns up at the agency. I will have to work for show expenses, but that can wait for a while. St Serapion won't sell to that boy—he bought a ptg. from the Mod. Mus. "new talent" show—greater prestige than buying a Hartigan, of course.

Anyhow I expect 30.00 from the other pictures this month plus 40.00 Walt will get on a photography venture, as well as his Xmas money. That should take care of paints, a few bills & maybe a darkroom in the corner of the studio.

Today I plan to work more on the "Oranges," also a charcoal study for Carousel.

Dec. 5
Work has been going well so far this week. The Oranges are about half done—I've made a few changes on some, and finished the lovers in bed (O the changing dialectics . . .)

Also have a grey Self-portrait, which with a few subtle changes will be quite good I think.

Saw "Dead of Night" yesterday for the third time, and was as absorbed as ever by the puppet sequence. The "split-personality" is my theme and my horror—I suppose it's a reason for the interest in self-portraits. Is this my face? and what does it look like, is it really I? "Is that the meaning of these faces in your eyes, these same faces though infinitely varied and colored and hung?"

Dec. 6.
Brought "Impressario" up to the gallery yesterday in a taxi, & picked up $23.33 check. The painting looked a bit strange up there, rather dramatic and more wild than I thought. Also well "surfaced". But I need more calm and architecture in my work, it's so difficult.

John spoke of a show that the Club will hold at the "Stable" galleries, and they want to include Al, Dzubas & Goodnough from De Nagy, altho they will consent to use Rivers. I felt depressed by this discrimination, for I think I deserve to be chosen. It seems as though everyone has powerful champions but me, this is mostly true of Larry of course, Al for instance is constantly criticized and ignored. I refuse to become involved or feel persecuted over these things, my doubts are great enough already without heaping on extra coals of fire. I believe I am the first woman of major stature in painting, and I feel that given a long life and sufficient courage and energy, I may become a great artist. Time is one of the cruxes, and I am as always plagued by fear of early death. Here in the peace of the studio I feel only the doubts and joys that come from grappling with the work itself. As soon as I go out in the world all these other things shout at me and confuse me. After all its not the hand that writes these words that paints the pictures—it is more mysterious than that, in a way I am only a medium.

I suppose I'm a complete autocrat in a way, I want undying devotion from people, I want them pledged to believe in me blindly, completely, and for ever. This is of course ridiculous, but I know I want it, and I feel for instance Frank's recent devotion to Larry in Larry's emotional crisis is nothing short of treason. I know I have the faith of several people—Walt, who started believing through love and now believes I think in my work for itself; John in spite of his weakness has really committed himself; Waldemar when he's able to think of someone but himself—only occasionally with him is friendship an exchange—and to a lesser degree Al, John Ashbery, Jimmy [Schuyler], Barbara [Guest] and Larry. Also two of my recent collectors, Pease [Roland Pease] & Jerry Goodman. Perhaps never in my life will there be any more than a handful of people. It certainly was all Cezanne ever had, I wonder if I'd have his courage. I have some of his ambition—an art of synthesis, I want to compose the world in my canvases, God give me strength and time.

Dec. 17
This has been an eventful ten days. I helped Larry hang his show, and it has been on for a week now and selected by Art News as one of the ten best of the year. It's a good show, stronger than last year, more disciplined, less dispersed and "splashy." He has good weights and volumes, especially in the large ptg of 2 figures. Some of the small heads are excellent, grotesque with little sharp teeth. In the weaker pictures the "background" sinks too far back, creating traditional space & isolating the "image" from it. This is not very

interesting. In the best ones the areas are dynamically inter-related, and hold the surface well.

I worked at a job at the Medical Society for four days filling envelopes with pamphlets and this morning I saw Mr Bocour & bought Bellini colors, 16 boxes of 3 plus 5 lbs of white for $20.00. I hated giving up those few days, but now with the paint here I think it was worth it.

I also have resigned from the Club. Friday night I created a small scandal by completely losing my head and accusing the panel (Ferren [John Ferren, painter], Soby [James Thrall Soby, trustee of the Museum of Modern Art], Goldwater [Robert Goldwater, writer on art] & Fitzsimmons [James Fitzsimmons, writer on art]) of being boring and pedantic, and stating that Greenberg no longer wrote art criticism because he has nothing more to say. I was livid with rage & almost incoherent, I could have said many better things if I had been more objective, but this has been storing up for a long time, this revolt against deadness and lack of feeling. (Also against "authority" I must admit). Whenever I go there I am either bored to *deadness* or filled with frightening aggressions. Since I dont care for either extreme the only solution is to burn all my bridges behind me and not return.

I made some enemies Friday I'm sure, but I may also have made some friends, that remains to be seen.

Dec 19
Started the Carousel to-day. I'm keyed up and confused about it, and sure it will take a long time to finish. I can't make any more "finished" drawings for it, all I have are those quick pen sketches. I'm afraid they must do, perhaps I can make studies along the way as the painting progresses.

Dec. 23.
Seems that my recent complaint that I have no ally was unfounded. I may have a powerful enthusiast in Alfred Barr. He & D. Miller [Dorothy Miller, curator at the Museum of Modern Art] were in the gallery Saturday, and he seemed to spend more time with my pictures than Larry's or any one elses. He picked out the recent "Still-life," 'Venetian Self-Portrait' & "St. Serapion"— said they couldn't be as good as he seems to feel they are, and asked John to bring them to the museum. Frank called at about 7:00 to gleefully say they

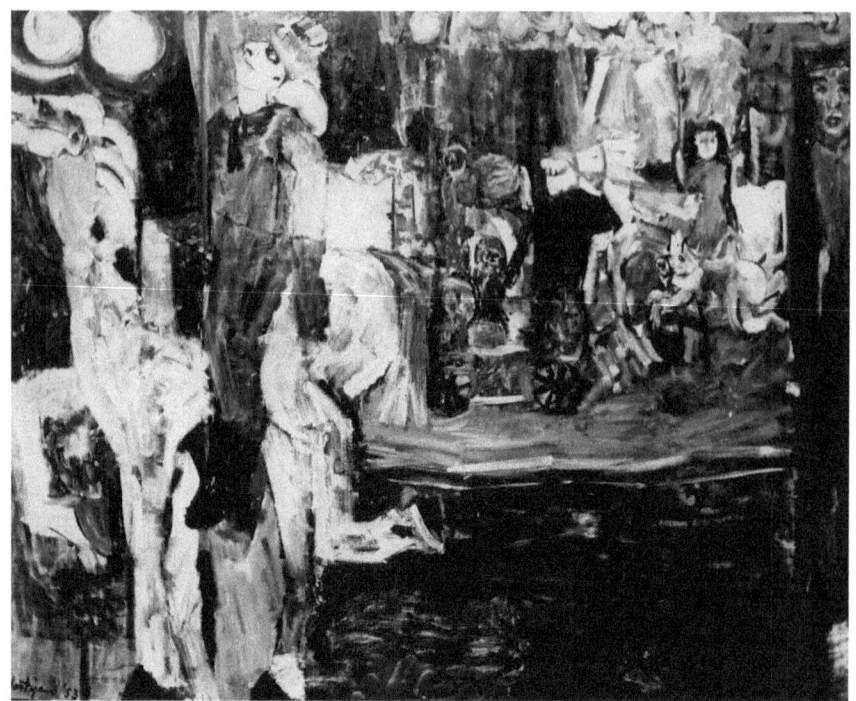

Photograph of the painting *Carousel*. This image is the only known one of this work because the painting was destroyed by Grace Hartigan. Photograph by Walter Silver.

were sitting in the office. I do hope the Museum buys one—but even if they don't, this has given me a terrific lift.

Dec 29.
I have two free weeks before I begin working at the "school of insurance" to get money for my show. I intend to work very hard on the Carousel and see if I can finish it in that time. Work on it today went well, it's more "drawn in" and the color key is pretty well set.

Dec. 30
I've been painting hard, really hard all day on my picture, and it's now at a stage that is so strained, so unresolved and disturbing to me that it upsets my stomach to look at it.

Dec 31
More on the Carousel. I want to make it so full, so fraught & it's still far from it. I musn't be so impatient, I must work and work till it comes.

Journal for 1953

Jan 2, 1953.

A new year. I'm filled with hope for this year, I feel I'm beginning to get some sense of myself in my work, as well as some glimmer of recognition. I also feel good about my relationship with Walt, and my friendships with Frank, Jane & Larry.

That devil of a picture is plaguing me. I think to-day I'll work a lot of detail in to give volume to all the areas then simplify later as it needs it.

All day on the Carousel, and I think it may be finished. At any rate I feel free from it for the first time in months. I can't tell yet how good it is, I must let it sit for a while.

Jan 5.

The "Carousel" is finished. It was a quicker birth than I had anticipated, but I've mentally been forming it for months. It's the most personal picture (in it's vocabulary) that I've ever painted, and in some ways it's painful to look at it. Walt is so far the only person who has seen it, and he was quite over-whelmed. I am most pleased with the handling of the "open" areas. That was really the greatest problem, and with the help of Manet & Courbet I think I solved it well.

I have in mind a few more things I'd like to do before the show. I'm working on a head of Frank. I'd like also to do one of Walt wearing a black muffler. I'd like to do a little study of Al & Esta from their wedding picture. Of course the "Oranges" will take a lot of time, but I'd also like to do more still-lifes, perhaps with flowers and fruit.

Jan 12.

I had expected to begin working this week for the Insurance School, but I've had a stay of sentence till next week. I'm just as glad, because I did very little painting last week, the Carousel seemed to empty me for a while. Now I think I can get something done, perhaps more of the "Oranges."

The big group show at the "Stable" opened yesterday. It seems a little more animated than the 9th St show, and begins with some of us to show a split in the ranks. My little self-portrait looked good to me, and I heard some compliments. Larry's sculpture held up well, and I liked Jane's little modest flower piece, Fairfields still-life, the Goodnough—also both the de Koonings had fine small figure studies. Of the "abstract" pictures I think Joan Mitchell's was one of the best—she has learned from Goodnough, much to her benefit. John sent a very insignificant Leslie, which should be an object lesson to Al—never let a picture leave the studio unless you feel it could represent you any place in the world.

This show has served to confirm my belief in my direction, I feel strong and confident.

I've tried working on the Al & Esta picture & I've given up the idea. It always turns out to look sentimental. Also the O'Hara head—I rubbed it out, may work on it when it becomes clearer for me. I've been reading Hawthorne, & I'd like to do a "Rappacini's Daughter"—I've asked Nina Castelli to pose for me—with flowers in her arms. I'll start it in February.

Jan 13.
I've just bought a chunky looking bunch of artificial flowers & leaves at the 5 & 10, also some apples. I feel very attracted to a kind of painting where the "subject-matter" is a cliché, there's something freeing about it. Rather than "pure" painting, I now like the thought of as impure a picture as possible— look at Courbet, he made his sentimentality his greatest strength.

I want to withdraw from friends & social involvements for a while, especially from John. This recent skirmish with R. (Roethe) [Theodore Roethe, poet] convinces me that John would willingly sacrifice me to satisfy his own lust for excitement—he'd like to lead me into a stormy Sand-Chopin deal, just to titillate his ennui. I hope I can always keep sight of what *I* need & what Walt gives me—peace, emotional security, and enough calm & inner aloneness so I can learn & discover myself.

Jan 21.
Working all this week and next.

Feb. 2.
Back in the studio again. The job wasn't so bad this time, I worked a bit evenings on the portrait of Walt, and managed to keep a sense of myself going all the time. I have 78.00 in the bank, which should just about cover show

expenses. It would help if I could sell a little something before the show, but still no word from the museum even though the board of purchasing met on Friday.

I went with Larry and Frank to see some shows yesterday. Helen's new work is terribly depressing, detached and uninvolved, the last gasps of the Newman-Pollock-Kandinsky thing, with Dzubas & Jackson thrown in. I believed her to be talented, but this show makes me wonder.

The only thing that really interested and arrested me was Lovis Corinth at Valentine gallery. He died a year or so after I was born, yet some of his things are uncomfortably close to what I've been doing—even closer to Larry & Jane. Makes me doubt myself, and once again I'm confused about what I want in my work now, I must be even more ambitious. This last still life has a nice denseness, and the head of Walt has a certain power, but I must do *much* more.

So far the only project I must finish before the show are the "Oranges". I don't know how I feel about Rappacinis Daughter, I'll have to see.

Feb. 4.
Oranges are going well again, I'm rather proud of my ability to sustain them over such a long period. I'm putting all my fervour into them, the night is coming all too soon.

Feb. 5
Well, the museum doesnt want to buy anything. The comittee thinks I have great "talent"—whatever that means, but they want to "wait a while." Of course that's always how it is—the artist is always ready long before the museum notices him—so ready in fact, if he's serious, that success comes as a rather silly anti climax.

In a way it's the same "wait and see" attitude that the Illinois men had. I understand in a way—it's risky collecting early works of artists who later on will go way out on a limb.

I feel a terrible sense of crisis about painting now. We saw Al & Esta in the Cedar last night, and spoke of the same thing—where to go now? Al feels he's reached the end with what he was doing. And Goodnough feels the same way.

I think this is why Larry is doing sculpture now—after all, you have to keep working if you have that kind of driving temperament.

I can't fool myself, these pictures since the Massacre are filled with the ecstatic passion of *re* discovery, not discovery. The Massacre summed up every thing of my former style, and now the almost naive enthusiasm for facing nature head on has left me. I'm putting the last fervour of "realism" into the Oranges, I feel the abyss yawning behind me.

I saw the work of Felix Pasilis yesterday at the Hansa, and felt a real sense of something strong. A good feeling, since the work of the older painters looks terribly tired to me. Pasilis hasn't hit on any thing "original," still-lifes in thick, intense colors, with an uncompromising nastiness that I enjoyed very much.

Feb. 10
The "Oranges" are finished, I think they came off with real verve—they also end something for me, the possibility of looking at nature "head on".

I feel tremendous anxieties and doubts about where to go from here, I must rest for a few days, and visit museums. This afternoon I intend to see the Morisot show & the Marquet show.

~

Why I Am Not a Painter

I am not a painter, I am a poet.
Why? I think I would rather be
a painter, but I am not. Well,

for instance, Mike Goldberg
is starting a painting. I drop in.
"Sit down and have a drink" he
says. I drink; we drink. I look
up. "You have SARDINES in it."
"Yes, it needed something there."
"Oh." I go and the days go by
and I drop in again. The painting
is going on, and I go, and the days
go by. I drop in. The painting is
finished. "Where's SARDINES?"

All that's left is just
letters, "It was too much," Mike says.

But me? One day I am thinking of
a color: orange. I write a line
about orange. Pretty soon it is a
whole page of words, not lines.
Then another page. There should be
so much more, not of orange, of
words, oh how terrible orange is
and life. Days go by. It is even in
prose, I am a real poet. My poem
is finished and I haven't mentioned
orange yet. It's twelve poems, I call
it oranges. And one day in a gallery
I see Mike's painting, called sardines.

The text of this poem is taken from pages 261 and 262 of *The Collected Poems of Frank O'Hara* (Berkeley and Los Angeles: University of California Press, 1995, by arrangement with Alfred A. Knopf, Inc.) edited by Donald Allen. It is used with the permission of Maureen Granville-Smith, administratrix of the estate of Frank O'Hara.

≈

Mar 5, 1953

The last few weeks have been indescribeable, and I brought myself so close to madness that it almost terrified me. Somehow I must find peace in the middle of all these machinations, lies, politics, deceits. I can't isolate myself physically, but I have to achieve it in some way, I need calm and quiet to discover myself.

I spent a quiet day with Walt yesterday, reading Delacroix's journal and found his wisdom just what I was looking for.

"Not only must the man who is greatest through talent, through audacity, through constancy, be also the most persecuted, as he usually is, but he is himself fatigued and tormented by his burden of talent and imagination. He is as ingenious in tormenting himself as in enlightening others. Almost all the great men have had a life more thwarted, more miserable than that of other men."

"'Independence has isolation as its consequence'—Alas, the alternative of being bored and harassed all one's life—or else of being abandoned by everything and everybody, because one would not submit to any constraint, that
alternative I say is inevitable."

He quotes from Balzac a passage which I feel applies perfectly to the John–
Herbert fiasco. ". . . To bring a mediocre man to success! For a woman as
for kings, that is to give oneself the pleasure which so carries away the great
actors and which consists of playing a bad piece a hundred times. It is the
intoxication of egoism. In a word it might be called the saturnalia of power.
*Power proves its strength to itself only by the strange abuse of crowning some
absurdity with the palm of success, of insulting genius, the only strength that
absolute power cannot attack.—*"

The following is a remarkable passage which I think sums up people like the
Brachs, Mike G. [Michael Goldberg, abstract expressionist painter], Joan, and
even Clem.

"Mediocre people have an answer for everything and are astonished at nothing. They always want to have the air of knowing better than you what you
are going to tell them; when, in their turn, they begin to speak, they repeat
to you with the greatest confidence, as if dealing with their own property, the
things that they have heard you say yourself at some other place.

As a matter of course also the mediocrities I am speaking of are well provided
with the kind of knowledge which everybody can obtain. The greater or less
degree of good sense or of natural wit which they may have is the only thing
that prevents their making perfect fools of themselves—A capable and superior look is the natural accompaniment of this type of character."

And this last, a note to myself—a remark of Boileau to Racine—"he had never
heard praise for the merest shoemaker without feeling the tooth of envy in
his heart."

And so to work, if I can. As for that, I have some few more words from the
journal for me to dedicate myself to myself—

"She (Mme. Malebran) was like the young people who have talent, but whose
turbulent time of life and whose inexperience always make them think that

they cannot do enough with it. It seems that she was endlessly seeking new effects in a situation. If one takes that course, one is never finished: *that is never the way of consummate talent*; when such a person has done his study and found his personal note he breaks away from it no more.—It characterizes the art of Rubens, Raphael and all the great composers. Outside of the fact that with the other method, the mind finds itself in perpetual uncertainty, one's whole life would be spent in trying over the same thing."

I must devote my energies toward finding my own expression, my best talent, what *I* must say, not what I like or admire or intellectualize about. This demands serious introspection, *calm* and time.

Mar. 6.
A grey March day, with a snow sky, and my violent depression has slowed down to a steady melancholy.

I have just written Virginia [Hartigan's sister] for sixty dollars. I have only enough in the bank for the catalogue & stamps, and the Oranges will cost about 20.00 to mount and present properly. I have no optimism about selling anything, but I do expect 67.00 tax return, with which I can repay her.

I am expecting Betty Holliday from Art News late this afternoon to review the show, and I've been taking out ashes, garbage and laundry to clean up the studio a little. On the way to the laundry I passed the stale bread store and the little stands that sell penny tomatoes, that foul market that has meat for 15¢ a pound, and I remembered how I lived three years ago with Al, that steady, endless poverty, when I felt bloated with bad food—could I ever go through it again? I hope that I will never need to, but it has given me a knowledge of what it means to be poor, really poor, and I have an intimate knowledge of these people down here such as someone like Helen will never know.

I started Rappacinis Daughter yesterday, will work on it for a few hours to-day. I don't know what I'm about yet, but I have an idea I want to contrast some tense, knotty areas against some broad, open ones—this is the answer for "detail" in the old masters.

Mar. 12
Been ill all week with a chest cold, what a bore—I have so much work to do

for the show I don't know where to begin. Displaying those damned Oranges is a headache—they're too big for art store cardboard, so I must use lumber yard panels for mounting & cut them down. And I'm not really sure that the first idea will work.

Then too I've felt a growing dissatisfaction with the Carousel, and I can't exhibit it as it is, I must work into it and make it richer and more fluid. The "figures" seem especially contrived to me—something in Delacroix set me thinking—to the effect that if the volumes are right, then the contours come right. And I think I forced the contours too fast. They are not "painted" enough. This may present problems—but what the hell, if I mess it up then I'll just have one less picture to show. It would be strange if Art News decided to reproduce it as Betty Holliday saw it—I gave her a photo. But I can't let that stop me. I bought some damar varnish and linseed oil to mix as a medium with turp as I paint back into it, it may help with that opaque richness I want.

Al's show opened Tuesday. It is terribly beautiful, heavy and full, and not as much "bravura" for its own sake as I had thought. Oddly enough he points up to me the need for rich, full color passages, not for sensual reasons but to give greater weight to the masses—his two biggest pictures pulse with fullness—it's going to be a difficult show to follow, but it's a good antidote for my too close associations with Jane, Fairfield and Larry. I need help now and then to be brave.

Mar 16.
The Carousel is a failure, I made a complete mess of it. All those months of thought and work gone. I couldn't have left it as it was, it was wrong—but I just don't have the capacity for carrying it through. It may have been a bad "theme" for me from the start, too specific and associative. I'm going to scrape it down now to keep the surface of the canvas to use again. I intend to spend the afternoon stripping the other pictures.

Mar. 18.
Saw the new de Kooning show yesterday, and I was overwhelmed. He's an artist with a great conscience. It's as though he not only had to make his own way, but that he had to invent a whole new world from scratch, with all the terrible struggles involved. Next to this show, Al's paintings all look like "ideas," not creations. I was struck by the wonderful tensions in the de

Koonings, and of course, as always, by the imaginative flow between the "background" and the "figure." He is a great seducer, for once you become wooed by that way of doing a figure, then you do what Larry did—tend to adopt the "mannerisms"—those wonderful teeth, the staring eyes, the painted fingers and round, pushed under the chin breasts—and miss the problem. To me one of the real "mysteries" is how she sits—she does, but doesn't.

One of my own problems occurred to me—and I think it may be the answer to why the Carousel failed. It has to do with human scale, and the physical size of a painting in relationship to the physical world. ie—the horse & rider were always the best things in the C., because they were near human size, so I could feel as though I were creating a true object, and not just "representing" nature. So with all my canvases, the small paintings are usually heads—"life" size. Or still-lifes, also scaled—true to nature. This is all by way of self analysis, I don't know if it's good, or if I'm stuck with it. But it's so obviously true that I must have been blind not to realize it before. The only way now for C. to work is to either bring the other "riders" in the same scale as the boy, or turn the whole canvas on end and make it one figure, a boy on horseback. I doubt that I have either the time or energy to do this before my show, but it will be a goal for me in the month or so ahead.

Mar. 25.
Stripping, mounting, framing sending out catalogues. I sent out 600 this year, perhaps thoroughness will do some good.

James Fitzsimmons from Art Digest was here Friday, and looked at the pictures and then took me for a late lunch. He is also writing a monthly column for "Arts and Architecture," a California magazine, and intends to write in May on Tomlin, Sutherland, de Kooning and me. He is an almost frighteningly restrained man, quite intelligent—and with my past knowledge of Bob [Jachens] I would probably say he is deeply and violently emotionally disturbed.

He seems genuinely interested in my paintings—how personal it is I have no idea. But I can't discourage a champion of my work, and the rest will remain to be seen. This is one of the bitter-sweet problems of being a woman and an artist, but I wouldn't have it any other way.

April 2
This seems like the first time I've been able to be quiet with myself for weeks.
Having a show is deeply upsetting to me, I must remember much that I want
to do impulsively during this time is due to some profound disturbance.

The show looks almost better than I thought—that is, the pictures hang
to-gether in a statement that seems to have authority and validity. It's not
enough, but I'm never satisfied. I do think there are lots of things there that
will lead to intensive work once I get my equilibrium again.

The opening was the most crowded and enjoyable I've ever had. I spent
several hours that morning doing oil on paper studies for covers—John had
100 copies of "Oranges" printed. I'm only getting a dollar for each, it's really
silly to do it but they look so nice, and it gets the poems around. I felt really
glamorous—Jim Fitzsimmons sent a huge box of gladiola anonymously—
later confessed—Jane brought blood red tulips, and lots of other people,
Jani, Nell [Blaine], John Ashbury—I wore Larry's long stem rose and Frank's
anenome, drank half a pint of scotch, and signed books of Oranges. I was
pleased especially that Goodnough and the de Koonings came. And then
Roland [Pease] had a marvelous cocktail party, and I got completely plastered
and came near making a fool of myself over some emotional opportunist
named Lansing Baldwin. I must remember what a serious girl I am and not
think I can flirt with impunity.

I have a horrible feeling that I won't sell anything. Herbert [Herbert Machiz,
playwright and partner of John Myers] is buying the "Impressario" for $150
on time, $20 a month—if I see a cent of it, that will be a miracle. Baldwin
wanted to buy the Artificial Flowers still life, but I think he expects it buys
special privileges, and once I slap him down I'm sure he wont buy it. Well,
who knows—Barr is back, and something may come there.

Today I'm going to turn out as many covers as I can—twenty or so, and perhaps next week I'll be able to get to work.

May 2.
(This entry refers to a brief "affair" with Jim Fitzsimmons)
I've just burned the pages of the last month. I needed to write them at the
time, but they were emotional outpourings of the kind that should never be
re-read. This last month has been incredible torture, for me and everyone

The cover of the catalog from Hartigan's April 1953 show at the Tibor de Nagy Gallery. Hartigan's handwritten notes detail the disposition of the works. For example, *The Persian Jacket* is identified as being at the Museum of Modern Art.

who loves me. And although I'm a little exhausted and spent, I've at last some sense of myself and my direction again.

James Fitzsimmons described Hartigan's work as Dionysian in the May 1953 issue of *Arts and Architecture* (on page nine of issue five of volume seventy) and proceeded to continue his analysis in this fashion: "Such labels need to be qualified, of course, and I call Miss Hartigan's art Dionysian merely to indicate that in feeling it is closer to (and more directly concerned with) the darker, instinctual side of life. The paintings and drawings in Miss Hartigan's third (and I think best) show are less abstract than those she exhibited last year. They include full-length standing and seated portraits, male nudes, still-lifes, and a large free interpretation in oil of Dürer's engraving, The Knight, Death and the Devil. Miss Hartigan's willingness to look with more than academic interest at the old masters—first at Delacroix and Rubens; more recently at the Venetians and Spaniards—and to be inspired by them, does not seem to have harmed her work and is in line with Malraux' thesis that art is based on art. Because she uses a certain amount of distortion and a rich, dark, dramatic kind of color, I would call her an expressionist. But she seems—wisely, I think—to be more consciously concerned with order, with composition, than the allout expressionist is apt to be. In the end, the coherent statement is always more expressive and moving than the impassioned but turgid gesture with which some expressionists attempt to whip up and dramatize their feelings. The progress Miss Hartigan has made during the past year is apparent in her use of color dictated by pictorial requirements, rather than by impulse or 'taste.' It shows, too, in her brushwork: bold and sweeping as always, but now more controlled, more effectively paced."

Two things have been accomplished. My independence has been established, and the relationship with Walt has been re-vitalized. I've hurt him, J. [Fitzsimmons] & myself, but perhaps some good has come from it all.

I love living here, being alone a great deal. And I feel more energetic, alive and intense. In spite of the real money problem, I think I can really start to get back into my work. I know it will go painfully for a long while.

All the rest was a dream.

May 3.
I've had a real boost in morale, just when I needed it very badly. Alfred Barr

was in the gallery yesterday. He apologized for not making my show, and asked to see what pictures John had. He went wild with enthusiasm over the "Persian Jacket," asked the price—John quoted $400, and he said he thought he knew someone who would buy it. So after he looked at the Oranges & the Tiepolo study, liking both, and John gave him one of the books, he, Dorothy Miller & Persian J. all bundled into a taxi & were off to the Museum. Dorothy M. also thought she might have a buyer for Art. Flowers & Apples. It would solve my whole summer's financial problem if this went through. And of course I'm terribly pleased at the quality of enthusiasm on Barr's part.

John asked me to do the decor for Jimmy Merrills play "The Bait," but I don't want to do it. I feel the need to be very introspective and quiet at this time, and I've been painting on the Landscape with Figures to-day, really beginning to get in it. It's in a good working stage of chaos, but I feel sure, not floundering, and I'm quite excited over it.

May 4.
Working all day on Figures in Landscape, it's coming well & all to-gether. It's beginning to be a bit too impressionistic, the fault partly of too much broken & naturalistic color. I find myself looking often at the Massacre for help, although I want this ptg. to be much more tense & contained.

May 5
I think the desire for, and the ability to make, total committments is one of my noticeable traits. I think I've finally brought off the gladiola still-life.

Frank, Hal [Hal Fondren, poet] & I at John Ashbery's last night, listening to music—Saint-Saëns Piano Concerto, Schoenberg, Couperin. I looked for some time at reproductions of drawings in Windsor Castle by Poussin, mostly magnificent tonal studies of figures in landscape, I think I learned something.

May 6.
I believe the Bathers is finished, I'm trembling with excitement over it. In some ways I think it's the most important picture I've ever painted. The palette is strange for me, almost pretty—but the picture's structure keeps it from being cloying.

I wonder if there is any relationship between suffering and creative profundity?

May 7
I was wrong about Bathers, there is much more that it needs. I've been carried away by these momentary enthusiasms before—I must try to remember to be more hesitant in the future.

John, Herbert [Machiz], Frank, Augusta [Augusta Rivers] & some wealthy woman were over, and having alien eyes on the picture helped me see it. Everyone praised the Gladiola Still life, I will show it in the coming group show. This woman wanted something like the Impressario—that is proving to be the most popular picture I ever painted. I am *profoundly* not interested in it, and said so, much to John's annoyance.

My personal agony reached a high pitch last night after everyone left. Fortunately I am much calmer this morning.

I am re-reading "Rilke, Man & Poet." Some of his feelings about psychoanalysis are interesting to me right now. "Can you understand—that I fear, should I avail myself of any kind of alleviating classification and survey, *to disturb an order of an infinitely higher kind*—to which,—I must acquiesce, *even if it should destroy me?*—"

He finally came to this decision, which I reserve also for myself—

"I now know that analysis would only be of use to me if that peculiar mental reservation with which I used to console myself,—during the throes of finishing "Malte"—namely *never to write again*—should become really serious. Then one would have a right to exorcise the devils, who are really only disturbing and embarrassing in every-day life—"

Later.
This time it's really finished. I almost feel as though I can't take any credit for it. I worked on it all morning in a blind, inspired heat, every thing went right. In color especially it is one of the most bold & brave pictures I've ever done. I still can't believe I did it—I learned tremendously from the last year of "study," and this is a strong departure from the show.

What am I being so humble about? "I" have a hangover, a vague nausea, and a throbbing sinus headache—but "I" am only the medium for my artistic genius, I can only hope for it to come & take over, and I can't take credit for any of it.

May 8
"Bathers" looks good this morning. I think for the first time I am using color as a powerful *structural* element. As a result this picture looks "French"—but who else has used color but the French? I'm sick of this American provincialism anyhow, childish rejections of all the lessons we can learn from European art. "Bathers" owes a great deal to Matisse, he has always been my master. I am more & more interested in a very formal, classical art, but an art which is also filled with a sense of irony.

May 9.
Barr & John spoke on the phone yesterday, and he said he felt disturbed by the upper left area in P. Jacket, and wanted me to look at it under the most favorable lighting conditions possible—a spot outside his office.

I went up there in the afternoon. P. Jacket looked good, more full and arrogant than I had remembered. I agreed about the area—it always was a difficult one to solve, partly because it is the most open area, and the one which in traditional painting would be the "background." The area bends in, so it doesn't sit right—and I'm going up on Monday with my paints to work on it a little. This was at Barr's suggestion—I thought it a bit unconventional, but we both remembered the incident of Delacroix touching up the "Massacre of Scio" two days before it was shown.

He was extremely pleasant and interested, and we discussed my background a little, and my switch from "abstraction" to "realism."

I feel no compromise is involved with my integrity in this affair. There have been times when the most casual observer can say something which would make me re-touch an area in a picture. Walt said something about a blue in the "Bathers" yesterday, and a few darks underneath it resolved the area completely.

May 12.
Took my paints to the Museum yesterday. They moved P. Jacket into Ritchie's

office, and I worked on it for about a half hour, brushing out the orange on the left side of the canvas, and working in sienna, umbers & black. Also touched a few other areas—it is a great improvement to my eyes, I don't know how Barr feels about it, although he did say he thought it "read" better that way. He said nothing about the future of the picture, and I left quickly.

Helped John & Tibor hang the group show. My Glad. still-life hangs by the window and looks good. I pray to God I sell it, or something, my money is almost gone already and I'll have to get a job.

Frank & I had dinner at the studio last evening—he saw Bathers completed for the first time and read me his "Second Ave" long poem. There is a part about me ". . . and when the pressure asphixiates and inflames, Grace destroys the whirling faces in their dissonant gaiety where it's anxious, lifted nasally to the heavens which is a carousel grinning and spasmodically obliterated with loaves of greasy white paint and this becomes like love to her, is what I desire and what you, to be able to throw something away without yawning "Oh Leaves of Grass! O Sylvette! Oh Basket Weavers' Conference!" and thus make good our promise to destroy something but not us.—"

Jane & Joe [Joe Hazen, Jane Freilicher's partner] & Al Kresh [Al Kresch, painter] came over later with talk of their sets for the next Artists Theater performance. Jane crowned Bathers with a typical remark "Oh, Matisse— that's what comes from association with Alfred Barr".

I didn't know that the influence in the picture of Matisse was so strong, but I'm looking now at a post card of the 1916 Bathers by a River, which impressed me so much last year in the big show at the Museum, and I guess it's true.

So now what shall I do.

May 13
Very depressed. Tomlin [Bradley Walker Tomlin, abstract expressionist painter] is dead, and will be buried this morning. Brings up all my fears of being stopped before I reach any real expression. Makes me think of Waldemars often repeated "Work, work, for the night cometh when no man may work." Very dismal opening of the group show yesterday, almost no one there— Larry in from country for a day. Thought J. [Fitzsimmons] might come, but he didn't.

Poindexter [George Poindexter, art patron] has offered to buy Persian Jacket for the Museum if they will accept it. I could paint all summer without working if this went through.

May 14
I think perhaps what I'm doing now is coming to grips with "modern art," which to me means Picasso and Matisse. In a way "New York School" or "abstract expressionism" avoids the issue, which is that of working within a frame of tradition. De Kooning is the only one who faces up to it, and he is still out of Picasso.

May 18
I'm waiting to hear from John whether Gertrude Fisher has decided to buy Venetian Self-Portrait—she had it on approval for the weekend. I'm down to thirty dollars, and if she doesn't take it I'll have to look for a job to-morrow. I can't get to work until I have this thing settled.

Frank & I went to the dress rehearsal of the Artist's Theater last night. They are doing Jimmy Merrill's The Bait, it's not bad but not very moving—Gaby [Gaby Rogers, actress and Frankenthaler's roommate] is terrific as the lead. Barbara Guest's Lady's Choice is mush—how few women artists have that core of objectivity necessary to make a work of art live by itself. Jane did a sweet garden for it. John Ashbery's Heroes is a little masterpiece, even better to see it than read it, and I've always loved it. Herbert [Machiz] tried to force it too much, but it has such quality that it comes through anyhow.

May 20, 3:30 AM
Something happened to-night—and I won't work to-morrow at that tabulating job for morons. It isn't that I am such an artist, but that I have value as an intelligent human being, and if I must work and move in the *world*, then I am capable of being more deeply engaged in what I do. I can give more than automatism, I refuse to submit myself to such degradation.

May 20
In a terrible state of melancholy to-day. Gertrude Fisher returned the picture and I *must* get a job. In the midst of my upset I thought "Mexico," and the idea of turning The Hunt canvas into a painting of a figure in a patio, with hot colors and a lot of Mexican light. I'm going to use some of those snap-shots of myself as a start.

Four-Color Illustrations

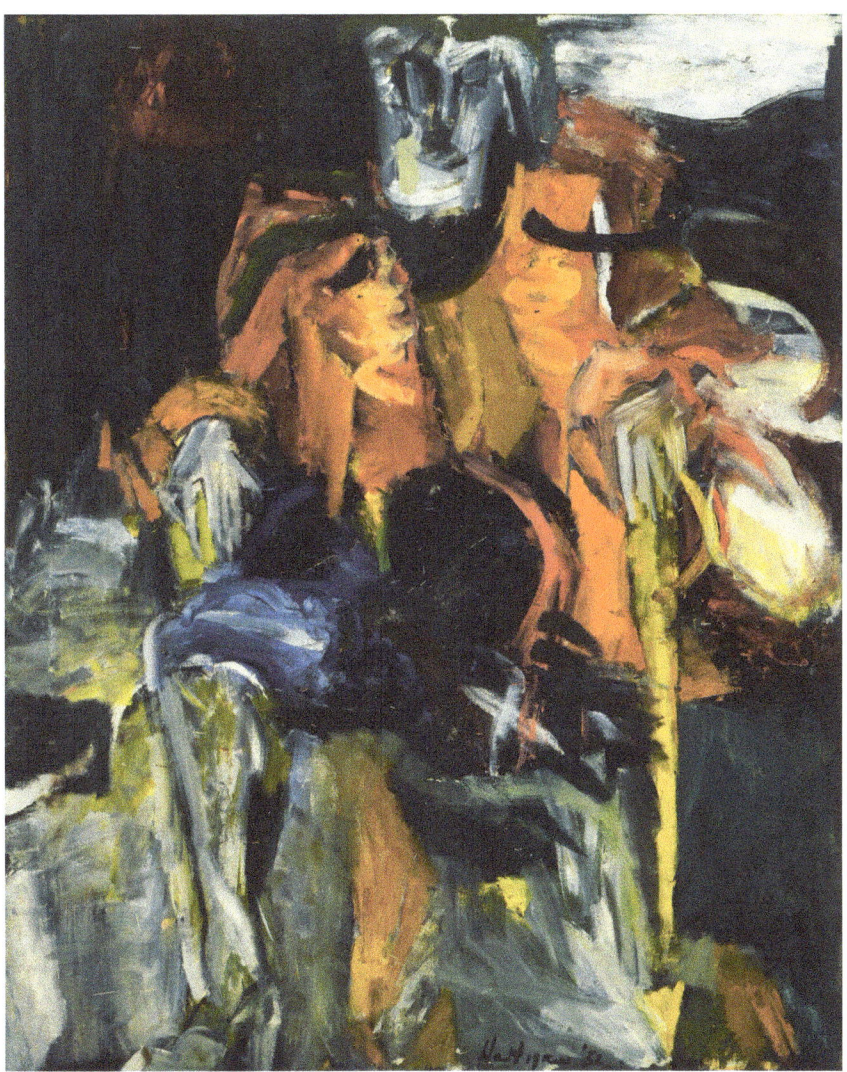

Plate 1. *The Persian Jacket* (1952). Oil on canvas, 57½ x 48 in. (146 x 121.9 cm.).
Gift of George Poindexter (413.1953). Digital image ©The Museum of Modern
Art/Licensed by SCALA/Art Resource, New York (ART367504).

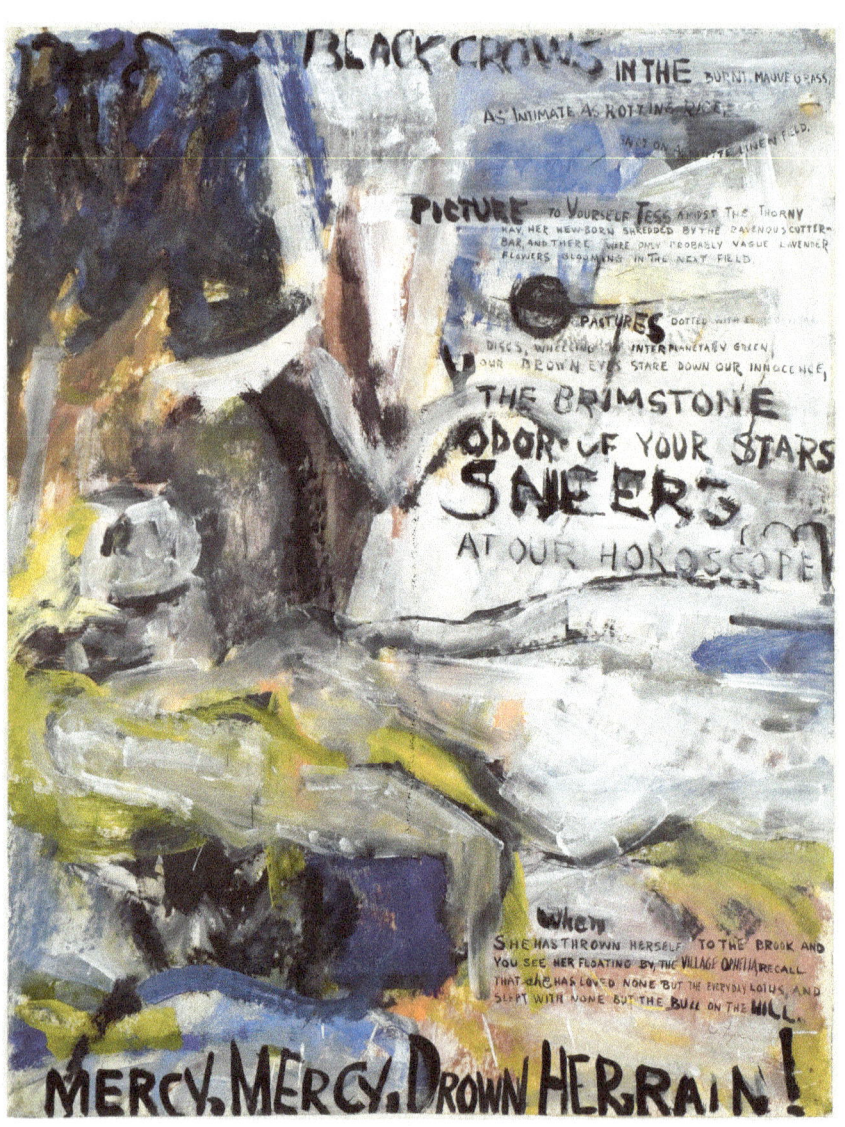

Plate 2. *Oranges # 1 (Black Crows)* (1953). Oil on paper, 45 x 35 in. University at Buffalo Art Galleries: Gift of the David K. Anderson Family (2000-001-061).

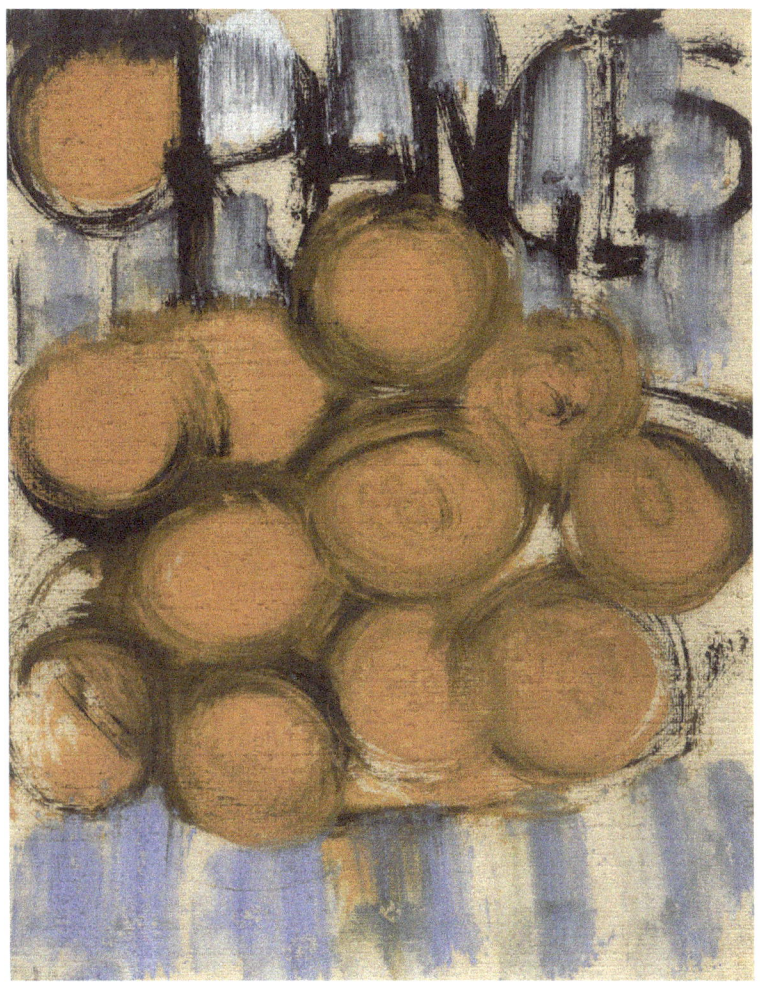

Plate 3. The cover image of *Oranges: 12 Pastorals* by Frank O'Hara (New York: Tibor de Nagy Gallery, 1953). This publication consists of nine unnumbered mimeographed leaves that have been paperbound. The illustration pasted on the front cover is an original oil painting by Grace Hartigan. Courtesy of the State University of New York at Buffalo Libraries: The Poetry Collection.

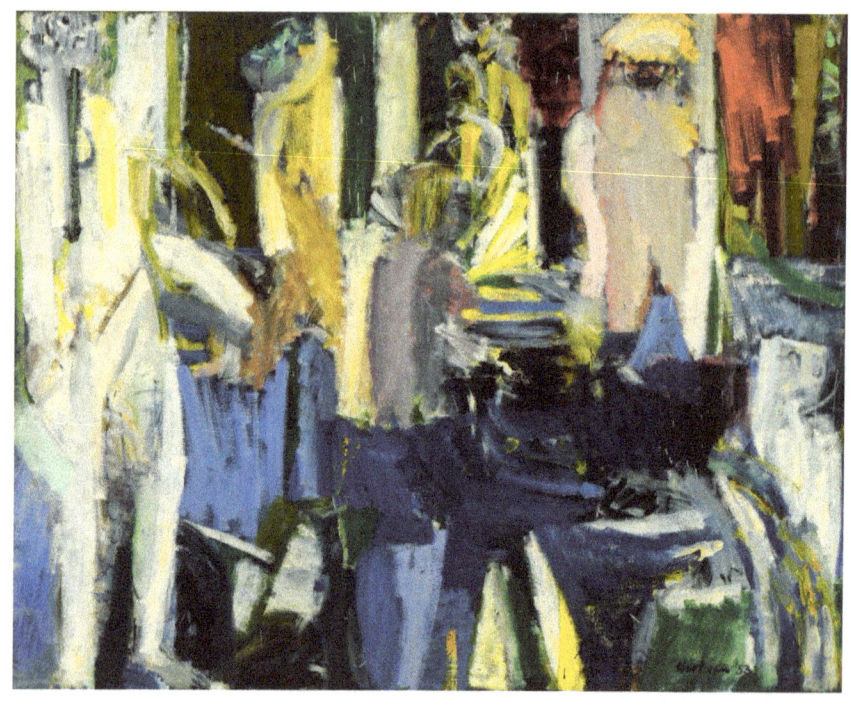

Plate 4. *River Bathers* (1953). Oil on canvas, 69⅜ in. x 7 ft. 4¾ in. (176.2 x 225.5 cm.). Given anonymously (11.1954). Digital image ©The Museum of Modern Art/Licensed by SCALA/Art Resource, New York (ART340049).

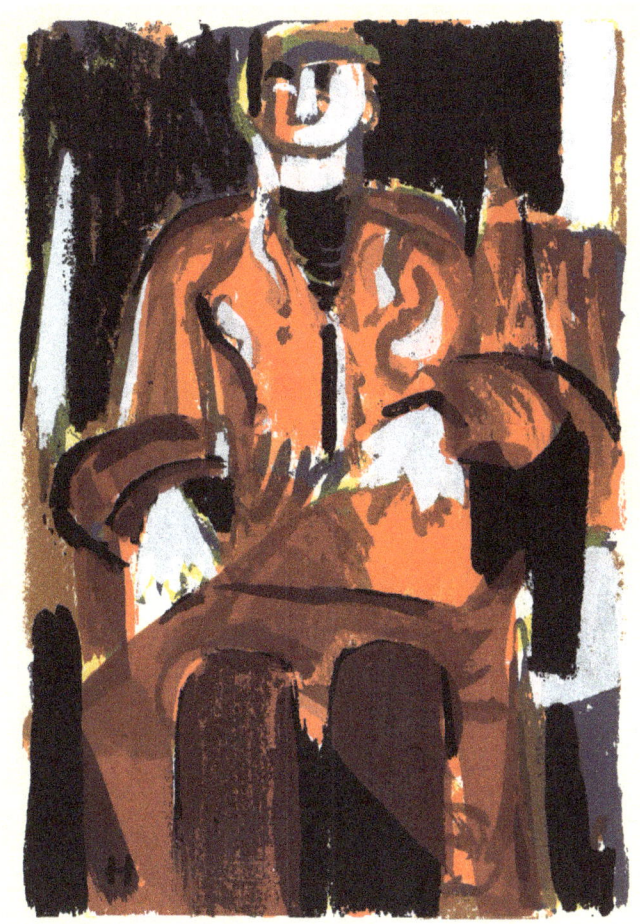

Plate 5. Silk-screen print that appeared in *Folder 1* (New York: Tiber Press, 1953).
It was based on the oil painting entitled *The Persian Jacket*. In her journal entry
for 27 July 1953, Hartigan made this assessment of it: "I finished the second print
Friday, 'The Persian Robe,' it is quite full and successful. It has an emotional
intensity that I wasn't sure I could get in that medium, so I am really pleased."

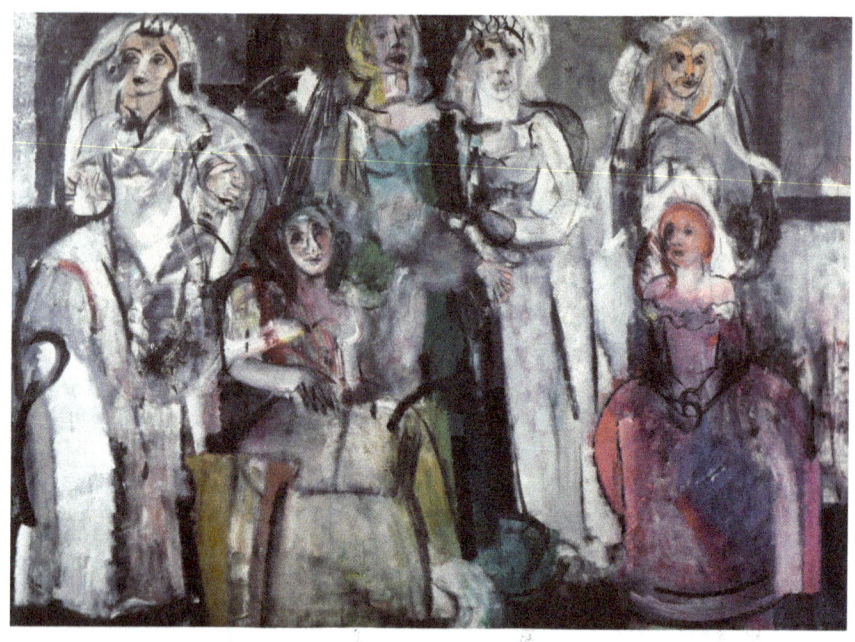

Plate 6. *Grand Street Brides* (1954). Oil on canvas, 72 x 102 in. (182.88 x 260.35 cm.). Collection of the Whitney Museum of American Art, New York. Gift of an anonymous donor (55.27). Photograph by Geoffrey Clements.

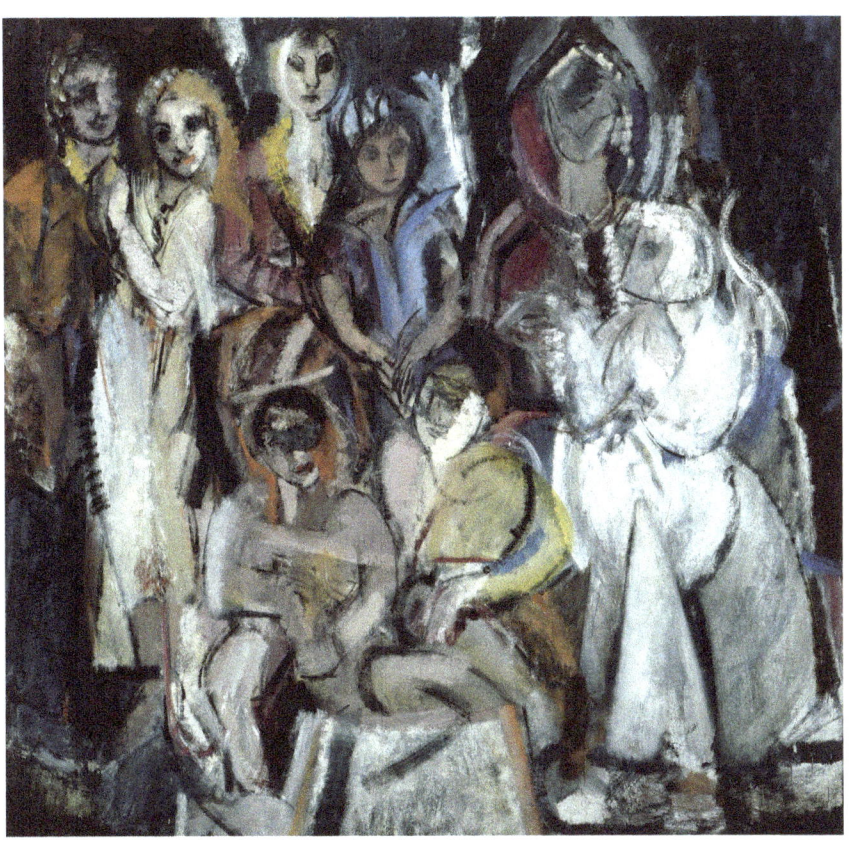

Plate 7. *Masquerade* (1954). Oil on canvas, 207.7 x 219.1 cm. Anonymous gift (1955.493). Reproduction, The Art Institute of Chicago.

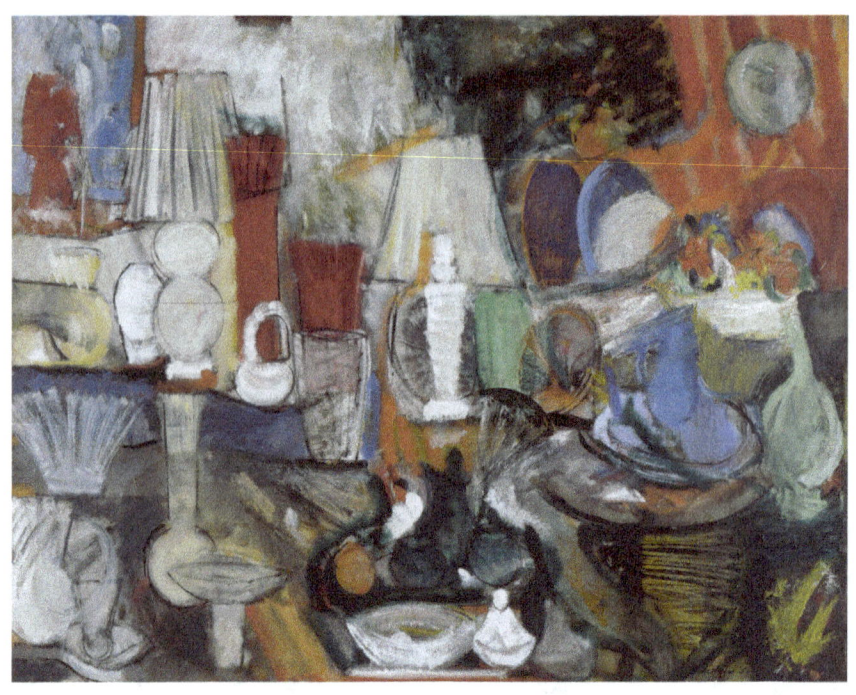

Plate 8. *Giftwares* (1955). Oil on canvas, 63 x 81 in. Collection of the Neuberger Museum of Art, Purchase College, State University of New York. Gift of Roy R. Neuberger. Photograph by Jim Frank.

These last few weeks have shown me that my most extreme emotional upsets don't bring on artistic sterility—almost the contrary, everyone who has seen the recent canvases feels they are joyful affirmations of life.

May 21
I intend to look for a job in market research this afternoon, and I was so filled with anxiety that I had that feverish, clammy hand—dry throat feeling. Reading my old journals has been a great relief, if only from the standpoint of knowing I've been through it before, and worse! This time I've not had my usual after-show painting sterility. My work is going, and I have a good start on the canvas "Mexico." I also feel I can have a job & paint at the same time, something I thought I could never do. If I could have painted so well in the midst of such emotional torment, a job should be nothing to contend with!

June 2
I've been working, editing research interviews ever since the last entry. I haven't painted at all yet, and I don't know what will happen—I can't go along like this indefinitely.

The museum comittee met to-day, I'll know Persian J's fate soon.

June 6
A full, hot, heavy summer Saturday afternoon. I've been painting and puttering, listening to jazz and thinking.

Nothing has been decided yet about P. J., and D. [Dorothy] Miller told John that there is so much delay and red tape involved in these things that I must put it out of my mind. Even if they do take it, it may be a long time before I get the money.

This job has been the best I've had yet. Mostly I think due to the freedom of coming & leaving as I please. I would probably have had a period of sterility after the Bathers anyhow, so it's good it came at this time. However I think I'm incapable of sustaining a painting mood while working 8 hours a day, and if I must do it I shouldn't even try to paint at the same time.

Ive put "Mexico" aside until I'm free, it requires too much sustained concentration.

Today I'm working on a still-life, the wash basin with two bananas on the Persian Print bed cover.

Larry was very excited about Bathers. He told Frank that he felt he & I, and to a lesser extent Jane, were the ones who were really finding their own style. I hope to visit him for a few days in Southhampton—when I'm free. I'd like to paint some landscapes in oil from nature. Jane is in Nyack for four months, Joe [Hazen] got a house, and I intend to paint there also. I feel like spending an isolated summer here, painting a lot, and seeing no one but Walt and Frank. I think I'm ready to do a lot of work now.

I intend to stay at this job through next week. I'll get a hundred dollars Tuesday, and then another sixty if I work 40 hours. That should carry me for a month, and Walt wants to help again on a new non-domestic basis, which will be fine for me at this time.

I feel that I'd like to do dozens of small paintings this summer, lots of still-lives and landscapes, rather quickly and then destroy and discard later. I've never worked this way before, but I think it might be right for me to do now.

June 16
To-day I begin working evenings, 6–10, which will give me all day to paint. I don't know how long this will go on, but I need the money it seems.

Made a small change on the left hand side of the Bathers at Al Leslie's suggestion—it keeps the tall figure from sitting forward too much.

Walt gave me Barr's book on Matisse, which I have been reading and studying with intense *interest for the last few* days.

John just called to say he sold "Trojan Horse" to Sylvia Remet for $150. I'm very pleased—I'll work through this week nights, and then this sale with my next check from Simmons will be enough to live on thru July or possibly longer.

I *must remember* the absolute necessity for me of painting or being in the studio every day, all day. This is the only way I can sustain the inner energy out of which painting comes. The problem of getting back in myself after these weeks of job working is always serious and depressing to me.

June 17
Sylvia Remet's husband just stormed into the gallery and threw the Trojan Horse at Tibor, shouting "How dare you sell junk like this!".

John is rushing to the bank to deposit the check before they stop payment. Fortunately I said nothing about not working next week at Simmons, I may have to continue. I'm always deeply hurt when things like this happen, I never expect my work to inspire violent hatred.

Tibor and John are having horrible quarrels about dissolving partnership. John wants to run the gallery alone, and *all* the legal papers are in Tibor's name. Goldwater [Robert Goldwater, writer on art] just bought a Leslie for $300 for Gloria Vanderbilt (Joan M. sold one also) and now Tibor wants the gallery himself, to stock with "saleable" painters. Some mess.

June 19
Mrs. Remet's check is good, and she will select another picture in the fall from the summer's work. I am not going to work at the job after this evening, and I will live & paint until the money runs out again.

This week has had a strange pattern—I seem to drink coffee, study the Matisse book and talk to friends on the phone until early afternoon, then I work two or two and a half hours on one of the three still lifes I've started. One of them, The Red Bowl, is finished I think. I rather like its simplicity, lord knows it took long enough to get that way.

I'm joining Frank at Larry's for 3 days next week—I'll pose with Frank for a sculpture Larry wants to start, swim & do some landscape painting. I'm eager to start working outdoors.

I feel optimistic about the way my painting will go this summer, as though last year's "experimentation" and intense study is over for a while, and I'm working in a way that is quite my own, though with an acknowledged debt to Matisse.

June 30
The Museum of Modern art has taken Persian Jacket, and George Poindexter is donating it. I am of course very pleased, but it still seems a little unreal since I've seen neither the money or the picture hanging in the Museum. I

will only get $400 for it less Johns ⅓, but if Poindexter can pay soon it will get me through the summer.

John just about ruined the whole thing by using Poindexter for a donation of a Goodnough to a Birmingham museum, and unwilling to ask for two donations. But I gave a party for Frank on Sunday and mentioned it to him (Poindexter) myself, in a subtle way. I can't usually do things like this for my own career, but this was too important to me not to.

I hope to keep Johns personal bitchiness and projected anxiety out of my life this summer, and also in the future preserve more distant dealer-artist relations with him, he's deeply destructive.

I'm a bit bothered that I haven't done more painting this year—five months—six! have passed of 1953, and all I have is The Bathers and this Red Bowl still-life. Of course half of the "Oranges" were done this year.

I tried a couple of landscapes directly from nature last week at Larry's—actually I painted them in Easthampton at the Castellis, on their rear lawn. I'm not at all pleased with them, but I intend to do more and find out if this way of working is good for me.

July 7
Back from four days in East Hampton with Walt at the Brach's—Joan & Mike [Goldberg] there too. They were most agreeable, and certainly more gracious and easier to be with than Larry or any of my friends. However in another way it was much less rewarding. I tried some painting at the beach on the bay, I rather like one of them.

I was terribly depressed this morning, I don't know why, I feel time slipping away and I'm accomplishing very little.

July 9
For the last two days I have been working on a silk screen print at the Tiber Studio—run by Daisy [Daisy Aldan, poet, editor, and cofounder of Tiber Press] & Richard Miller [cofounder of Tiber Press], two young people who are putting out a small magazine called "Folder" in the fall. I expect to have two or three prints in the first issue. They are using poems etc by Frank, Jimmy [Schuyler], Kenneth [Koch], John Ash. [Ashbery] & Bill Weaver.

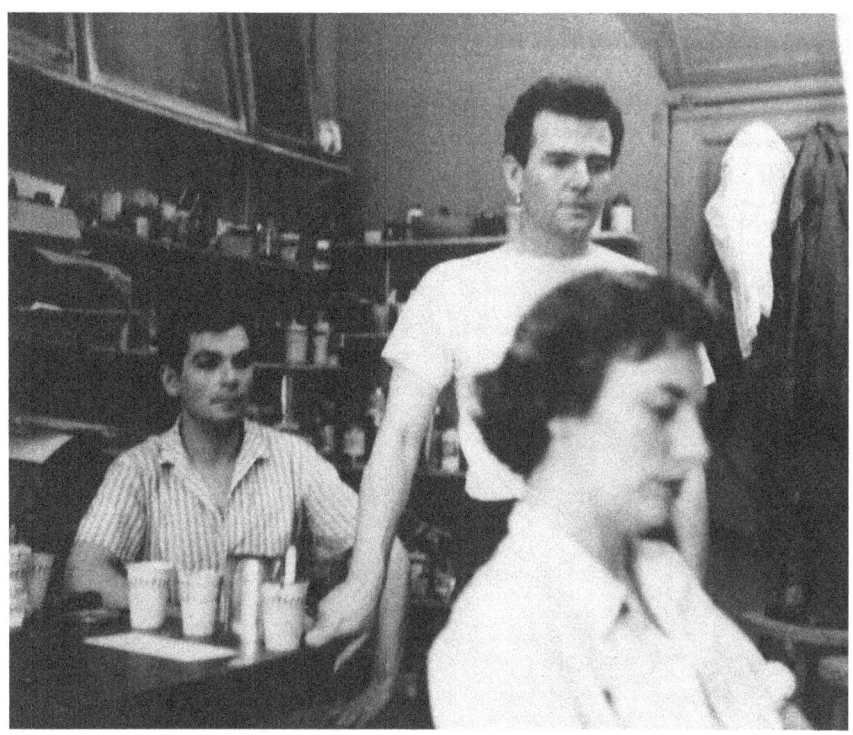

Richard Miller, Floriano Vecchi, and Grace Hartigan (left to right) working on silk-screen prints for *Folder 1*. These were Hartigan's first prints of this type, and she learned the serigraphy process from Vecchi. Photograph by Walter Silver.

The print process is interesting. I'm making 600 and my arm aches so I can hardly move it—and I've only pulled 2 colors & 100 of the third. I had intended to use many colors, but I've started a "still-life" in primaries, and I have experimented with opaque white on top of the third color, which is red. It seems to work well, I'll try it in ink tomorrow & it might finish this one. Then I intend to do a study of the Persian Jacket, from the drawing for it.

July 11
The first print "Still-life in Primary Colors" is finished—it's rather nice, fresh and open. I think this may be of help in the future, the nature of the process has made me more analytic about my "technique" or procedure in constructing a picture.

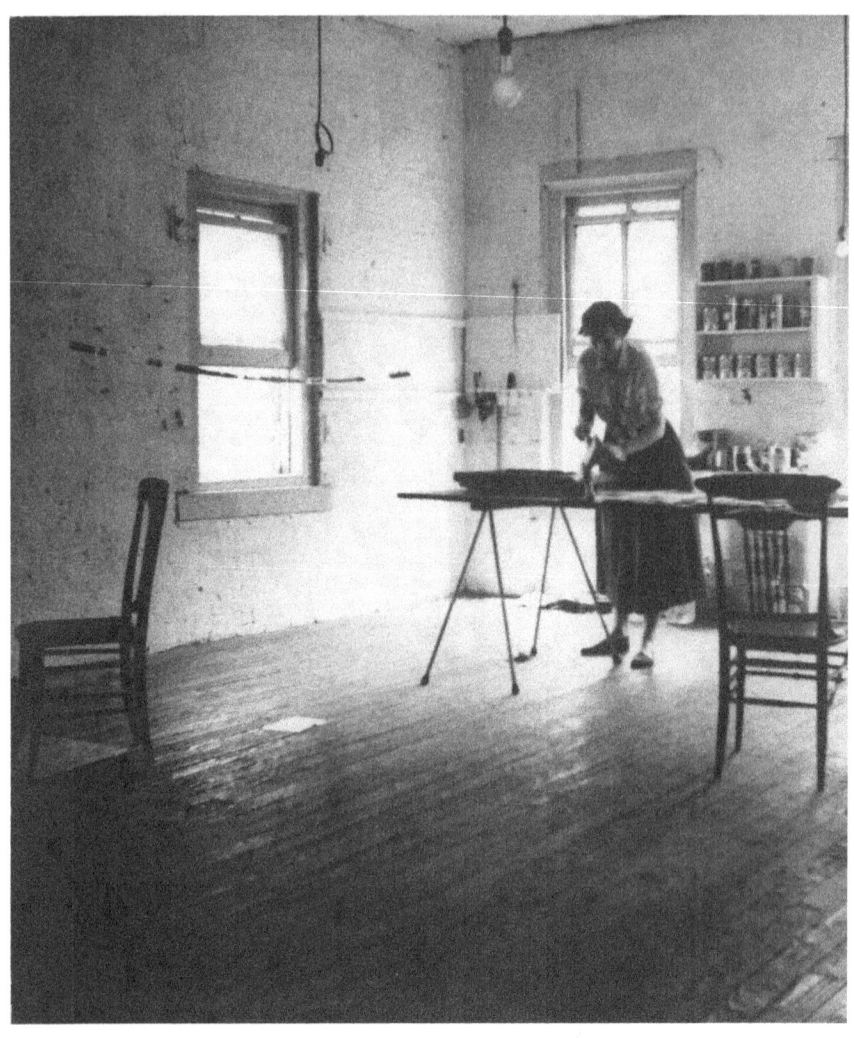

Hartigan making silk-screen prints for *Folder 1*. Photograph by Walter Silver.

July 13

At Westfield yesterday to see Arthur [Hartigan's brother]. I went over all my early drawings and paintings. Most of them were incredibly bad, really its difficult to understand how I could have gone on from such work. I destroyed almost every thing, 1944 through 1947 gone on a summer's afternoon. There are some examples left—as I just said to Frank, they indicate only too well the nature of my direction at that time. Most of the ones done under the

Muse-Avery (& misunderstood Matisse) influence were especially awful. The two I like best I remember painting very clearly, in Newark in that apartment on Clifton Ave opposite the cathedral. One of them was painted from an eggplant on the window sill with the garden in the rear. I remember hating it after it was finished. The other, a bowl with fruit, was painted when I was pregnant (with the never-born child) and at the *utter* depths. I think life could never be so black again as it was in those years, at least I have the comfort of facility in painting, even when inspiration fails. Then I had nothing but continual frustration, it's a miracle I survived.

July 21
To-day I ran the ~~third~~ fourth color on the second print (another version of Persian Jacket) with almost disastrous results. It's a penetrating orange which flattened everything out. I am quite upset to-day anyhow. Time seems to be rushing by and I'm getting so little done. And Bob's [Jachens] father died last night of lung cancer. Jeff is with my family till Sunday, I don't know yet how this will affect his life.

July 27
I finished the second print Friday, "The Persian Robe," it is quite full and successful. It has an emotional intensity that I wasn't sure I could get in that medium, so I am really pleased.

I intend to do a third, but I want to rest and think for a few days.

I felt filled with panic and anxiety until I got to the studio this morning, now I feel much better.

July 29
Humid and sticky all day, but I worked some oil on a few unfinished prints, variations on the seated figure. Also painted on the sea bather picture which I had originally started as a "Mexico" idea. It's nothing yet, but the vague beginnings are there.

July 31
I feel once more that I am getting into myself. The Sea bathers is getting to the point where it is painful, a good sign. And I have done several rather quick oils on paper over various stages of the silk screen Persian Robe.

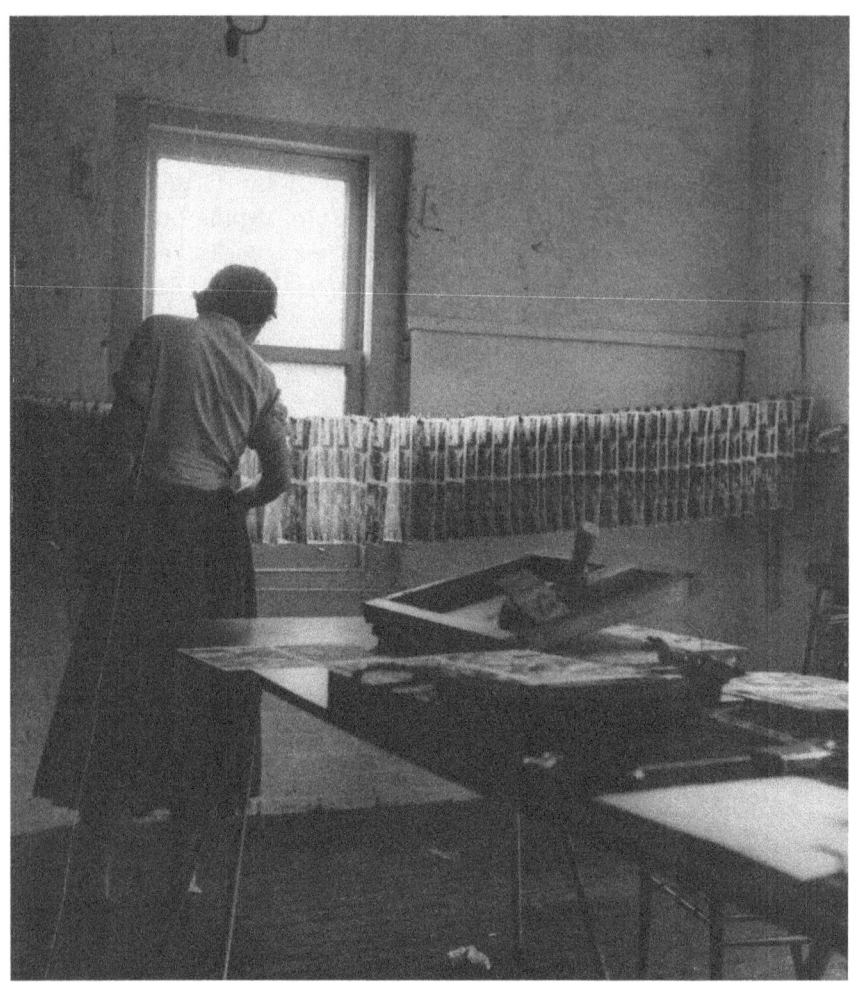

Hartigan hanging silk-screen prints for *Folder 1* to dry. Photograph by Walter Silver.

I want to keep this working feeling going and I've broken a date to visit Jane for a few days. Also if I do the 3rd silk scr. next week, I intend to work on it only for part of the day, and paint each morning.

I believe the Museum purchase has affected me more than I realized. I feel a sense of pressure and responsibility. I can't feel that it means nothing (as it has been bitchily suggested) because they have purchased so much mediocre work. Did the Louvre mean less to French artists because it embraced Messoniers [Meissonier?] & others? I cut my artistic teeth in the Mod. Mus., and when I think of it I think of my first seeing Matisse, Picasso—even my first Cezanne I saw there!

This means above all, an enlarged audience, and that I will be identified with this one work, The Pers. Jacket, almost exclusively. This is a subtle pressure to paint more of the same, or for me to identify with the same work. Of course I know this won't be a trap for me—my talent is too much out of my hands. I couldn't paint another P. J. even if I tried! But, as I said to Frank to-day when he asked what my reaction was going to be to "success," I said "retreat."

I will learn soon how to live with my aloneness.

Joan Mitchell said she admired my courage in making ugly pictures. I'm always hurt when anyone thinks my pictures are ugly, I make them as beautiful as I can.

August 3
To Nyack yesterday, saw Jane's new pictures. They are entirely lacking in drama, and seem timid and fearful. We all know that nature is over-powering, but the least we can do as artists is try to match her wonder with our passion.

August 4
Worked furiously all day yesterday on the Sea Bathers. I haven't painted this intensely since I finished the River Bathers. It's strange, I felt drained last night, but this morning I feel I know what to start doing to it. It has gotten too closed, I need to free it a bit, however I am pleased with the way it is coming along.

August 5
Struggled all day yesterday with this damn picture, nothing now but difficulties. It just won't work right.

August 6
Finally brought the Sea Bathers to a point where it is near completion, at least I feel almost free of it. It's a little too soft in places, I've blended color on the canvas in a way that's new for me.

Walked all the way to the studio this morning, this has been so far a gloriously cool summer.

August 7
The "Sea Bathers" is finished. There are many things about it which please me, it has a certain order & calm in spite of the color intensity. I feel exhausted, I had to give so much to it. I wonder if I'll always have to "go under" in this way to get a solution?

We intend to go to the Brach's this weekend, I may stay an extra day, I have some water color sticks to do some sketching from nature.

Aug. 11
I've been reading Quennell's two volumes on Byron, which John assures me will change my life. In just what way I am at a loss to understand. If J. wishes me to dissipate my talent in self-destructive wandering & promiscuity, taking Byron as a model, is the surest way to do it. J. is an idiot, he doesn't understand my temperament in the least.

I had no feelings of identification with Byron—far more with a spirit like Rilke, shy, but at times powerfully sure, mystical, misanthropic—I feel also for Cezanne, his outward desire to fit into a conservative life, his antagonisms, etc. Or even I'm more like Melville or Hawthorne. I can see in the future more and more withdrawal from everyone but a few trusted friends.

The only area in which I felt anything with Byron was his romantic idea of his own beauty, & his desire to stay thin! I do have a picture of myself as pale & willowy & poetic instead of this big strapping creature that I am. I've been struggling to lose weight, but I can't seem to get below 150, even tho I haven't touched bread, potatoes or any thing sweet for two weeks.

I still haven't gotten the money for the Persian Jacket from Poindexter. The Goodnough donation is holding everything up, since he wants to take care of both things at once for tax deduction. I have no money, no paint & my rent is due in four days. Walt has been feeding me, but I'm getting concerned.

Aug. 25, 1953
Spent a nerve-wracking day in Brooklyn court, waiting for my annulment case against Harry to come up. It went in a few minutes after it was called,

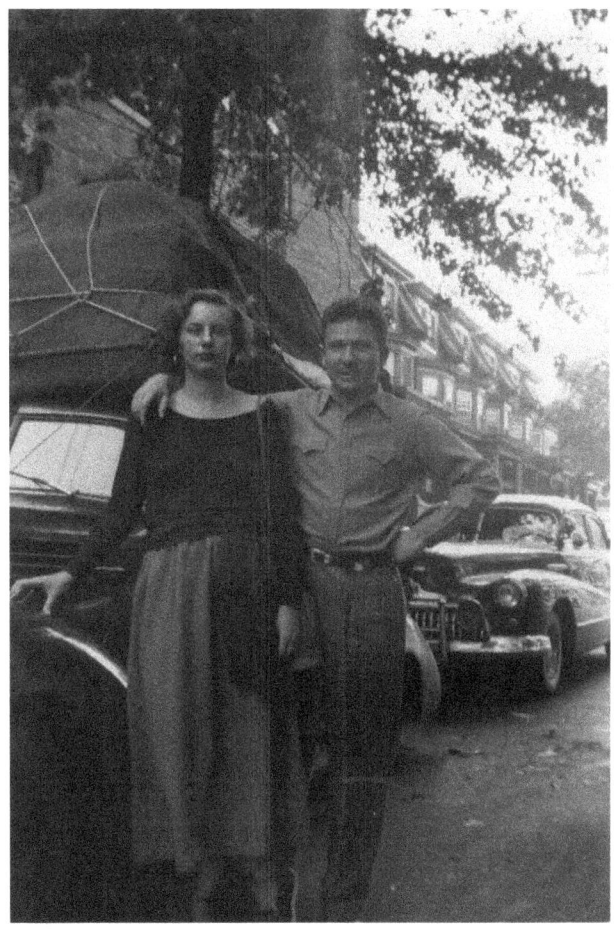

Hartigan and Harry Jackson leaving for Mexico in
1949, soon after their marriage. Hartigan returned to
New York, alone, a few months after this picture was
taken.

and I'll know in a few weeks if I'm "free." It seems so absurd, as if people
should know when a marriage is over & not be forced through such a
charade.

I have finished the third silk screen for "Folder," it is crisp & nice, but more
trouble than it was worth.

Richard wants me to do another, a double page in black and white, but I think the medium is really not suited to my kind of drawing, tonal drawing, and it would be wiser if I could be firm and refuse.

Aug. 27
John and Frank here yesterday, Joan for a few hours to-day. I get little from anyone these days, I feel suspended and lethargic.

Joan's visit was the most pleasant, oddly enough. We discussed the Sea Bathers, and it's relationship to my recent interest in Roman wall paintings —(Pompeii).

I haven't been able to get energy to do anything, even draw. It's terribly hot, and I haven't a continuing sense of myself yet. I want to get into the rhythm of being in the studio, working day after day.

Larry's new work impressed me very much, it is full, calm and truly original.

Aug. 30
The heat for the last five days has been in the upper nineties, and although I had planned to start on a seated figure from Johanna, I simply haven't had the energy. I did buy linen (!) canvas & some paint. The linen was a bargain, 14.00 for 45″, 6 yd roll.

I'm impatient for the summer to end, for the rains & clarity of autumn. I feel I haven't worked enough this summer, though the only one who has done more than I is Larry.

We visited Al & Esta Friday night—he has done nothing since his show, I'd be filled with anxiety if it were I. Of course they spent all their money on the trip, and now he must work at jobs to make more. As time goes on I realize how important day after day painting is, or just being in the studio, reading or looking at reproductions, it is the only way to keep in touch & sustain one's efforts.

I have been thinking of a talk I had with Mimi [Schapiro, Paul Brach's wife] on my "subject material." I think I work with emotions of loneliness, alienation and anxiety. The pictures ask "What are we doing here?" and "what do we mean to each other?" The figures never touch, never look at each other, but still have some intense meaning for each other.

This is what I am attracted to in Hopper, it is very "American" this kind of gigantic aloneness. Only he "represented" it too much, I want to really paint it.

Sept. 3
The heat goes on and on. I have been working on a still life of plants, and made a strained drawing of Frank, but it's difficult to work in such an oven. I do feel in touch with myself, and I intend to do a little each day until cool weather comes & my energy returns.

I've been reading the life of Chopin, with great interest & sympathy. He spoke of giving "birth" to his work in the same way I have thought and spoken of my own. I feel very close to him and to Rilke.

Sept. 8
Labor Day is over, and another summer. I have some work I feel good about. The two large bather pictures, two still-lifes—"Red Bowl" & "Flower Pots." Three little landscapes, some drawings (one, done yesterday from Johanna, which pleases me) and a good beginning on the seated Greek figure & the head from Jo.

I am unhappy about my life to-day. I feel I am a coward, I fear loneliness so intensely that I submit to emotional chains. I am grateful for peace and security, but freedom seems so desirable, and so unattainable.

Sept. 9.
Everything changes.

I will be quite alone now. Frank has moved to Sneedens Landing with Bobby Fisdale [partner of Frank O'Hara and a musician]—it should be good for him and his work, a kind of isolation he couldn't do for himself in the city. Larry will spend his first winter in Southampton. Al has been in Hoboken for so long it seems he always lived there. Waldemar doesn't exist for me any longer, we have nothing to say to each other, he'll never write a novel, he's too afraid of failure. Jane will be returning the end of this month, but I am so embarrassed by the weakness of her painting I can't bear to see her.

Well, who knows, maybe there are others.

Sept. 10
Work went well yesterday, and I finished the head of Johanna [a model]—
"Greek Head"(?) Maybe that title has too many classical connotations. I seem
to be working more with a palette knife than ever before, scraping down in
some places, adding impasto in others.

I'm going to work on the seated Greek, but I find it hard to begin, it's such a
good start. One must beware of beautiful beginnings, and feel free to destroy
them. What comes eventually is better and more true.

Sept. 14
Finished the seated Greek figure to-day "Cephalonia "Seated Greek." I can see
it will be one of my most popular pictures. John, Tibor & Larry all praised
it before it was even finished. It's too blended, and not "painted" enough to
please me, but I learned some things I can apply in future works.

Sept. 17
I realize what I hated in the "Seated Greek" was the face, it was too timid
and underpainted. I worked on it over & over & it wasn't right. Al was here
this morning for several hours, looking at pictures & talking. He liked this
immensely but for the head. After he left I rubbed it out, and in ten minutes
put in a head that would please Manet I think. Now it's really complete, I am
pleased with the handling of her left arm & hand.

The gallery opened Tuesday with Nell Blaine. I have never seen such a
crowded opening, I think the season will be the best so far, there seems to be
enormous interest.

Larry was in town & took a large dose of heroin, I spent most of yesterday
spooning him chicken broth & ice cream. He felt better late in the afternoon,
and we went to see Bob Stone's paintings. They are really peculiar, nutty
three dimensional Gorky figures cavorting in violet clouds. I enjoyed them
immensely.

Al always has a good effect on me, I feel very vigorous and stimulated. He
liked the two still-lifes, the older bathers (River Bathers), the seated Greek
(but for the head) and the little oil on paper seated figures. He's working,

painting now. But he & Esta have great battles, she's only happy when he's making money & seeing none of his friends. It's so necessary to one's work to have a calm, uncomplicated emotional life, I wish Walt were wiser & would let me feel more free.

Dorothy Miller called John. The Whitney is interested in seeing my paintings, John will bring ten or so over next month to show them.

Sept. 21
". . . Those trivial delights, those shameful agonies, which the ordinary man suppresses, but which the artist hoards as unconsciously as the seed secretes those elements within itself from which the growing plant will draw its nourishment." Maurois on Proust.

"Proust held that an artist's most pressing concern is to arrive at the closest communion with a reality which, in the last analysis, is the reality of himself."

Sept. 25
Returned to-day from three days in Nyack with Jane. I feel as though I got more from this visit than any other all summer. The weather was glorious, fall-cool with beginnings of leaf-changes and deep shadows. I read some Balzac, and Jane and I worked hard each day, she in pastel & I in pencil, and I did a few good drawings. I got a different idea of her work through such close contact, and insight into my own. I think she is working honestly and directly from her own experience & observation, with *no* preconceived attitudes towards composition, style or "art." This leads to stumbling, but it is a brave approach. I think I work too often from my knowledge of other art, and I wish to simplify and become more stark and direct in my experience as I paint.

Sept. 28
Brought "Seated Greek Girl," "Greek Head" & ~~Potted Plants~~ "Flower Pots" to Gallery. Dorothy Miller is bringing Whitney people there next week to see my work. I'm going to send up the River Bathers just in case something important happens.

I finished a peculiar still life from the beets, squash & red peppers that I began some days ago. It is all palette knife, and is along with my new ideas of working with nature all the way through the painting, observing closely and directly.

I intend to begin pastel studies & drawings for a nude self portrait. It's too cold to paint nude, but I should know my own figure well enough to use it.

This was a good month of work for me, I hope October goes well, my money should last till the first of November if Herbert [Machiz] pays me for the Impressario as he promised.

Oct. 8
I haven't seemed to be able to do any painting since I finished Still-life with Beets and Peppers. All who have seen it think (Larry, John, Walt, Jane, Frank) it is one of my best pictures. It seems to have emptied me for a while. Frank told me Pasternack said that the artist is not a fountain, but a sponge—so I haven't enough to squeeze out yet.

Social life and personal upsets have kept me busy—"Folder" is out & seems to be having a small success. Everyone likes my silk screens, Leo Castelli says they are the best he has ever seen in America.

Mike' [Goldberg] show is up, it looks nice, but isn't very ambitious. He is quite content to follow that De Kooning-Gorky abstract line.

I think seeing Al's new seated figure which John brought to the Museum has upset me quite a bit. It was so powerful, so bold that it made my Greek Girl look fussy to me. I must find what *I* must do, and not be so impressed by others whose work I admire.

My anxieties about money are beginning again. I did get the check for the Impressario, but this is the end of what is owed me & no sales are in sight. I don't really care about money, but I need time desperately. I don't want to give up my solitude for the nightmarish intrusion of a job.

What I really need is a patron, someone who will either regularly buy pictures or send me $100 to $150 each month.

Al Bing [Al Bing, real estate investor and art patron] could do this easily enough if he cared to, but I feel too involved with him as a friend to even suggest it, or to let that be a touchy point at this stage of my relationship with him. I am going to his country place for the weekend with Ann Ryan [collage artist], perhaps something will come of it. Fortunately he is too old to have the added complication of sexual attraction confuse things further.

∿

Hartigan's relationship with Alexander M. Bing was ambiguous. The ambiguity was appreciated by Bing, as this excerpt with run-in paragraphs from a letter dated 17 September 1955 from the Hartigan papers demonstrates: "I intended to bring up the question of your possible need for a loan, the other evening but forgot about it & am enclosing a check for a little more than you suggested as it may be a little while before funds start coming in. You exaggerate the amount of help I have given you. Whatever I did, I was very glad to do both for personal reasons as well as my judgement that you would probably become an important artist—one as to whom it would be a great satisfaction to have been of any assistance—anyway I did not feel it. So please do not feel under any obligations I do value our friendship very highly & could become more sentimental—but that would be foolish—"

∿

I feel that my life is going to change drastically soon. I think certain things will remain constant, my intense concern with my painting, and the relationships with a few people—John Myers, Frank, Larry, maybe Al & Jane. But the milieu of the Cedar Bar, of the Brachs, the Club people, all that seems to do nothing but *drain* me of my energy and enthusiasm.

Oct. 12, evening
This is the first day of my new life. I hope I have the strength to remain isolated and quiet. I feel about to take a "giant step" in my art or life direction, and Walt seems to have no place with me now. All I would do is destroy him— if we continued. I hope I can bear the sexual frustration, and not become involved in a new relationship.

I feel fairly calm, I've spent the whole day in the studio, resting & thinking. I made a solitary dinner and I've been drinking dark beer and watching a bold grey mouse invade my privacy.

The WNYC broadcast last night was a complete fiasco, half of us sounded like frivolous children & the others (including me) unbearably pompous. I regreted leaving the calm luxury of the weekend at Al Bing's to come for such a farce. The situation there is complex. I had underestimated the emotional capacities of so old a man, and I don't have the temperament which would enable me to play a game in order to use someone. He intends to buy a painting this week which eases my mind considerably—I'm entirely on my own now. I would like to go with him to Europe, I feel the need to travel and learn from old culture now. But the only way I could do it—if he indeed decided to ask me—would be as a companion, not as a mistress.

Another thing I must do is see fewer artists, I seem to be so vulnerable and I am being bitterly attacked, even by my "friends" Part of it is jealousy, part resentment of my willful attitudes & opinions. I am happier with people who admire me and don't challenge me, like Al Bing and Richard Miller, than I am with a group of my "best friends" who can be vicious when they get together, knives drawn.

Oct. 13
Slept well, poached egg, toast, coffee, still calm.

Oct. 14
Terribly upsetting experience, yesterday. I had asked Harry if I could see his new pictures, and he came by & picked me up at noon—we walked over, his studio is beautiful and I was most impressed with an intensely full large picture he calls "Family." As I was looking at it I heard the crash of something in the kitchen—he ran in and soon I heard loud slaps and things being thrown—he and his girl friend were having a violent battle. She came rushing in the studio like a mad thing and screamed at me "I consider you Harry's worst enemy". Harry offered to "beat the shit out of her," there were more blows & she left. He showed me a flat iron and said "I saved you from being hit with this".

I was shaking with nervousness, and left soon, what insanity!

Oct. 15
I've started a full length self portrait that I've had in mind for a long time. It's coming in an impossible way, but I intend to stay with it until something begins to happen.

I'm reading Maurois' life of George Sand, it's comforting beyond belief at this time.

Her bravery and ability to live alone with herself for long periods are inspiring. I am deeply in myself now, and I feel strong, with a sharp awareness of my destiny.

Exit Walter. "Happy are those who, having been caught for a while in the white heat of a brilliant destiny, have been able to escape from the danger zone before they have suffered too much damage".—Maurois on Sand

I may take Edi as a lover in time, if the situation presents itself easily. He is the only man I know who is attractive & gifted enough to interest me. It would be odd to be wooed by a very old man, and love a very young one! [This passage was heavily crossed out but was decipherable. Hartigan granted permission for its inclusion.]

Oct. 17
I called Frank at Sneeden's this morning, and one of the things we discussed was the way art seems to fail us when we need it most.

Then I worked all day in a white heat of fury on the "self portrait with Jack-o-lanterns." It is all palette knife, and a strange picture for me—I suppose it looks "uncontrolled" and as though I "can't draw". But I'm proud of it's directness and blunt passion, and if it's not one of my best pictures it's certainly one that gave me the most joy and release while painting it.

The pain of being without a lover is beginning to set in, but everyone has been marvelous to me, John and Herbert have had me to dinner twice, Richard took me to dinner and the new Italian film "Overcoat," Jane & Joe [Hazen] brought dinner here, and last night Frank and Bobby [Fisdale] came in town & we drank with John Ashb. [Ashbery] at Jane's, a hilarious time with them all giving liberal advice about my relationship with Al Bing.

Al B. was here yesterday and bought three small things for $250.

Nov. 2.
I've been reading the previous entry a bit sheepishly. I ran into Walt in the gallery the day after writing it and I was overwhelmed by the intensity of my feelings for him I have never found any special virtue in fighting my emotions, so we are to-gether again, with new resolution to try and understand what we need from each other more clearly.

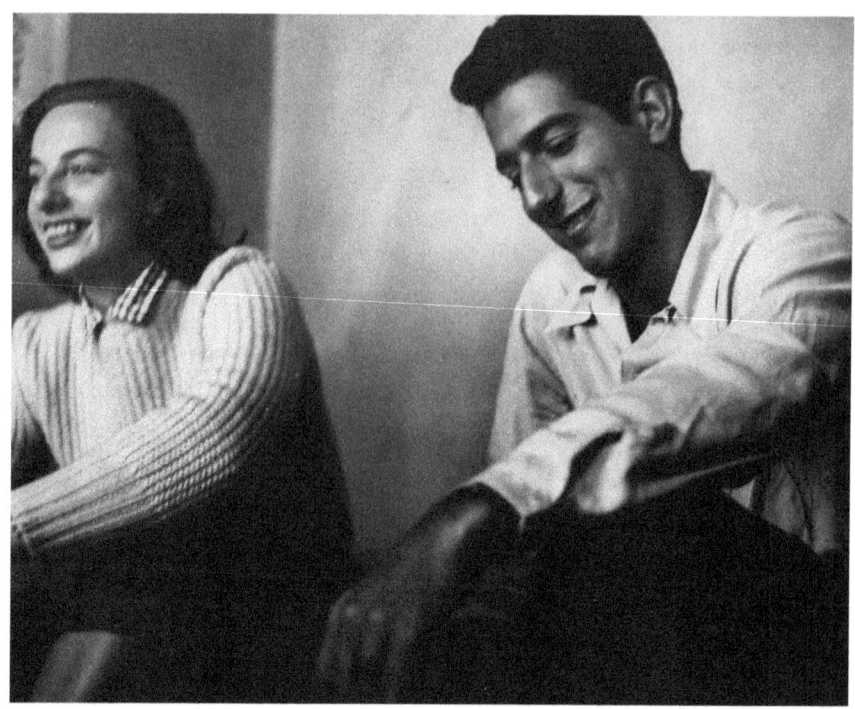

Hartigan and Edi Franceschini in 1952. Photograph by Walter Silver.

One thing that I must have is more time alone, days and nights both, to get into myself and sustain my painting. This is far easier to do with the knowledge that I love and am loved, it gives me a deep security that helps me be strong.

"The self-taming process was not always comfortable, and the aftermath of each crisis was likely to be a bout of melancholy. "The evil of isolation"—as he termed it—In short ennui: Ennui was simply energy quelling itself, waiting for an outlet—not merely an explosive discharge, and seeking fulfillment through coherent expression in lasting forms. The chain of impulse is logical: daemon, self-control, impatience, ennui, "rage for order": art."
Barzun on Berlioz.

Nov. 4
Complete fiasco at the Artist's Theater last night. They did Lorca's Don Perlimplin and a Lionel Abel play, sets by Al Leslie—it was all too

embarrasing and depressing. I never make any particular stand for "art"—I just assume that I and some other people are involved in certain principles. Obviously it takes unusual theatre people to be interested in these ideals, and Herbert's [Machiz] aims have nothing to do with mine. I intend to withdraw from all theater activities, it would be a useless waste of energy to do the Ghelderode sets.

I just called John to console him for his disaster—he is absolutely blind, thought it was a bit clumsy here & there, but generally went charmingly. I don't know why I should be burdened with this horrific honesty—what do I care, why should I be so appalled at loss of ideals? I'm such a self-appointed guardian of conscience! I make such enemies this way—no one wants to hear "truth"—I should perhaps be like Frank, who after telling me he thought Herbert had no talent, not even commercial talent, called John to say how much he liked it!

Nov. 5
Long letter from John, defending the theater & Herbert. I wrote him some of my feelings, but my position is so difficult, and the only answer might be—what I do is art, what Herbert does is not. And that is such a stupid point of view.

Of course I doubt myself all the time, but I must obey my instincts, they are the only things I can trust. I was thinking last night as I sat by the stove reading the journals of the last year how suspicious I am of whatever "procedure" I'm involved with at a certain period in painting. When I was working from "master" reproductions I was afraid I'd never do anything original. When I was painting from photographs I was afraid I'd never work from nature again. When the work was more agitated I hated its "expressionism" and wanted more calm. And now that it's more calm I fear it's not emotional enough. When I take a long time on a picture and struggle a great deal I hate the agony and suspect I'm over-working. And when it comes easily I fear facility.

This all would be almost funny if I didn't suffer so with it. Now that I'm working more directly from nature I'm terrified that I'm chained to it, and that I'll never be able to work out of my imagination again.

Nov. 10.
I'm continuing to lead a withdrawn life—no Cedar Bar, no artist's gatherings,

it's so peaceful I wonder why I never did it before. I've been working a bit, finished a rather strange still-life of flowers & bananas, it has something I think. Done a couple of drawings from David. Working now on a large painting of my plants lined up almost in a row. I have some idea of white, green, grey, black that I'd like to carry out.

I feel that my art is becoming more public, and this will increase over the winter. I want then to have my life more and more private. I feel so vulnerable.

Spent a warm and pleasant evening with Al Bing last night, a fancy dinner out and then a few hours looking at some of his magnificent books on art. He loaned me a book on Berlioz with original lithos. by Fantin-Latour, to look at along with reading Barzun's Berlioz. He gave me a check for the other fifty dollars, plus another hundred for a "future" picture. He makes it so easy for me to take a gift, which is what this last amount really is, that I have very few qualms. I'll be able to buy now a cheap winter coat, and some paints & canvas for a painting of Walt in the costume of a matador.

Nov. 12
More Barzun on Berlioz—"The price he paid was to experience bouts of his dread "isolation" which we may translate as the child's sense of being bereft. In the grown man, it took the form of feeling that "life escaped him" that he could only catch shreds of his own existence, which may have unconsciously spurred him to fashion works in which life is caught, pinned down, held forever. But hence also, at times of intense composing which brought elation, he experienced moments of inexplicable anxiety—".

This "inexplicable anxiety" is what I've been feeling all week, it's almost too much to bear.

Nov. 13
For some time—I guess from the return to N.Y. after Mexico in 1949 until just recently I had a feeling of a group, an artistic milieu that I identified with, some feeling of work in common with three or four painters and some poets. I think perhaps the "giant step" I spoke of a month ago is the realization that I am a solitary artist, isolated, and that my painting is not part of any "movement" or group but a thing alone. I still respect the talents of a few people,

but my work has nothing to do with theirs, and it will help me know myself better if I realize this once & for all time.

I have an old copy of a Cahiers d'Art in which there are photographs of Picasso and his studio at the time when he was a cubist. I find myself looking at the studio photos, in which you can see such over-flowing energy and greatness, such *abundance*—drawing on drawing pinned up, paintings by the dozen, stacked against each other every which way, and I have such feelings of envy and impotence! Will my art ever flow for me this way? Now the "self-taming" process is so painful that only one picture comes at a time, I sit & brood with it like a hen on an egg until finally something happens and it begins to break through. And there's always the fear that the "something" won't happen this time, or ever again—!

Nov. 18
Received notification this morning from the Museum that "Pastorale" was accepted for the Young Amer. Printmakers Show. It will open next week & run for two months. I had hoped to sell out of this show, but they have requested only two extra prints—perhaps they see if those sell & then request more.

If the Museum shows Pers. Jack. next month, and then the magazine Art in America comes out in January, my show should be at a good time—Feb. 2 to receive attention and perhaps sell.

I've been working the last week on "Row of Flower Pots"—I think it may be finished. I rather like the use of black in it.

I'm a bit tired of working from still-life. I'd like to start the Matador picture soon, but I don't really feel I can afford the costume, canvas, stretcher & paint I would need.

Dec. 1.
The "Black Still-Life" is finished, and it ends my interest in still-life for a while. I intend to try a small studio interior, and the Matador picture is in my mind, although I havent really any money to start it.

I've been anxiety-ridden lately, for no observable reason. Some of it may come from the questionaire sent me by the Mod. Mus. It made me feel crowded in some way. Then, too, the horrifying results of foolishly letting the News Inquiring Reporter print my name & photo with remarks of his invention—the intrusion of phone calls from sex maniacs, nuts & cranks, what a lesson to me, I must always keep guarded from the outside world.

Larry is here in town stretching paintings and preparing drawings for his show. The pictures didn't look as good to me here as they did in South Hampton. They are too much like huge stained drawings, and they make no use of the surface, they dont project.

Harry's show has been on two weeks now. He takes almost shamelessly from Matisse, and the results look easy and almost too beautiful. However it's better than most everything that's being done these days, and it should have attracted more attention.

I feel at loose ends to-day. I don't know if I have the energy to begin a new painting. Barzun talks acutely of this feeling—"The overcoming of inertia at the beginning of a great work, that psychological dead weight which has nothing to do with the nature of the task, the author's preparation for it, nor even his desire to be at work, but *is an emotional resistance due to the disparity between the world of created things and the world of the uncreated.* The conception on its way to birth—is unreal and, as it seems, superfluous— *reality being complete without it.*"

Dec. 3
Discouragements, discouragements. Went to the reception for Young Am. Printmakers Tues. evening—it was pleasant & champagne flowed. Only one of mine sold, and I went back yesterday after several museum staff people promised to buy—and they haven't.

The New Acquisitions show this month is only for design & architecture, so God knows when they'll show lady Persia.

The new show Young European Painters is so free-form non-objective, slanted, tasteful and weak, that I'm sure Sweeny will never select one of my pictures for the coming American show.

I am down to my last twenty-five dollars.

John just spoke with Clem, who is so vicious about me. He told J. that he is the creature of G. Hartigan, that "everyone" is boycotting the gallery because J. makes Cabals, intrigues and plays a horrifying game of art politics. Helen left the gallery, & is suing John for a picture of hers that he can't find. Clem also says I wooed Alfred Barr, because I know who is "important" It's so absurd—I would woo him if I could, because he *is* so bright, so *important*, and admires my painting. A delightful combination. But I've met the man only three or four times in my life. Everyone wants "success" and "power". And everyone tries and fails. The only time you are ostracized and condemned is when it looks as though you are successful.

On top of all these worldly concerns, I am worried about my painting. There was a time—including last year—when my energy overflowed, and I'd be involved in a constant stream of work, several pictures coming at a time, drawing, sculpture. Now it's more & more painful to even begin a small picture, and until the point when it starts to "flow" I almost have to force myself to work.

This has been increasingly true, ever since River Bathers. I hope it is a temporary situation, due to a high standard I've set for myself & the difficulty of achieving it. If I could be more like Larry, for whom drawing is such "fun" that he could go on for hours with it. For me to do even a small drawing takes such an effort, that it exhausts me.

Dec. 4
Harry dropped by here yesterday, and we talked for two hours without stop about one's audience and "subject material." In some ways it was similar to a conversation Larry and I had in Southampton, ideas float in the air at certain times.

Harry feels that the reason the "de Nagy" artists are hated & boycotted is fear that we will make painting more public, less art for artists and so revolutionize the whole "special" ivory tower position of an artist in America. We talked long of what to paint—that artists for so long have been portraying only the essence of art, it's skeleton. If one's talents and imagination are huge enough, that will always be there, and one can present it with many faces.

We both liked Larry's painting a "Washington Crossing the Delaware". It's completely his own style, but think of the audience possibility on the basis of the subject material! Plus the incentive of enjoyment in painting what is interesting, and the rewards of attention and sales!

Harry is thinking of painting the West, big cowboy and horse pictures, which should find an appreciative audience in wealthy ranchers, cattlemen, Texas oil men, etc.

This whole idea interests me more than anything since I "discovered" Spanish painting. What I must do is find *my* world of reference. I have some vague ideas, and I'd like to note a few for future reference. Landscapes & Still-life is out. It must be people to interest me.

I admire Velasquez & Goya, the portrayals of kings, queens and court life, costumes, etc. with the *irony* they use in these interpretations.

I admire Manet's Spanish period. Also some things such as the opera pictures & Folies Bergère. ["Cezanne's baroque pictures" is added in the margin.]

Delacroix's Algerian exoticism. Renoir's & Matisse's exoticism. So—as I can vaguely begin to feel it, I am interested in a certain kind of romanticism. The pictures I have painted which come near to this are Persian Jacket, Greek Girl, and oddly enough the Impressario. I think the reason I hated it so was it's over done "expressionism." However it may contain a lot of possibilities for future reference when I learn greater control and discipline.

I will need a tremendous amount of simple, plain FACILITY for these ambitious ideas. I must draw much more, heads, figures, anything human & preferably from life, not reproduction or photograph.

Ideas—
Haut monde? Opera, ballet, theater—audience or participants.
Restaurants—diners in evening clothes. Elegant homosexuals.
Parties, openings
High fashion world—do drawing, from photos in Vogue.
Movie world—glamour.
People with extravagant ideas of dress (Judith Malina in black with her Egyptian jewel-look)
Dancers—Spanish.

The matador thing fits in beautifully with this—

I'm going to not finish the studio interior & perhaps work on a thing of John Myers with a fur robe on his shoulders.

This of course will take *years* to digest, discover and express.

Dec 10
Bought canvas duck—prepared, heavy weight & wood & screws. Walt has hired a matador costume & I intend to start the picture & drawings this weekend. I have $15.00 left in the bank, but what the hell. I have to get started on this.

Larry's left to go back to South H. His show opened Tuesday. I helped hang it—we are very compatible now, and I feel closer to him than ever before. There is no doubt, in spite of what personal disagreement I might have with the "drawing" in the pictures, that he is one of the most exciting painters I know. He also is way ahead of everyone in stating his own uniquely personal style and point of view. This is part of the reason for his abundant flow of work, he is so clear about what he wants.

I have an uncomfortable feeling that I haven't enough work for my show. There will be a big "vanguard" show in Feb. at the Stable, and John wants me to show Ocean Bathers They intend to have a fully illustrated catalogue. This will leave a gap in my show, but if I dont have to work for the next month I guess I can do some more paintings. Mel Pitzele [art patron] has Coffee-Pot & Cucumber on approval, Richard is paying a first payment on Still life with Blue Wall so that will carry me till January if all goes OK.

Dec. 16
I've been ill for the last three days, and Walt's been nursing me in his warm apartment. A touch of virus, I guess.

I have so much to do I'm mad with impatience, but I do feel a bit weak. Over the weekend Walt posed in his hired red velvet matador suit—it was so stimulating that I started four pictures, one of them 3 ft x 6 ft, I hope to carry it off with the red figure against white, a tough problem. Got a rather nice charcoal drawing which only needs a few touches in the jacket to finish it. I feel pleased with what I got, we took photos and I can refer to them as I work more.

Pitzele did buy the still-life, and Richard came by Mon. evening with Floriano [Floriano Vecchi, Italian printmaker who taught silk-screening to Hartigan and others, including Andy Warhol], bringing violets, chartreuse, a gingerbread man and a hundred dollar bill. I don't think I've ever been so touched. He is a real friend, and one of the few people in the world devoted to my work. I think we will have a close relationship for many years, possibly he will be the Vollard of the future it's too big a role for John to handle.

Mother & Dad sent me a 25.00 check, so my finances are better, and with my rent & phone paid, the commission for John and 10.00 for the Stable, I have $129.00 in the bank and 20.00 to spend on Christmas presents.

I intend to put Seated Greek Girl in the Stable show, they've pleaded for "reasonable" size pictures, it's one of my best pics & a nice size. The art world is buzzing with the show—they've invited 130 artists. I don't see how they can hope for high quality with such lax invitation standards. Bob Stone is flipping over what to send, he's so unsure and so attacked, he wants to put in a 9 foot canvas. He's become so involved in art politics & careerism that he'll land in the hospital again if he doesn't calm himself somehow.

My prints are selling a little now, there are four or five stars I've been told. If I'm lucky I may sell enough to pay for my catalogue. [A star represents a sale of a particular print.]

Dec. 17
Last night with John to hear Berlioz's "L'Enfance du Christ". I got a great deal from it, even though the conductor fell far short of getting a "divine fire" into the work. I was impressed by Berlioz's desire to incorporate many elements into a work—using an organ for perhaps five minutes in a two hour work seems remarkable to me. And I am confirmed again in my thoughts that nothing is extraneous or "impure" in art, if the creator has enough ability to sythesize [synthesize?]. I'm re-reading Barzun's chapter on this work, and I am impressed by these lines:

"The very element of life implies *will*, and it is will that links nature on the one hand to moral choice, and on the other to art. The will to create—or procreate—is spent asserting that it's forms shall not perish; art is conscious-ness scratching it's mark upon matter; *love of fame is love of continuity, of sur-vival*, and all these require energy which desires form and attains worth. His dominant trait as a man, energy, is for Berlioz one of the tests of art—only notice in his music the vigor of most of his opening phrases. Even tenderness must be strong, masculine, never languorous or mawkish, and love must be supreme awareness, not (as in Wagner) Nirvana or death. For life to Berlioz means vertebrate existence, brain and sinew. Here he is at one with Stendhal, Balzac, and Nietzsche, all of whom find the essence of beauty in the excite-ment of the will and the enhancement of being."

Dec. 21
Suffering from the annual Christmas-time depression. These holidays hold nothing but horrors for me—empty sentiments, spending money for gifts I can't afford, constant nagging pressures about what I should be doing that I cannot do, guilts about Jeff.

Frank was terribly drunk last night in the Cedar—my first visit there in weeks. He was vicious to Larry, made a scene of quiet ugliness as only he can do. He's so close to madness, it frightens me sometimes. I can't bear his switches in loyalties—of course I change too and now my feelings of friend-ship for Larry make me defend him, and I can't feel close to Frank, Jane, or Jimmy and the other boys.

I think the reason I feel estranged from Frank is that he doesn't give me that final, deep allegiance that I need from my friends. I am more vulnerable than ever, the outside world seems cruel, and I want that deep blood vow from those I love.

That kind of devotion can be given by very few people, and maybe for only periods at a time. Now I get it from Walt, Richard & Floriano, John Myers in his nutty way, Bob Stone (he came up to me drunkenly at Larry's opening party and told me I was the best painter in New York) and Larry. I get it from Bob & Larry partly because I return it, loyalty & admiration.

What a horror, that even in our "group" we are all at each other so bitterly, what a lonely life!

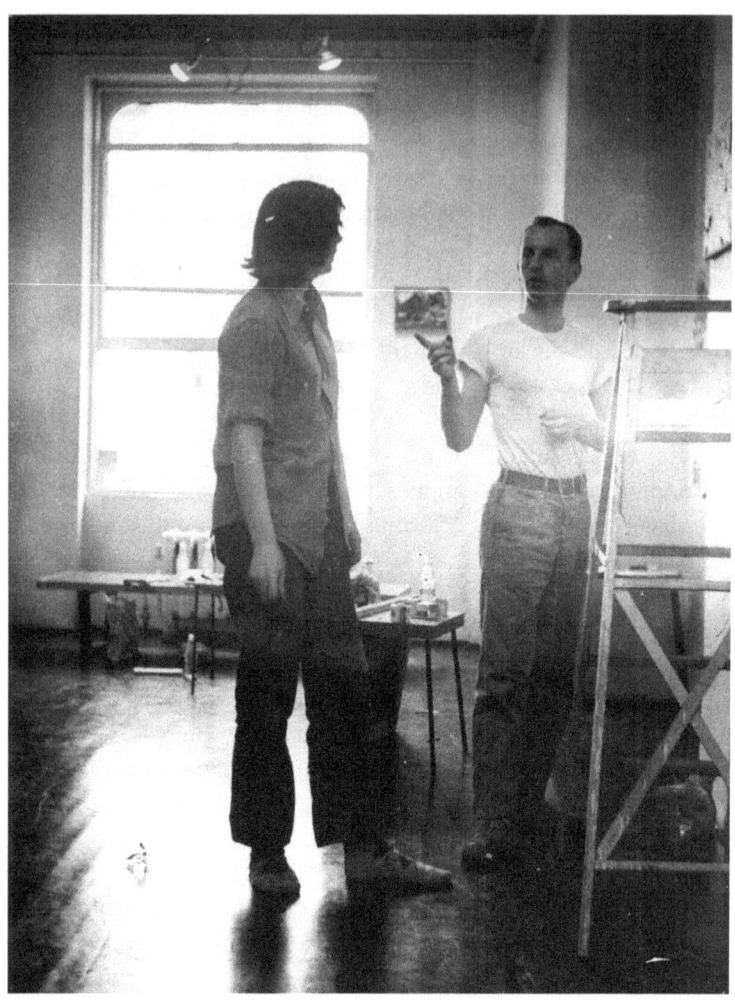

Hartigan and Frank O'Hara hanging paintings at the Tibor de Nagy Gallery. Photograph by Walter Silver.

~

For Grace, after a Party

You do not always know what I am feeling.
Last night in the warm spring air while I was
blazing my tirade against someone who doesn't
interest

             me, it was love for you that set me
afire,
        and isn't it odd? for in rooms full of
strangers my most tender feelings
                                    writhe and
bear the fruit of screaming. Put out your hand,
isn't there
            an ashtray, suddenly, there? beside
the bed? And someone you love enters the room
and says wouldn't
                    you like the eggs a little
different today?
                And when they arrive they are
just plain scrambled eggs and the warm weather
is holding.

The text of this poem is taken from page 214 of *The Collected Poems of Frank O'Hara* (Berkeley and Los Angeles: University of California Press, 1995, by arrangement with Alfred A. Knopf, Inc.) edited by Donald Allen. It is used with the permission of Maureen Granville-Smith, administratrix of the estate of Frank O'Hara.

≈

Dec. 30
I'm simmering Poindexters French Onion soup on the coal stove and re-reading the entries so far. Walt and I will leave on the early train for South Hampton to-morrow, and stay through the New Year till Sunday, when we'll drive back with him for the opening of his sculpture show.

I've been thinking about this year, and speculating on the next. I believe I have many things clearer than ever before, both in my life & painting, and I am filled with optimism about 1954.

Finished Berlioz, and I am in love with the nineteenth century. I think I've learned through reading on Chopin, Sand, Balzac, Delacroix, Byron and Berlioz many clues to my own personality—not to fight romanticism and "excess," to become even more ambitious for an all-encompassing art, and to keep contained and strong.

I will bring Stendhal's Memoirs with me to read, also some sketch pads and my new journal. Walt intends to photograph the sea, he has made great leaps in his own work during the last few months, and although giving up his job will mean financial hardships for us both, I think it will be worth it in harmony.

Journal for 1954

Jan. 2, 1954

I always experience a certain thrill on writing the date of a new year
for the first time. I am writing this first entry of 1954 in Larry's home
in Southampton. It has been a quiet and easy few days. I've read a bit of
Stendahls memoirs, his style has clarity and interests me a great deal. He
spoke of the "vanity" involved in writing a journal, and excused his efforts on
the grounds of self-analysis. I can't claim that as a basis for my own words, all
I know is that it gives me pleasure and some kind of peace to write a bit every
few days, and may add a bit to self-knowledge, not in the psychological sense.

Walt and I walked to the sea just now at about sunset, the ocean was grey and
self-assured, the sky flagrantly orange and beautiful. He took some pictures,
it is good to feel free enough from nature to be only a lover

Jan. 6

I've been spending the last few days attending to various businesses for the
show. Al & his little truck & I picked up all my scattered pictures Monday—
but for "Greek Girl" which will be in next month's Stable show & "Studio
Interior," now at the Remet's [Sylvia Remet, art patron]. The bastard, he
would choose my newest small picture.

Yesterday J. [James Fitzsimmons] was here to look at paintings and probably
write something for Arts and Architecture. He still has the power to affect me.
I was disturbed for a long time after he left.

Everyone praises the unfinished Matador, I'm getting afraid to go on with it,
very bad thing to have happen. I should remember never to let anyone see
unfinished pictures again. I hope to work on it to-day before Walt comes to
photograph and Frank to review for Art News.

Larry's sculpture show opened yesterday at the Stable, a strangely quiet opening, no one had a word to say, and stood in little groups, very few people, I
wandered around like a sleep-walker. The work is very good, the best sculpture I remember seeing in a long time, but recognition outside of a small
loyal group seems an up hill struggle.

This is the first opportunity I've had to see all my work since last spring together. I think I have achieved my aim of bringing more "architecture" into my painting—sometimes to a degree of stiffness and arbitrary areas that are awkward. I now want to loosen my brush again, I'd like my paintings to be more fluid, to look almost wet. I still want a formal art, but I'd like it to be not so obvious, to be there to be discovered under the form, and I'm working on the matador with this in mind.

Jan 7
As I had feared—I was so intimidated by the praise, the pressures and the beauty of the unfinished Matador that I have ruined all its best qualities. It's a relief in a way—a picture shouldn't get so much out of my hands until I decide I'm free of it. Now it's like beginning again, everything is potential.

I feel more leisure to work now. Walt has taken the photographs, Frank has taken his notes, and I'll see Nell [Blaine] to-night about the catalogue—all I need is money for expenses, which I hope to get from Al Bing.

Jan. 8.
Worked hard all day yesterday on the large Matador, and it looks good to me to-day. I am pleased with the tension of the stance, and that I brought it off with as much red against white as I had imagined. I think it's the best figure since Persian Jacket.

When I finished painting at about twilight, I felt such happiness and fulfillment! Such a rare feeling, but so intense that it could be only rare.

The catalogue is on it's way, I'm using the drawing of the seated woman from David. It will cost about 80.00, but I want something special this year.

I ran out of oil white and I've been using the new white plastic paint that Bocour gave me to try. I find this, mixed with my regular oils gives me a very fluid mixture, a little faster drying than regular oil, I like it very much.

Jan 11
There has been a large snow and everything seems muffled and small-town-ish, the studio is light and snug. Walt and I slept here the night of the storm, it was like a cabin in the woods with the coal stove going all night.

I asked Bing for 150.00—it was agony for me to do it, but he was warm and wonderful, and immediately made out a check for 200.00, which he says will count as a picture for him or a museum. He has been enough of a help for me to feel the slight amount of security to keep going without panic and constant worry that I'll have to take a job. My show is a gamble, if I don't sell a little I am done for, I couldnt ask Al for help again.

He also gave me the new Velasquez book, and loaned me some marvelous books on Manet, to whom I'm turning again for inspiration.

Richard brought Cesare Brandi, an Italian museum man to the studio to see my work. He really seemed to respond, each picture brought forth an absolute stream of Italian, quite extraordinary.

Jan. 20
Nothing but show preparations, now stripping remains and addressing catalogues. I've done no painting since the matador and head. Drawing at Bob Stone's to-night.

When I begin work again I'd like to do Marian Jim [a model] in a white dress against white with a black fan in her hands. I must work now with more subtlety of color and less obvious "composition"

Jan. 22
Worked through last evening on stripping, then made a late supper with Walt and spent the night here. I get such joy waking in the studio, if I had a more comfortable bed we'd stay here more.

For a while yesterday I had the feeling that my paintings were very good. I would like to keep that sensation as armour for the weeks ahead. I do wish I could continue painting during the show. I passed a store window jammed full of mannequins in cheap white lace bridal gowns, with a seated figure in a bilious violet maid of honour dress. It would make a marvelous group picture, a kind of modern court scene, I would need to photograph the window & work from that.

I have been rereading some of Delacroixs journal since breakfast, it is inspiring as always. I'd like to own this book and abundant reproductions of his paintings. Also a book of Goya's work. A most beautiful Goya print of Senora Garcia is on my wall, I may copy it.

Jan. 28
The Stable show opened yesterday. I am depressed by it, I knew it would be a prejudiced hanging—my Greek Girl is in the badly lit unheated basement along with other unpopular, disliked or less well known painters such as Pasilis, Jane, Fairfield, Bob Stone and Gandi [Gandy Brodie]. I realize I am disliked by the club group, but I try not to think of it most of the time since I brought it on myself by my willfulness and spleen. The only thing to do is become so famous and powerful that they don't dare mistreat you. They all loathe Pollock but they wouldn't ever put him in the basement!

I haven't any memory to-day of any picture which I consider outstanding least of all my own, and that depresses me even more. All those shouting pictures cancel each other out and you can't see anything and you come away with disgust and a headache.

Olga, Daisy's friend, said there was little in there that "inspired" her, a rather sweet old-fashioned idea of what painting should do that I found wise, and I certainly must do much more intense work to justify my opinion of myself.

Larry has been in town for the last few days and I have spent a lot of time with him and Frank. I feel so happy that they are close friends again, I care for them both so much. They seem stimulated by each other, and Frank let me read his new poems which are marvelous, full, restrained, and mature.

Jane's picture pointed up as Frank says "the danger of painting from experience (or observation) instead of talent or *style*." I thought of this as we went thru the Metropolitan. I think Manet has great "style" and I even enjoy his pastel portraits of women which Larry says look like fashion drawings. They are too "chic," but I love the arrogance and elegance. I felt enraptured in the "Spanish" room, I think they'd have to carry me out on a stretcher if I ever saw the Prado.

Larry likes the English, and also the Tiepolo—I remember above all the Goya balcony and the Manet funeral landscape.

We then went to see the "Zero le Conduit" at the Museum. I have eight stars on my print.

In the evening to the "Artists-Theater"—that name is a joke—to see V. Langs "Fire Exit." I liked the play, she has a great deal of talent. I think the set is the most nauseating I've ever seen. And Herbert utterly lacks subtlety. However, much came through to me in spite of the handicaps. The memory of this play is dimmed by the Jane Bowles [a playwright] In the Summer House which we saw yesterday afternoon. I don't think I've ever been so moved in the theater. When the daughter cried "dont leave me, I love you!" Frank, Larry & I all burst into tears at once.

All this activity is too much for me and I intend to spend a few quiet days in the studio finishing the work on the stripping to calm myself before the ordeal of my opening Tuesday.

Feb 1
Hess [Tom Hess, art critic], in his article on the Stable show, seems to regret that the younger artists don't ask of a blank canvas "What is a painting?" I think that is no longer the question to ask. Must give this some thought.

Feb. 3
The show [Hartigan's show at the Tibor de Nagy Gallery] opened yesterday, the day was like Spring and all the poets brought violets, daffodils and carnations. It was a nice crowd, all seemed to admire etc, but I feel let down and fatigued to-day. What I really want above all this time is to sell, so that I can be relieved of financial worry for a few months.

Moore [Herman Moore] of the Whitney was in to-day, and wants the Standing Figure (self-portrait with hydrangeas). Goodrich & Baur [Lloyd Goodrich and John I. H. Baur, Whitney Museum officials] need to give their approval. This seems a strange choice, but who can tell, it may be the best picture.

Feb. 4
Looking through Art News Annual, I was struck by my lack of interest in the artists they featured—Vuillard, Vermeer, Miro, and a horde of trompe l'oiels-ers. I am not attracted to the enclosed, the intimate, the private world.

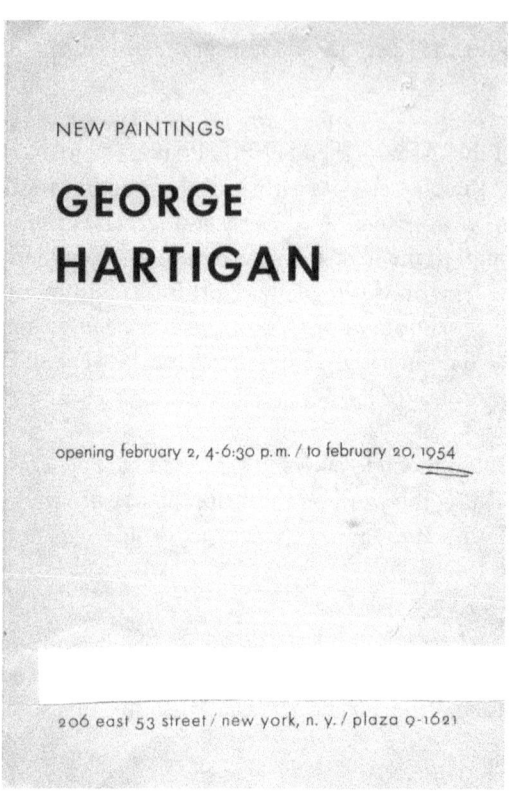

NEW PAINTINGS

GEORGE HARTIGAN

opening february 2, 4-6:30 p.m. / to february 20, 1954

206 east 53 street / new york, n. y. / plaza 9-1621

Cover of the catalog for Hartigan's one-person exhibition at the Tibor de Nagy Gallery in February of 1954.

I am deeply disturbed to-day. Art in America is out, and John read me Baur's article on me, also Soby's remarks. I fear all this official approval, and I'm sent into self-questioning and doubt. I must ignore this kind of attention in order to feel free to change and grow. Also John's remark "Face it dear, your "Matador" is not "going over"' is upsetting, since it is the picture that interests me the most and presents a challenge for future work. If I didn't need the money I would like to abstain from showing for the next year or two.

Worked a bit more on the Goya head, it may be finished. Thinking of my bridal window composition. Would like also to do a double portrait, full length, of Olga & Daisy.

Feb. 5
I feel almost ill with anxiety to-day. I am trying to blame it on money worries, but I know it's deeper than that.

Al Leslie just called with apologies for missing the opening—poor boy, he spends his days consumed by envy. He fed my fires by saying he thought it criminal where they hung Greek Girl at the Stable. At least it convinces me that my feelings were not just paranoia. He said the hanging committee all hated the picture. Well fuck them, its reproduced in Art News, Art Digest and Art in America.

Stuart Preston wrote a brief commentary on Hartigan's exhibition in the *New York Times* on 7 February 1954: "Grace George Hartigan's new paintings at the de Nagy Gallery make no bones about dealing with figures, indoors and out, themes that had been sternly banished from her earlier work. She approaches them obliquely and with skillful ease, now losing touch with them in a sort of honeycomb of luminous color and again pinning them down with the decisive stroke of the portraitist, and seeing to it all the while that her abstract manner keeps pace with the feelings of visual enjoyment that they arouse in her."

Feb. 8
Very active day at the gallery Saturday, John sold the drawing after David to the Simons for 50.00, the first drawing I've ever sold.*

Restless and faintly melancholy. I am going to force myself to work a little each day, if only for an hour until it begins to flow again.

*—Not true, I sold one to Peggy Osborn from my first show.

Feb. 10
Soby in the gallery yesterday, John says he was filled with enthusiasm. He intends to urge Baur [actually John Myers was discussing the painting with Alfred Barr of the Museum of Modern Art] to take the "River Bathers." If they only would! It is a "museum" picture—and perhaps Al B. [Al Bing] would pay $1000 less the $200 I've already received.

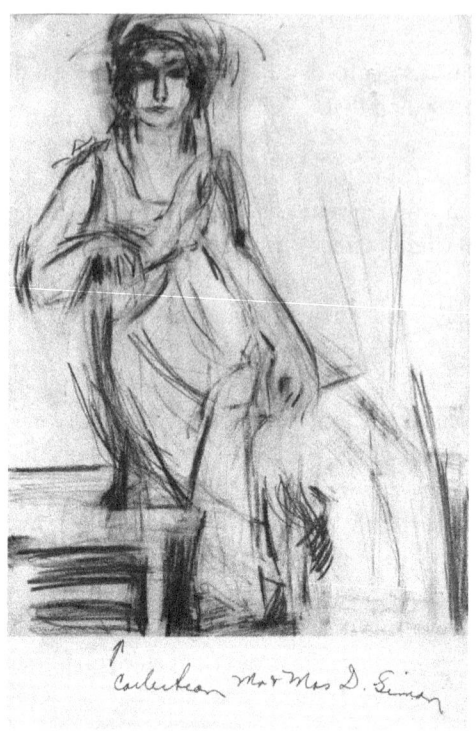

Hartigan sketch in her February 1954
exhibition at the Tibor de Nagy Gallery.
The annotation reads "Collection Mr &
Mrs D. Simon."

Terribly funny & sweet letter from Larry, he says he has just "not finished a
head of Augusta that makes Gainsborough look like Al Leslie."

I wish I would *sell* something!

Been working on "Self-Portrait as a Matador". It's going very slowly.

We ran into Edi last night while walking on 8th St. He seems to believe
his destiny lies in acting, not music—I asked if he also imagined he was
Napoleon? Another example of my foolishness in attributing genius to people
simply because I know them!

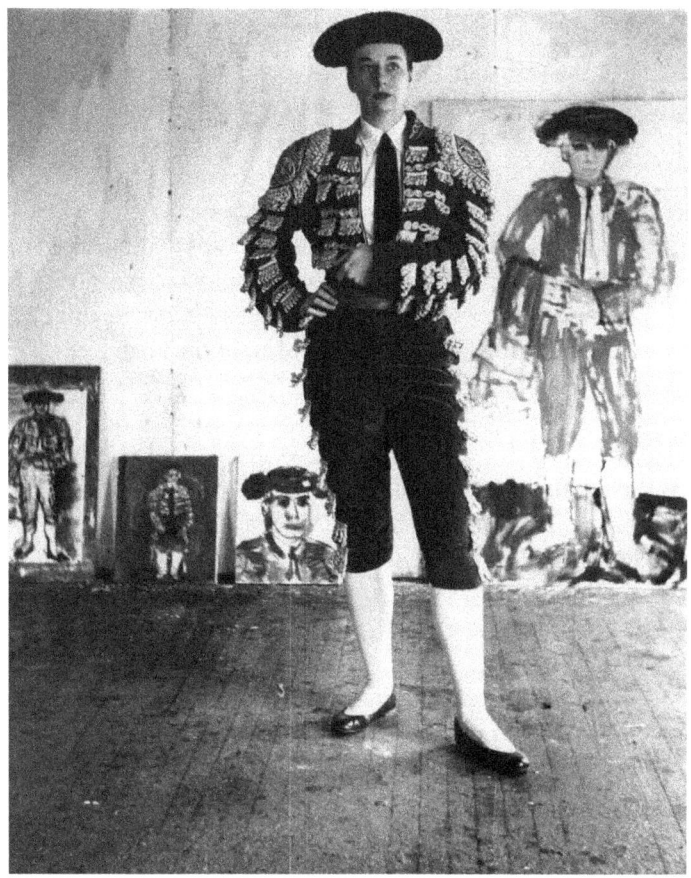

Hartigan dressed as a matador and posing in front of several
works on the matador theme. Photograph by Walter Silver.

Feb. 11

Jeff will be operated on for appendicitis next week. He's been having pains
for some time, and of course Bob [Jachens] had to take him first to a psycho-
therapist before it occured to him that there might be something wrong
physically!

As usual I am dropped in to a pit of suffering and guilt—Bob is too, I know,
that's why he behaves so foolishly.

This comes at a time when I am hitting the low level anyhow, morally, creatively. If one of the words that might characterize my previous paintings is "strength," then surely "weakness" is the best way to describe these recent efforts.

I have definitely decided not to show next year except for group shows. I won't tell John yet, his interest level is so fickle. I want the freedom to try many things, with the hope of stumbling on some way to reconcile "architecture" with a somewhat representational figure idea. Of course this could be a life-time search, (Cezanne for instance), but I want the luxury of feeling that I won't be interrupted for over a year.

Feb. 15
It looks as though the Whitney will take "Greek Girl." Since "River Bathers" is too large for them to consider, I'm just as glad. It will be $500.00-200.00 I have already received.

     134.00 Whitney
      72.00 Museum Mod. art
     <u>34.00 David drawing</u>
   240.00—That will take me through April. It's just a dream to suppose I'll ever be free of nagging anxieties about money, that I'll ever have the little extra for such things as full canvas & paint supplies, dental care and all those items that most people consider necessities.

Feb. 16
The weather is like spring, Jane and I went to Central Park yesterday and drew. Every thing I do lately seems so timid and undynamic. I am in a very bad state of melancholy lately. I have the perpetual sensation of grief, as though I am suffering, without knowing why. I have no energy, no enthusiasm Jane says she has felt this way for about six months. Worse of all, my painting is an accumulation of half-hearted dabs, with no magic. If this keeps on much longer I'm going to run out to Southampton to see if it does me any good.

Jeff will be operated on to-morrow, so I will want to be available until he leaves the hospital. Also I am completely broke, *no* money. I am expecting the check for the prints each day, but it doesnt come. So Walt is feeding me on his unemployment check—he also just sold a photograph for 25.00.

catalog

Mrs. Mod. Art

	river bathers	1	1000
Arizona Museum	black still-life	2	400
	coffee pot and cucumber	3	
	(collection Mr. and Mrs. Merlyn Pitzele)		
Jay Steinberg	ocean bathers	4	500
Mrs. Hartfield	standing figure	5	500
Ethel Hartfield	still-life with blue wall	6	estate
	(collection Mr. Richard Miller)		
	Dr. Mel Keller		
	hydrangeas	7	300
	red bowl	8	estate
	(collection Mr. Alexander Bing)		
	studio interior	9	
	(collection Mr. and Mrs. Murray Remet)		
Kenward Elmslie	matador	10	600
	drawings		

50 & 75

Hartigan's annotations on her February 1954 Tibor
de Nagy Gallery catalog indicating the disposition of some of her paintings. *River Bathers,* for
example, was purchased by the Museum of Modern
Art.

My show has been extended another week, Goodnough wasnt ready.
Something more may happen, but I'm losing hope as far as sales are concerned. The attendance has been good, however. I hope Barr gets to see it. He
is one of the few people whose judgement I respect completely.

I've played Scriabin's Etude #12 over & over again this morning, and it seems to say that life without courage is nothing. So I attacked the head from Goya with my old conviction, and now I think it really lives, with light in the blacks.

Feb. 19
I've spent every day for the last three days visiting Jeff in the Orange Hospital. He is recovering fast and will go home to-morrow, so I feel less anxious.

Barr & Dorothy Miller were in to see the show yesterday. John says he was most enthusiastic, and insists that he wants "River Bathers" for the Museum if John can find a donor for it. I find this all incredible, and I wont think too much of it until it really goes through committee, etc. Evidently Barr called the painting "a work that shows genius."

Aside from the implications of two such close museum acquisitions, the money would be so welcome, I could live through the summer if John gets $1000 for it.

I've been paid for 6 of the 8 prints from the print show, and received my income tax return of $46, so my situation has eased considerably.

Feb. 23
Everything has worked out very well, the Whitney is taking "Greek Girl" and the Modern "River Bathers." It's being donated by a fund called the "Plymouth Fund," set up by Al Bing to use up profits from a housing project. I'll get $500 for G. G. and $1000 for Riv. Bathers. Al insists the $200 he gave me is a personal thing, and he will take a picture for it one day.

It would be impossible to describe my feelings, so I won't even try.

All that I can think of is the time it gives me, freedom to work without the pressures of financial worry. Since I'll have $1000 for myself [the rest would go to the gallery], I could go to Europe, but I feel at this time I'd rather stretch it out and just live and work. I think I have some good pictures in me. I'm going to get a roll of linen! And a *lot* of paint! And all the little things that I complained I'd never have (Feb 15 entry).

Feb. 27
John sold "Ocean Bathers" to Mr & Mrs. Steinberg from Chicago, for

$500. They also took a large painting of Larry's. They have the "Attic" by de Kooning, and I am most pleased to have the O. Bathers in their collection.

Rec'd $1,000 full payment for "River Bathers" & "Greek Girl"—
To receive:
334.00	Ocean Bathers
33.00	drawing from David
18.00	2 more prints
33.00	R. Miller
418.00	

[The following two expressions are printed in the margin.]
WEALTH AWAITS YOU   .
FACTS IN WRITING

Mar 1.
Helped John straighten out the mess that was Goodnough's idea of how to hang a show. He is almost pathologically sloppy, and I am feeling very annoyed and taken advantage-of.

I am very disturbed by the pictures. He has included almost every idea that anyone ever had about abstract art—it is one of the most eclectic demonstrations I've ever seen, but curiously authentic and strong, and so *plastic* so many of what Hess called "ideas of what a picture is." River Bathers was sitting around—due to John's inefficiency it wont go till to-morrow—and it looked so soft and romantic I was amazed. And depressed. No doubt, "open" areas look easy next to detailed, crisp ones. I know *exactly* how Matisse must have felt with all that cubism going on around him.

Goodnough's work always has the same effect on me, it always makes me question myself. This may be good.

I must get to work soon.

Mar 8
A furious past week of money going, going—out of $1000 I have 487.00 left. What madness.

25.00	loan repaid John M.
26.00	studio elec. bill
60.00	loan repaid Virginia [Hartigan's sister]

55.00	Bob for Jeff operation
40.00	Walt rent (owed him this)
35.00	Walt gas & elec.
27.00	„ phone } these he will repay
30.00	trench coat
10.00	shoes
6.00	Kabuki tickets
11.00	2 bottles Scotch
32.00	paint
52.00	canvas
12.00	2 bottles champagne
30.00	loan John Reed (to be repaid)
451.00	

62.00 went? dinners, lunches, taxis, Marian J. gown, stool, umbrella.
25.00 loan to F. O'Hara

I had hoped to do a great deal more with this money—at least I have a lot of paint, Bellini, 50.00 worth at 40% off. And some great canvas, a half roll of 7 ft Belgian linen & a half roll of 6 ft. English double primed linen. On the latter canvas I started the large picture of Marian Jim, in a $2.00 white bridal gown from the thrift shop on Third Ave.

I worked furiously yesterday, and besides the big one I have started a head and a smaller figure, all of them going with great energy and passion and in a peculiar direction

Mar 9
So intimidated yesterday by the beginnings that it wasn't till dark, after a stiff drink of Scotch that I really got into it again. I was exhausted at ten, and went right to bed feeling that I could never add another thing to it. As usual to-day, with the new light I find much more ahead.

John tells me of a conversation with Clem. He found my show "better than he expected," he liked the small seascape best (!!!) and the Bathers not at all —John said "Barr likes it" Clem—"Everyone knows Barr is a fool and knows nothing about art." Also "Goodnough will be 'up there' when Hartigan is gone and forgotten" Good old Hartigan—Le Brun—Bonheur [women artists]. How sad this all is, but funny too. It would have upset me so much at one time, how much more confidence I've gotten in the last two years. Naturally Barr's approval has a lot to do with this. Clem is a bitter man, tragic.

Mar. 12
My work on "The Bride" interrupted for the last three days by visits to the hospital on Welfare Island to see Frank. ["Frank was shot in his hallway by a robber."] How odd and terrifying to see my great poet in a sordid ward, with a bullet in his hip! We had talked that very day of violence, and his fear of being murdered. I must say he is far calmer and more ironic in this calamity than I, I am filled with horror.

Mar 14
I have brushed plastic white into all dark areas on the Bride painting. It was too arbitrary and done with *my* knowledge, not the deeper knowledge of the work itself.

Money on hand—	285.00	
Simon picture	33.00	
loan to Frank	175.00	
" to Reeds	30.00	repayed
" to Walt	60.00	
	583.00	

Mar. 15
My "Bridal Portrait" is finished, except possibly for a few final touches.

There are several factors that contributed to its solution. One was Larry's visit, and his comments on the "lovely" color of the unfinished picture. It recalled the look of my show, and my resolution to work without pure color. He also made me feel that I was leaning on my "style," which is a great hindrance for further growth.

I cant underestimate the importance that rereading part of Barr's great book on Matisse played in the solution of this picture. I read on the years 1913–1916, and of Matisses grey and "architectonic" periods. I resolved to become more severe in my form, more austere in my color. And to rely more on line and chiaroscuro than before. This picture recalls Matisse, but I hope there is enough of my hand there to still make it my own.

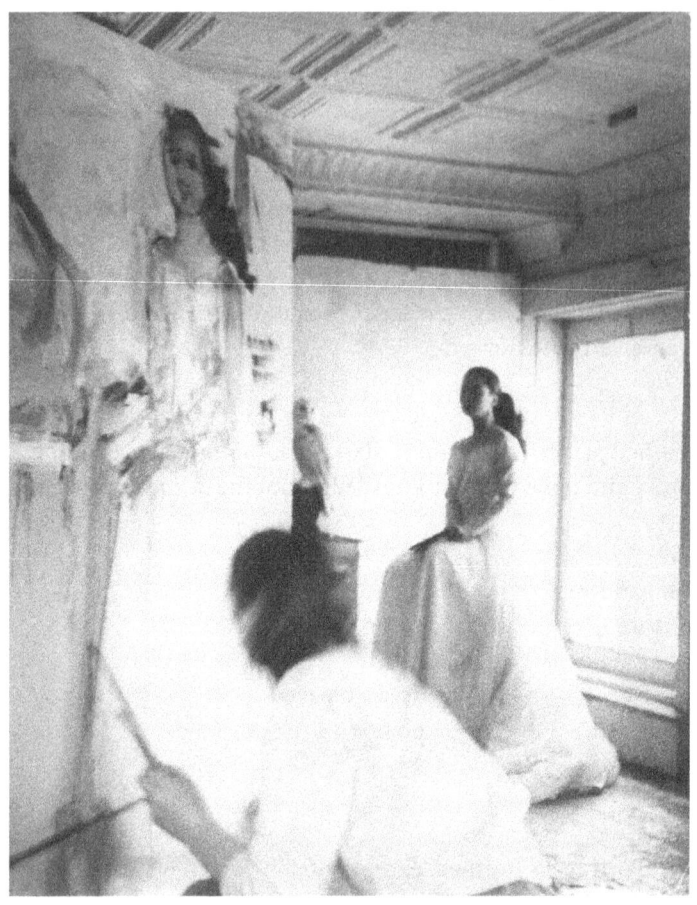

Marian Jim posing for *The Bride and the Owl*. This is a rare image of Hartigan working on a painting. Photograph by Walter Silver.

money on hand—	241.00
	20.00 Walts
	221.00
Frank owes	175.00
Walt owes	60.00
~~Simon owes~~	~~33.00~~
Steinberg May 1 payment	167.00
	656.00

Took a late afternoon walk by the river to see the gulls. Now that the picture has resolved the beast has taken its fangs from my throat and I am peaceful for a while.

Mar. 25
"Bridal Portrait" wears well, a few—Larry, Richard, Walt, think it one of my best pictures. I worked and worked on the small version, but I seem to have exhausted all the possibilities in the big one, so have abandoned this.

Walt has photographed several bridal windows for me, and I intend to start on the large composition soon.

Read Maurois' "Disraeli" with great interest.

I'm offered a one-man show at Vassar in November, and a hundred dollars to attend the opening, and "speak informally to the girls." I think I'll show my new bridal pictures.

Mar 26
For some reason I can't involve myself in any "small" work. I am unable to concentrate on even a drawing, and I continually dream of another large canvas as a battle ground. I intend to make the Bridal Window 6 ft by 9 ft, the largest work since River Bathers.

I walked a bit this morning, looking in bridal shop windows. I want to use, beside grey, white and black, some acid pink, sky blue and a kind of moss green.

Mar. 30
Began Bridal Window to-day, everything loosely brushed in, the kind of beginning that shows nothing of the end.

I have been thinking over my paintings of the last year, and I think I have some perspective now, especially with "Bridal Portrait" on the wall. I believe my best pictures—River Bathers, Persian Jacket, Greek Girl, Bridal P. all have one thing in common.—A strange combination of "nature" and "abstraction." It is that combination that makes each area relate and "jell." In "Bridal Portrait," for instance, the head as nature is made more powerful by the enclosure in a black square. The upper body surges with the lines across it. The hands hold their space by being tied with a blue line, the owl's head pierced with black line, etc. And the large black areas add to the mystery as well as the structure.

My feelings now are that my pictures haven't been too formal, they have been too "constructed." The Matador is a semi-failure, partly because I wanted each area to find it's solution in a naturalistic way, and for me, at this time anyhow, that's impossible.

It seems also that the working method used in Greek Girl & Bridal P. suit me—one all day session with the model, photographs taken, and the rest of the work looking at & not looking at the photographs. With the Bridal Window I have only photos, I may walk out occasionally to look at windows. And I have the thrift shop bridal gown hanging in the studio.

I intend to add detail to this picture, more and more, until its logic begins to assert itself.

Apr. 1
Spent the morning writing a letter to Clem which at last throws down the gauntlet. Also answered a questionaire from the Whitney about Greek Girl. I defined my philosophy of art by quoting Maritain "Art is the work to be done."

~

Hartigan's papers include the following letter to Clement Greenberg.

April 1, 1954

Dear Clem,
     John tells me he has asked Helen [Frankenthaler] to return to the gallery. This increases the possibilities of meeting you socially, and I feel I must say a few words about the polemic that exists between us. I have no real quarrel with Helen. Each time I see her I am reminded of the affection I had for her, and it makes me sad.
     Admittedly my attitude toward you is loaded way beyond the point of intellectual disagreement. I had unreasonable respect for you and your judgement. Plus whatever complications always exist between a man and a woman. Even understanding this, there is something to be said.

In your discussion of me and my painting I think you have been fla-grantly irresponsible. You must know that your remarks have been repeated to me, and that I helplessly fuming hear you think I am "not even a painter." To my face you toast my success, say "nice show." Then behind my back I hear a grudging remark for my most febrile effort, that Alfred Barr knows nothing about art (what implications there!) and "Goodnough will be 'up there' when Hartigan is gone and forgotten."

Whatever opinion you have of my work, you must respect my seri-ousness and energy. When an artist presents a show, he backs it up with his life. You are a coward, because you back your words with more words. *Conversation is not criticism.*

I must ask you to "put up or shut up." To undertake in writing the re-sponsibility of your ideas, or to accept the consequences of being condemned as frivolous—a "cocktail critic."
Sincerely,
G.

~

Apr. 2
All yesterday afternoon and all day to-day on Bridal Window. The paint is beginning to tug, like a physical presence, a good sign of progress.

Apr. 6
Feverish work for the last four days on "Bridal Store Mannequins." It may be finished. I'm letting it set for a while. It certainly is an odd picture—traces of Larry, Francis Bacon and Demoiselles D'Avignan. It has a sinister calm.

Apr. 7
This devil of a picture is plaguing me. I'm not satisfied with it, and its gone so far that it is almost lost. I'm going back into it with drawing.

Apr. 8.
Yesterday was the turning point with B.S.M., what agony. I wonder if I'll always have to "go under" so with painting to arrive at a resolution.

To-day was a joy, just touches here and there, and enjoying the picture like a spectator.

Received a life pass to the Museum, which pleased me immensely.

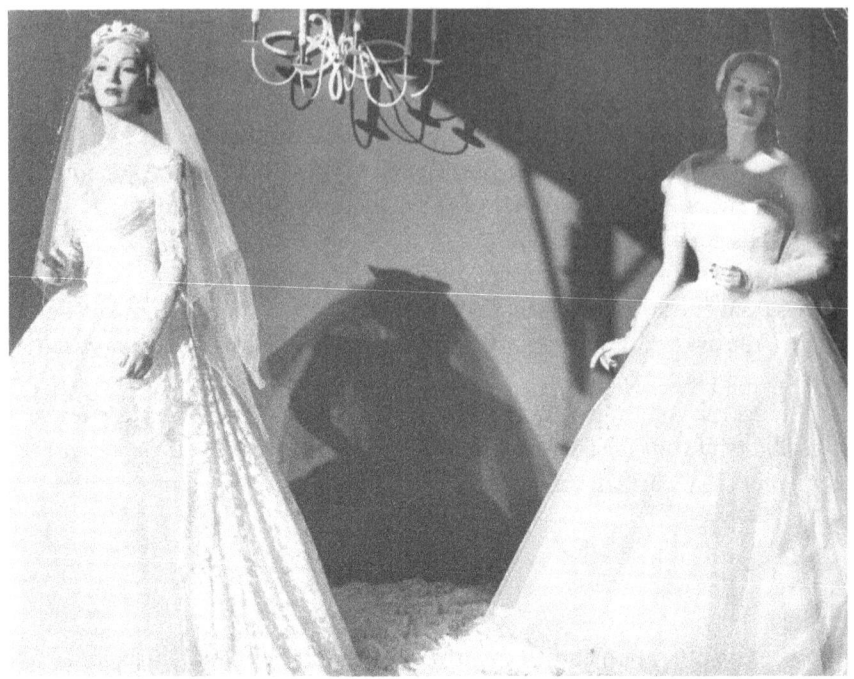

Bridal shop window on Grand Street in New York. Hartigan developed her painting *Grand Street Brides* from photographs such as this one. Photograph by Walter Silver.

CEZANNE! Every time I take another step, I see more to learn from this great genius.

Apr. 11

Living now with Bridal Store Mannequins, I alternate between great pride and great doubt. It is a departure, and what bothers me is that the resolution came with wiping down huge areas with rags & turp. So now it doesn't look "painted" as my previous pictures do.

What I think I mean is this—that it is an extraordinary painting, but that in the fire of creation as the areas began to resolve, they came in a way that is blended, and looks soft. And now that the heat is over and the picture finished, it is not in a manner that intellectually I admire most. I believe that tension in a painting should exist down to the tiniest area, and that such an area as [image] should look something like [image].

The second portion of Hartigan's journal entry for 11 April 1955
relating to the painting that would be renamed *Grand Street Brides*.

April 14
Everyone who sees BSM seems moved—and upset—by it. Frank saw it two
nights ago and then came again last night to look some more.

I am working on a still life with a Greek head in it, but I feel spent and melancholy so it's going very slowly. Every large work uses me up for a long time
after. I intend to go to visit Larry for a few days next week.

Read Jim F.'s [Fitzsimmons] irritating remarks on me in Arts & Arch. He
finds "Hydrangeas" (my *most* unimportant work!) most worthy of praise.
And criticizes River Bathers composition!

The manuscript journal entry for 14 April 1954 discussing "Bridal Store Mannequins" (it will be renamed *Grand Street Brides* in the entry for 26 April) and a review by James Fitzsimmons that Hartigan found most irritating.

Mike [Goldberg] said about BSM that in it I am beginning to combine all my painting "styles"—in a way this is true, for it resembles The Massacre as much as it does Persian Jacket.

I'm not in such a dilemma about my sources as I was last year—and the year before. I'm establishing a working procedure, and even though the painting itself continues to present great obstacles & problems, at least I'm not torn between old master reproductions, photos, and nature as I once was. This makes me much less a victim of my talent.

I must still work on a picture until it is "right," and I only know this point, when I see it, I can't anticipate it. But at least I know it is some kind of a stage between "realism" and "abstraction," where both things speak fully and with meaning.

Also I am working again with anger—at what I don't know, but the canvas is a foe, or it is a battle ground.

I am surrounded with *mediocrity*! All my fellow painters seem cowards to me but for Larry.

Apr. 15
I think of all times this is the worse, between works, used up, sterile—waiting, restless and bored for my creative energy to be renewed. And wondering if indeed it will ever return again.

Apr. 16
I've been thinking to-day that there is no reason why art must exist for itself alone. Why can't it be used as a powerful voice for comment or instruction, as it was often used in the past? I think I am a crusader, or a missionary—I have the voice that can speak to thousands.

April 26
Back from a few days at Larry's. It was both restful and stimulating. His new pictures have extraordinary authority, although they are in a direction far from my own.

I feel vigorous and ready to work again, I intend to start the picture of Daisy and Olga as soon as they can pose for me. I also have in mind a picture from a bizarre Hungarian woman that I met at John's. Also an outdoor canvas of Walt, a warrior, nude with sword & helmet.

Took the "Tribute Money" after Rubens up to the gallery. It will probably travel with "Black Still-Life" in a Modern Museum show. And "Bridal Portrait with Owl" is going to the Iowa annual. I have very little of my "figurative" work left, either for shows or sales.

Renamed the large picture "Grand Street Brides."

"River Bathers" is hanging in the Museum penthouse. Walt and I went to-day for tea to look at it. It looked small to me on that large wall, smaller than I remembered it. But I liked seeing it again, it seemed rich and full. It seemed more myself than I am, and reminded me that I am only a medium for my gifts.

May 3
Daisy & Olga posed all yesterday afternoon, and I got a good start on a painting. Also worked on a charcoal drawing which I don't like. I don't know what I want from a drawing now. Walt took pictures, and I'll work some this rainy afternoon from them.

May 4.
Hard work on "Daisy & Olga" to-day. I think what I feel for is the point where the paint seems to resist me, to come from the canvas outwards instead of being "layed on." I work slowly until things seem to become inevitable, and then it all speeds up so fast I can hardly put it down. Perhaps my sphere of interest or "subject material" could be called "façade," the empty gesture, the dead ritual, the costume, the mask. Painting is not putting on a mask, but taking it off. That's the difference between Italian and Spanish high art.

May 5
Progressing on D & O. Seem to be wiping down a great deal in these recent pictures. Odd how different times bring different technical approaches. I never touch a palette knife now.

Nagging money concerns. I have 75.00 left of the $1000.00! Frank owes me $175.00, and intends to pay me when Arthur Golde pays him, but Arthur claims poverty. Looks as though I'm stuck. Still no money from the Steinberg's.

Let this teach me to be more careful next time I get a large sum.

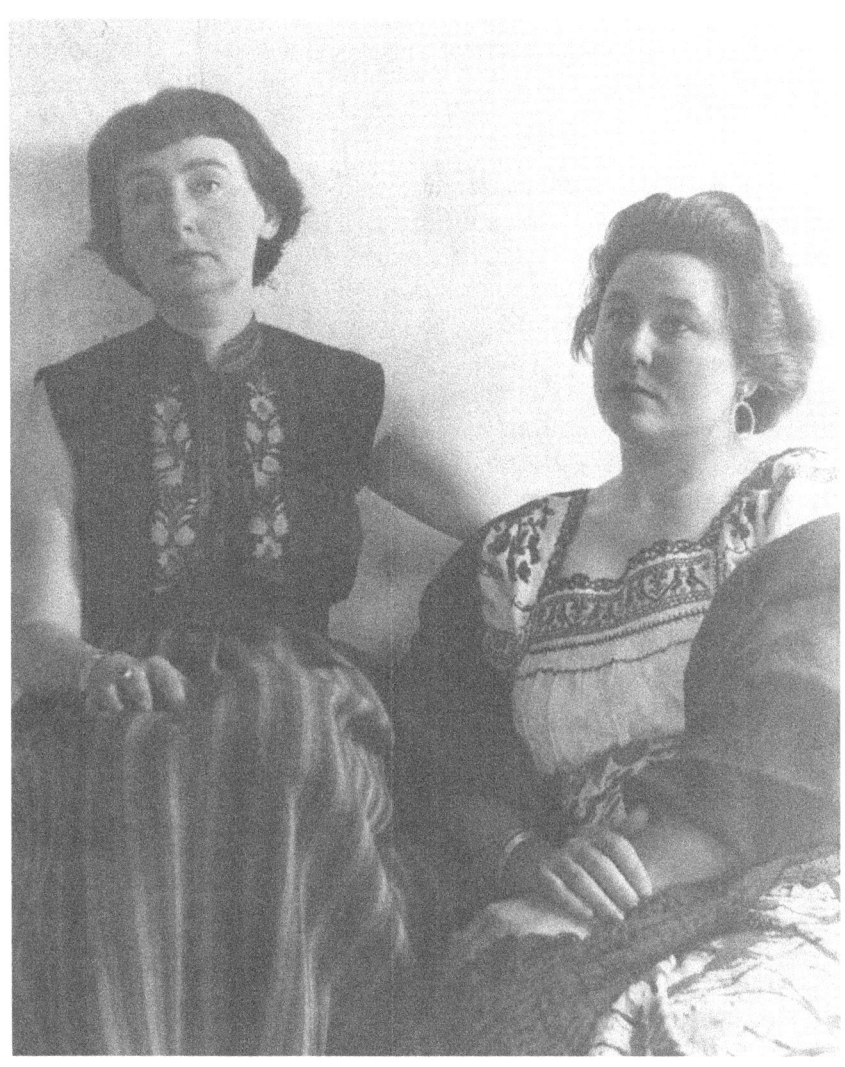

Daisy Aldan and Olga Petroff posing for Hartigan's *Two Women*. Photograph by
Walter Silver.

May 7
Yesterday and to-day on D & O. It seems complete now, with a kind of ara-
besque ease and subtlety new to me. The discipline required to achieve this

look of grace has left me nervous and tense, with indigestion and long hours of wakefulness at night.

May 10
Bob [Jachens] & I, if we had stayed married, would have our 13th wedding anniversary to-day. How little a sense of myself I had at that time, nothing seemed clear.

Generally now I feel the inevitability of my own way, even though I am distracted and very upset at times. I was very depressed by a series of shows I saw Friday alone and again on Saturday with Walt. Leslie, Kline, Soulage and Briggs, all "power" drivers, with almost frantic impact and surfaces, makes my recent concerns seem fussy and foolish. Al's pictures are mostly too un-resolved & not "formal" enough, but as always I am moved by his talent and energy. All the rest seemed to be in the realm of "action" painting, and truly made me believe, for a while, that they are right and I am wrong.

I am this much advanced over a few years ago however, that I can't be dis-tracted from my own involvements and direction, I must do what I must.

May 18
A week or more where life's urgencies and complexities blot out everything else.

I found out accidently that this Steinberg payment which Larry so graciously let me have in full was the second amount, not the first. He and John decided not to tell me & to let Larry have the whole amount. I haven't discussed my knowledge with either of them yet, but I am so hurt that I dont know how I can not let Larry know.

~

[Grace Hartigan provided this additional information about the sale: "Steinberg bought a Rivers and a Hartigan at the same time, to be paid in installments. The first installment, which I didn't know had been paid, went completely to Larry. Then, when the second installment arrived, Larry 'gra-ciously' let me have it all."]

~

John is something else—I know he is vicious, and works on my nervous-ness and anxieties like no one else can. Thank the lord for the end of the art season, sometimes the intrigues, cabals and politics are more that I can bear.

I made a nasty scene at John's in front of the Steinberg's, De Kooning's & Ben Heller. My hatred for him seemed to pour out.

It seems to me I am too much a child, too open and vulnerable. I must learn to guard myself better in this jungle, to remember who my few true friends are, and to be more aware of those who are really destructive.

May 19
Saw Larry yesterday, and I couldn't help telling him that I knew of his deceit. It was all very depressing—he just said it was offered to him, and he took it.

I feel such sadness.

May 24
Just made a stretcher & stretched the canvas for a nude & interior. I had wanted to paint the Hungarian or Midi in one of her dance costumes, but Midi won't pose for me, & the other woman is busy. Such is the irony of being dependent on nature for one's start. At least I always have myself for a model & Walt took some nude & semi-draped photos for me to work from.

May 25
The days are quiet now no phone calls, little mail. So that as a result the ups and downs come from inner fluctuations, not from the outer world. I think I must have this peace to develop fully as an artist. It means some loneliness and boredom, but actually all I get from worldly politicing and involvement is a nervous titilation, which makes me feel anxious and unreal.

This break with John may cost me some painting sales—just how petty and vengeful he can be I dont know yet. I cant sacrifice my energies to him any longer, no matter what he does.

I am reading Flaubert's letters, some of them seem extraordinary to me. The one to du Camp on success seems so acute—"'To be known'—is not my chief concern—that can give complete gratification only to very mediocre vanities. Besides, is there ever any certainty about this? Even the most widespread fame leaves one longing for more, and seldom does anyone but a fool die sure of his own reputation. Fame, therefore, can no more serve us as a gauge of our own worth than obscurity.—

I am aiming at something better—to please myself. *Success seems to me a result, not a goal."*

I have been dissatisfied with my work lately. Not only don't I work enough, but the Daisy & Olga picture seems to me to be thin, and not to have enough excess in it. Flaubert says some things about this in a letter to Louise Colet—". . . you can judge the excellence of a book by the strength of its punches and the time it takes you to recover from them. And then the excesses of the great masters! They pursue an idea to its furthermost limits. In Molière's Monsieur de Pourceaugnac there is a question of giving a man an enema, and a whole troop of actors carrying syringes pour down the aisles of the theatre. Michelangelo's figures have cables rather than muscles; in Ruben's bacchanalian scenes men piss on the ground;—I think that the greatest characteristic of genius is, above all, energy. Hence, what I detest most of all in the arts, what sets me on edge, is the *ingenious*, the clever. This is not at all the same as bad taste, which is a good quality gone wrong. In order to have what is called bad taste, you must have a sense for poetry; whereas cleverness, on the contrary, is incompatible with genuine poetry."

May 27
Work for the last two days on the Nude with Reboso. Nothing there yet but detail, no magic.

I truly loathe this picture now. It contains not only all of my worst faults but those of Matisse and Picasso too. I dont know what can be done with it now—perhaps to-morrow.

May 28
Well, I've worked the Masters out of this picture until now only my disgusting hand is left. I must say it has that quality of "excess" Flaubert spoke of. I hope it has a little something else too—at this time I can't tell.

June 4
I suppose I'll always remember this as the time when I drowned myself in German popular music of the twenties—Die Dreigroschenoper, Deitrich, Zarah Leander. I am consumed with nostalgia for something I never knew. I spent all afternoon in Yorkville listening to & buying records, then to Richard's for a few hours of his records—a great one by Pola Negri. I'd like to

find photos of café singers and actresses of that time, perhaps for a painting, or just study.

I gathered up courage to ask Lotte Lenya to pose, but she said she hasn't time. Of course I mean nothing to her, so why should she bother?

I'm always making people uncomfortable with my excessive enthusiasm or my excessive indifference.

June 8
Much talk and drinking with Daisy, Richard, Floriano and Frank the other night. They are going to expand Folder to make it more vital, with more art topics, letters or essays. I'm trying now to work out a new cover for them, but the combination of hay fever, antihistamine pills and life interests makes me confused and distracted. I wonder if the years will bring greater work capacities, less distractions?

I have vague plans for a large night club painting after I do Lilla, but nothing is clear yet. I have some nutty & stylish photos of Pola Negri & Dietrich that interest me, but I'm not clear about it either. It must all have something to do with finding my world, my subject material, what must I paint?

June 9
I'm in love with life to-day, full, happy, glad I'm young enough to feel glad, in love with a bouquet of red red roses surrounded by a forest of fresh tarragon in a white vase, I must draw it.

June 14
Started a painting of baby's breath and dying red peonies. I don't know where it will go.

I feel far from the mood of the last entry—Life, what cauchemar!

June 19
The flowers are finished—it is all right, but seems not important enough, not vital.

June 20

"Artistic creation, it would seem, represents such fragments of this fantasy world as he (the artist) is able to retain and to impose upon society."

"The neurotic obsessions of artists are often a clue to their greatest gifts." —Angus Wilson on Emile Zola.

In the Ludlow Market Thursday I came upon piles of old clothes and costumes, and I bought some that excite me—a long black hooded coat, harlequin shirt and blouse, a red hunter's coat, a beaded twenties dress. Since then I can think of nothing but a large painting called "Masquerade," for which I want all the Folder people and Jane, Frank & John Ashbery to pose. I think of them in various attitudes around a table, a feeling of strangeness, madness.

June 24

My tableaux has been posed and photographed, and I have an almost 7 foot square canvas tacked on the wall. I intend to begin to-day drawing in charcoal. I want to work this picture in a lot of detail if I can, simplifying toward the end. I also hope its look will not cause people to say "Bechmann" as they seem to be saying recently. I hope it is only the surface similarity of drawing in black line. Certainly there are many artists I would prefer being compared to.

I pray that someday my painting will lose that look known as "expressionism."

June 28

One day drawing in charcoal, another day in flat washes of oil & turp.

So far it shows less than nothing, inept and amateur.

I am a mass of bruises from falling into a brook while picking tiger lilies.

My pictures may be called expressionistic in those times when the formal values are overcome by "expressive" ones—personal and emotional. To keep this from happening requires intense self discipline—which I am incapable of at times.

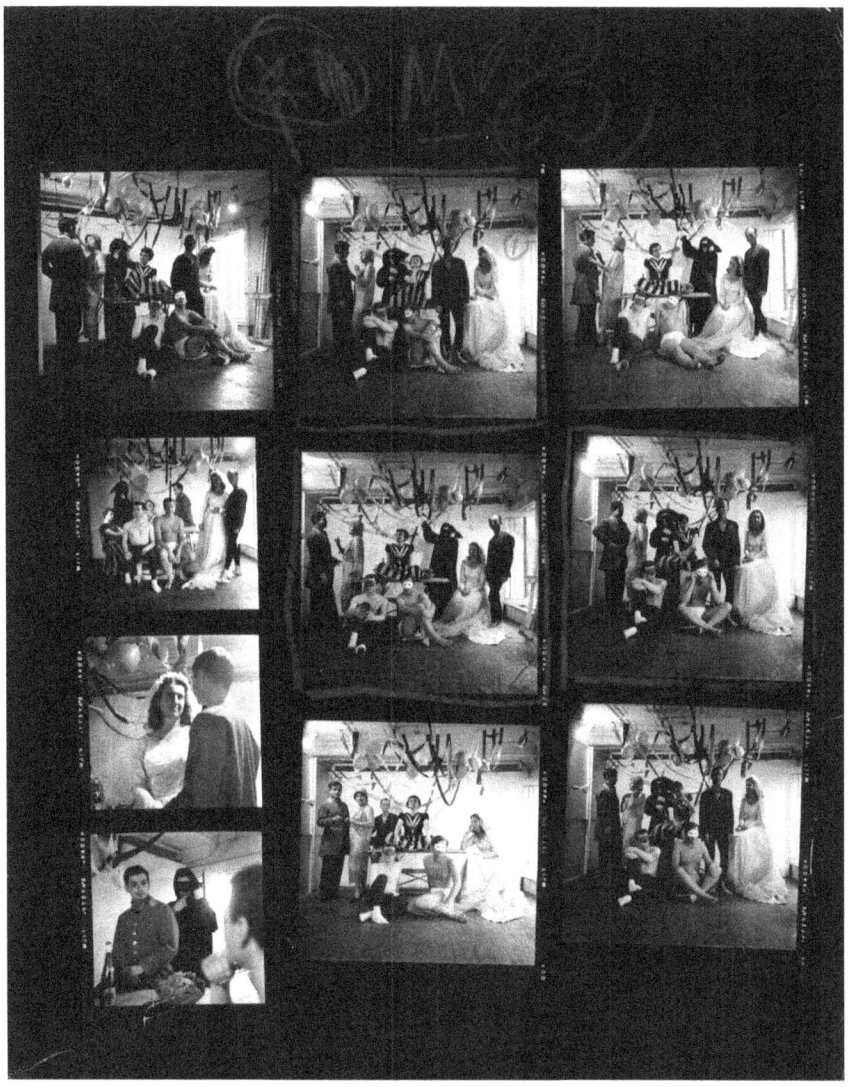

Contact sheet with photographed poses for Hartigan's painting entitled *Masquerade*. Hartigan assembled many of the people associated with the publication *Folder* for this purpose. This included John Ashbery, Jane Frankenthaler, and Frank O'Hara.

It seems the only way I can have the architecture I want in a picture is to maintain some attitude towards cubism and to almost *deliberately construct the picture in planes.* Remember this while working on Masquerade.

[The following entry is a marginal pencil note that was written several years later.]
This anticipated the '56 & '57 work

Worked all to-day, more openly and loose.

My last two paintings (Nude with Blue Stole and Peonies & Baby's Breath) are very unsatisfactory to me—they were self-indulgently painted, and I can learn nothing from them.

June 29
All day on Masq. Some flashes of what it might be, then muddles. I thought of ochres, blues and blacks.

July 15
Work on Masq for some days, then away to Lavallette [New Jersey] with the family & Jeff. Spent the time in bed with an attack of virus.

Now I am faced with Masq. again, I seem to have no sense of it, or myself, or art or life or anything.

July 17
At last it's beginning to come.

Don't force a complete articulation of the facial features. They should be explicit only when the inevitability of the form demands it.

July 20
Three days obsessed with this picture, close to it, then loosing it—I've given up everything on the way, all the early stages of skill and brilliant color. Now its almost gone, just big wiped muddy areas, I've lost all the magic.

July 21
Ferocious work yesterday and to-day on Masquerade. I think it's finished but for ending touches.

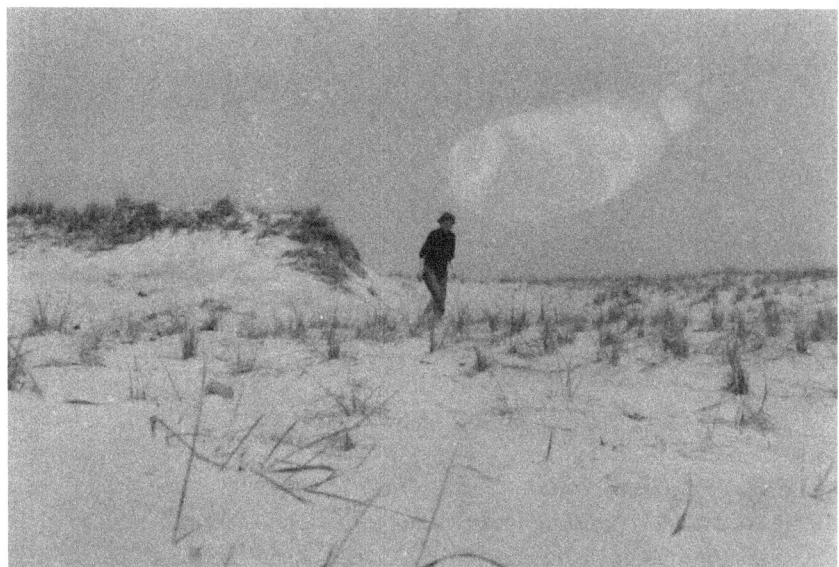

Hartigan in the dunes on Long Island. Photograph by Walter Silver.

I don't know what to think—it shows my study of cubism certainly.

Surely no other picture has cost me so much as this one, I am weak and spent.

July 28
Southampton
This is the third day, we are here for the rest of the summer. This morning I rode Fairfield's bicycle to a deserted beach, passing potato fields, and stretches of wheat, then high dunes and grasses. At last I felt connected with the landscape, and there is something I may in a little while be able to paint.

This house satisfies a certain "lady of the manor" side of me, those huge and much painted Porter trees are outside our window. I am cooking for us, Frank and Lawrence [Lawrence Porter, Fairfield Porter's son], so far I like it.

Aug. 5
The days are going by, I have the feeling I always get in the country, a sort of preoccupied stupor, no tension, feeling very physical. I've begun to work a bit, two charcoal drawings done in the studio while listening to Scarlatti

harpichord sonatas. And yesterday a small oil from the golden wheatfields and umber barn, I was so contented doing it.

Aug. 11
Frank said to-day he thought we were the opposite of the previous generation who left the distractions of the city in order to be alone with themselves & their work in the country.

On the contrary there seem to be so many diversions out here, even to lying in the sun and turning over—I think I won't get anything done until I return to NY. Nature, if you love her very much, is infinite in her diversions.

Sept. 9
We've been home a week now—a week of furious house painting, used furniture buying, scraping, painting. After the graciousness of living in Southampton I couldn't bear the discomfort of the studio—now it is quite attractive and liveable.

I have returned with five landscapes, all of which gave me extreme pleasure to paint. This was a feeling quite foreign to my entire painting experience. Now that they are here in the studio, they all except the Southampton Fields seem worthless in comparison to my city work. Richard says that I "fall apart" in front of nature, and this may be true. Certainly I had none of my usual fierceness in the execution of these, and it may be that the "profundity" of my work is based upon personal unhappiness, and that when I feel complete as in the country I have nothing to say in paint. What irony it would be if as the years go on I must either stay in the tensions of New York for the sake of my "art"—or risk living out of town—as I dream of—and paint relaxed and sentimental works!

Sept. 13
"Bride and Owl" back from Iowa. I am most distressed by the long tear in it, although it is well patched it hurts me to see it so damaged. Also the cobalt violet bled through that damned plastic white all down the center of the picture, and I've just been retouching it. Never will I use plastic paint again.

Just been going over old reviews, letters, journals etc. Struck by my intense pompousness at times.

Sept. 15
Yesterday was a day an artist dreams of—Richard brought Frances Pernas to buy a picture, and she ended up taking Bride and Owl—in spite of the tear—for 750.00. Then John called to say Al Bing is willing to donate the Masquerade to a museum—and I made the price on Daisy's picture 300. so she can afford to have it.

Of course all of this made me terribly excited and nervous, and I'm quite exhausted to-day after a sleepless night.

Sept. 17
Today building a stretcher and stretching canvas for the painting of Frank in his "Masquerade" costume. He will pose to-morrow, and I am planning a setup with a ladder back chair and the black cloak hanging from a nail. I think of it with deep darks and blacks, the jacket brilliant, the face pale.

Future paintings—
Lilla Van Sahr—seated in patterned chair
Marcia Pania, white hat, lace dress, black ladder chair
Frenchie & monkey, high stool
male nude (Walt)—others, in landscape

Sept. 22
Have some kind of a beginning on the Poet (Masker) painting, but there have been too many distractions to really get to work. Helped hang the Fifth Season group show, it looks good.

Received the Pernas check and John has the Bing check, so I'm financially secure for a while.

Sept. 23
I don't know which is more frightening, failure or success.

I feel the world pressing in on me to-day, and I can't sense this painting yet and I am morbidly depressed.

Sept 27
Ill with pressures and tensions, I must find some way to keep isolated,

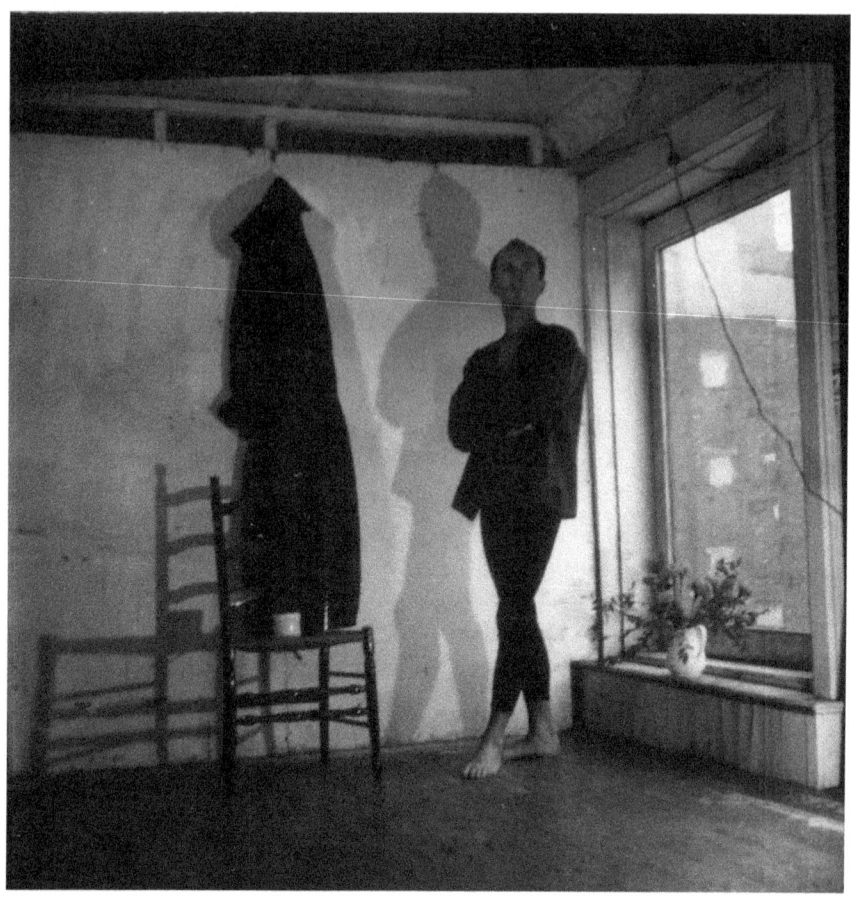

Frank O'Hara posing for Hartigan's painting entitled *The Masker*. Photograph by Walter Silver.

especially while I'm working. I've taken a private phone, and have decided not to answer the ringing while I'm working.

Terrible scene with Frank Sat. night at the Lansners, where he lashed out at me viciously, accusing me of being jealous of Larry, because I am obscure and unknown. Sent me into tears and then withdrawal.

We put Masquerade on a folding stretcher and Walt took a color photo for Life. Probably nothing will come of it.

5:00

The studio is filled with a quiet golden light, and I am content. I have a lot on the canvas that I can work with now, how sad it is that I must be so extremely misanthropic in order to be alone with myself.

I am trying to work with loaded brush now, and scrape instead of wiping down in order to get more fullness in the paint. I'd like to have every inch of the canvas tense.

Sept. 29.

Three days of intense concentration has finally resulted in "The Masker" I like it quite well, although it represents no radical departure from this year's other work. Much of it is wiped down, I find this is necessary in order to get the details I need.

At the finish I thought perhaps this picture was too derivative of Matisse, until I put Harry's "Dancer" (which I'm storing here) next to it. I must confess a malicious satisfaction at the comparison between this work and his.

I'm drinking a little Scotch and listening to my German records while writing this. And I am filled with that enormous sense of completion, rest and satisfaction that lasts for about one or two hours at the end of a work and makes all the sweat of it worth while.

Oct. 10

I am trying to gather to-gether from my confusion of emotions on seeing the "River Bathers" finally hung just what I am feeling.

It was quite by accident that I was able to see it yesterday—I had no idea that the third floor was completed until I ran into Hugh Koppel. I rushed up, through the rooms, from the great Picassos to the cubists, futurists, supremists—a room of mediocre European "abstract expressionism," then a lot of American mush with the beautiful red Gorky,—the Pollocks & DeK's in a room not open yet—and the final room, Kline, Rothko, Still, Baziotes and me. The picture was a shock, especially the color intensity. Still and Rothko looked pale by comparison. It is a beautiful picture, it has everything that is young in me, and ecstatic, but I pray that I am capable of much more, greater depth of message and emotion as well as a more profound and original painting form. I am proud that Barr feels what I know myself, that I am the equal—and more—of most of my American contemporaries. He is one of the few to see this, and I'm sure the bitchery from my fellow artists, art world, even friends will reach new heights.

I regret sometimes that this great gift has been born to me, a woman, with the countless flaws of vulnerability, worldliness, fears—what all! that I have. But so be it, I try to live the life that is necessary for it to flow. If fame is to come to me, it will require great strength to continue to work and keep the proper distance, the correct understanding in regard to my inner or spiritual self and my outer or worldly one.

I am reading Virginia Woolf's Journal with oh such tenderness, as though she were myself. How she did fret over the world and what it said of her! Perhaps my schizophrenic tendencies are my greatest protection.

There was one moment there to-day with Walter of such joy for me—as I stood there in the room, completely anonymous, and watched crowds of strangers wander in and stop before the Bathers, to shrug and go on—and many to stay and look a long time, one man explaining where the figures were to his child—to think of that picture in the world, with thousands of people seeing it, while I am safely here in the studio with Walt, listening to Ravel, and drinking the last of the Cointreau, all this is new, heady and confusing!

Oct. 12
I've been thinking for the last week or so of an interior, the studio corner with the Masquerade and costumes hanging. I'd like it silvery grey and white, with flashes of brilliant color from the costumes, the picture tense in the heady color and open in the whites. I'll begin it to-day on a newly stretched 48" x 60" canvas.

Oct. 13
I'm struck again by the difficulty I have in getting into a new work, how each stroke at the beginning is disgusting—Virginia Woolf calls it the problem of living in two worlds at once—When I am *in* the work, even though it drains me, the rewards are greater.

Oct. 14
Thinking this morning, while reading more of V. W Journal, on those

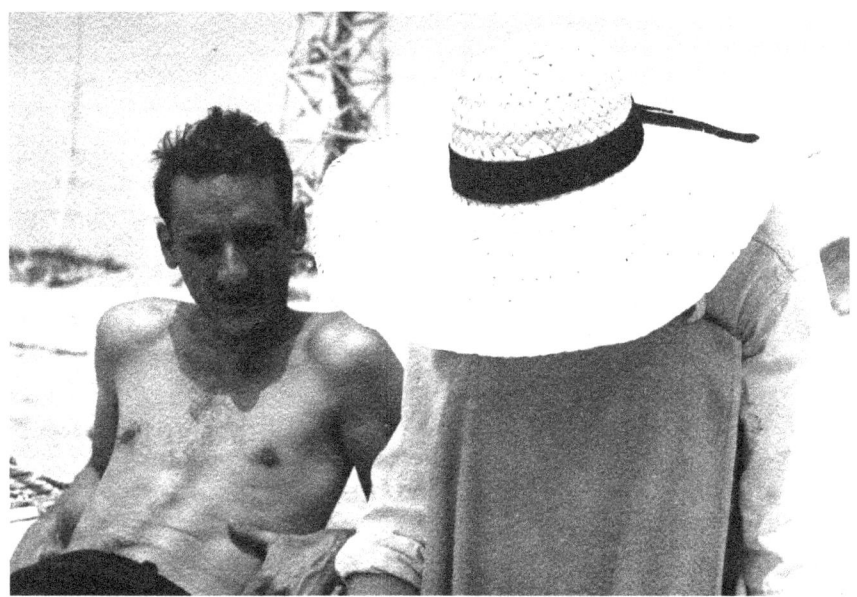

Larry Rivers and Hartigan with her Italian straw hat on the beach at Southampton.

exquisite passages describing her river walks and London storms and skies—how little "looking" I've been doing lately. I seem to have used up that part of me in Southamp. as though I had looked and looked so much that now I can draw from it—sort of an inner bank deposit.

It may even have been a mistake to paint there at all—but no, I enjoyed the sensation of sitting in nature, under the hot sun in my Italian straw hat so much, and even though the pictures themselves are worthless, who knows how much I stored up for the future?

Oct. 15
A gale wind is hitting the studio windows hard but nothing like the hurricane in Southampton just before we left. I'm cooking dinner for Frank, Hal [Hal Fondren, O'Hara's friend] & John M while W. [Walter Silver] is off to a photo discussion, and I'm calm now after an upsetting afternoon. I have borrowed "The Persian Jacket" from the M. M. Art for my show at Vassar, and it arrived here to-day. It is so close to what I'm doing now, and it seems I've made no

progress, so I dived into a typical swoon of depression, self doubt, where am I going?, how can I do more, be braver, better, stronger, more original, etc etc.

In fact P. Jack. is so similar to "The Masquer" that it might be a mistake to show them to-gether. What is wrong with me? I thought I had grown way beyond what I'd done two years ago And above all I must avoid getting stuck in a "style"—one look, one way. Remember my recurrent nightmare about my pictures changing into Baziotes'.

Oct. 20
Mrs Claflin [Agnes Claflin] was here from Vassar, and chose pictures for the show which opens Monday. She wants to show some older things as well as most of the new. She seemed to have a well bred interest in every thing I showed her.

The mod. mus. opening was yesterday—a big confused thing, not at all fulfilling my dreams of glory on such an occasion—No one knew who I was, so we wandered around like anonymous spectators, and if it hadn't been for Rich and Flor. [Richard Miller and Floriano Vecchi] & the Lansners, I would have had no sense of an *event* at all. I am still such a child, to hope for so much from life. Moments of delight and feelings of power never come on demand—and often never come at all. It is only in the work—that one feels glory of achievement.

Oct. 26
Whitney opening yesterday, in a new building—it looks like an art nouveau apartment house. They did not show my Greek Girl, and the whole thing plus my own state of confusion depressed me terribly. Nothing but interferences, I began again on the interior, it is a madness of indecision so far.

Apathy, mediocrity, indifference—these are the things we meet everyday, not hostility which is easier to fight.

Oct. 29
At last a day in the studio. It's becoming so that time here has to be fought for. Lord knows what I was working for in this interior I've been so distracted with Vassar catalogues, the new silk screen cover for Folder 3 and dentist appointments.

PAINTINGS

by

GRACE GEORGE HARTIGAN

⌒

OCTOBER 25 THROUGH NOVEMBER 24,

1954

⌒

VASSAR COLLEGE ART GALLERY

POUGHKEEPSIE, N. Y.

The cover of Hartigan's October 1954 one-artist exhibition at
Vassar College in Poughkeepsie, New York.

Dwight [Ripley] called John in great excitement over the Vassar show, he &
Rupert [Rupert Barneby, botanist and companion of Dwight Ripley] loved it
& he is buying "Southampton Fields" which he says he likes better than his
Dubuffet landscape.

stolen

1. ROUGH AIN'T IT. *Oil Collage.* 40" x 53".   1949

AGNES R. CLAPLIN -
2. SIX SQUARE. 60" x 65".   *300 .00*   1951

3. PARIS 1920. 50" x 48".   1951

4. THE MASSACRE.   *Robert Keene*   1952

5. THE INFANTA MARGARITA AFTER VELASQUEZ.
   30" x 32".   *Mrs Reynolds Silsby*   1952

6. THE PERSIAN JACKET. 57" x 47".   1952
   Collection Museum of Modern Art

7. STILL LIFE WITH CUCUMBER. 29" x 30".   1953
   Collection Mr. and Mrs. M. S. Pitzele

Whitney Museum
8. GRAND STREET BRIDES. 72" x 102".   1954

Vassar Museum
9. THE MASKER. 72" x 42".   *500.00*   1954

10. BRIDE AND OWL. 72" x 54".   1954
    Private Collection (Frances Pernas)

11. ODALISQUE. 52" x 42". *DR. Hoffman*   1954

12. INTERIOR WITH BRIDAL GOWN. 24" x 20". *de Yewin*   1954

13. SOUTHAMPTON FIELDS. 36" x 32".   *300 .00*   1954
    Dwight Ripley

14. MASQUERADE. 81" x 84". *Private Collection _*   1954
    Col. Chicago Art Institute

Exhibition arranged with the co-operation of the

TIBOR DE NAGY GALLERY, NEW YORK CITY

The list of artwork in Hartigan's one-artist exhibition at
Vassar College in October of 1954 with her annotations
indicating the disposition of some of the art.

Walt is attending his photog. discussion group, and I have just finished dinner
alone, with a Schumann symphony. I had a loin lamb chop with kidney, a
beefsteak tomato, Lacrima Cristi red wine, a brown pear with port salut

cheese, and a new blend of mocha-french coffee. I record this just in case, in retrospect, life at 25 Essex seems hard.

The interior went better to-day.

Nov 2
It is an odd, dark day of rain and thunder, and I am filled with inertia and melancholy. Every thing seems to interfere with my sense of inner flow, the joys of seeing the Vassar show, and selling a bit, and the Mod. Mus. thing seem just as disruptive as the annoying money quarrel with Al or my intense disappointment in Frank, both as a friend and a critic of my art.

Nov 4
Matisse is dead, what a gap is left! Soon they will all be gone, and what is to become of art?

For the last few days I have been working on this painting with one hand, and trying with the other to keep my door closed against the outer world— phone calls! interview with Newsweek, lunch with Glamour mag. feature editor, Vassar business, and now a big reproduction of River Bathers with a quote from me in Arts Digest, so John tells me, I haven't seen it yet. Good God, how do the Famous ever find time to do any further work?

Nov 5
The Interior is gone, wiped out, a complete mess—victim to my distraction, worldliness and weakness.

Nov 10
Who am I?

Nov. 19
It seems an eternity since I last finished a picture, although looking back over these pages I see its only a little over a month. I suppose these distractions which have upset me so terribly are no worse than any of the other times when life has loomed so large and important that I lost myself. I think espe-cially of man problems, Jeff worries, and money.

I was wondering to-night, as the Vassar visit is over and the demands on my energies seem to be dying down for a while, how people can live who have to depend on the world alone for their fulfillment. What I miss above all when I am not painting is the sense that I am concentrating and ordering all the tiny sufferings, sensations and nakedness of each second I live into some kind of form, and the resulting feeling that for the time, at least, I have triumphed.

Nov 23
I got the idea that I'd like to do something with the black feather fan—a kind of edgy "portrait of a lady". So I posed for Walt's camera in the eternal bridal gown, which turns out in this to have a kind of Victorian splendour, and to-day I am happily and busily at work with it, incommunicado, no phone answering. At last!

Nov. 24
Painting went well and fast yesterday. To-day more difficulty, no light, the seventh day of rain and fog.

Nov. 27
All day on "~~Woman~~ Lady with Fan" and I think it is finished.

It is a "charged" picture, with some good tensions and some that are just flashy, but I can't do anything about that this time. The expression on the face might be called "anguish," and if so it certainly expresses my state of being these days.

Nov 28
As has happened before when I thought prematurely that a picture was finished, I was wrong. This continued to haunt me all evening and night, and I worked myself into a terrible nervous fever and chill.

To-day more work, and it is much better—I'm still not completely satisfied with the face.

Nov 29
The pictures back from Vassar, minus three. Had to take Masquerade half off the stretcher and roll it, already it's cracked down the center.

Having these home again makes my new picture look monstrous, so shallow. I think I'm worrying too much about finishing a picture. As long as I work steadily, day after day, eventually something will happen. I musn't be pressured by the evident demand for my work.

[The following note is in the margin and is heavily crossed out, but it is still legible. It appears to refer to the 1 December entry.]

Mar. 23.
(This is the last picture that had any real value)

Dec. 1
I've done "Lady with a Fan" or it's done me. It has some things that interest me, and some that are puzzling—it's really an "off-beat" picture. I like the transitions, from one area to another, the way it moves.

Starting a still life of all my favorite white crockery, the composition based on a beautiful Zurburan which is in the Prado.

Dec. 6
I like Lady with Fan more as I get used to it.

Some work on and off with the still-life.

A long week of fears, helped by Walt, staying home and reading Mill on the Floss and Adam Bede. Now I feel a little less as though I were on the edge of a precipice.

Dec. 7
All through the ages artists have either been pulling art all apart or putting it back to-gether again. It seems as though ~~we~~ I have to put it to-gether—that makes ~~us~~ me a classicists, I guess. It's a sometimes unfortunate position for one of a revolutionary temperament.

One of the reasons for Cezanne's greatness is that he not only put art all to-gether again after the impressionists, but he gave all the clues for a future tearing apart—the cubists.

Dec. 8
Just finished what is probably my most "beautiful" still-life to date—"Spanish Still-life." I am pleased with the greys, they are so liquid.

Much praise last night for "Lady with Fan" from Frank, John Ash. [Ashbery] & the Weinstein's [Arnold Weinstein, writer and composer].

Minnesota wants 5 pics from me—large ones—& 5 from Larry for a Feb. show—"Emerging Reputations" or something. I can't decide what to send, all my new pictures seem to go as fast as I finish them.

Dec. 13
Brought the Lady to the gallery, John bewildered by it—so he says were Barr & D. Miller—I really shouldn't be surprised, it took me quite a while to like it too. Now I think of it as one of my best pictures.

More [Herman Moore] chose "Odalisque" for the Whitney Annual—in spite of John's dislike of the head in it—his favorite complaint. Damn, why do I let him irritate me so?

I am thinking of sending these to Minnesota—The Knight, D. & the D 1952, Standing Figure with Hydrangeas 1953, and Grand St Brides, Two Women and Lady with Fan—they will be back about March 1, and my NY show has been pushed on to April. This relieves the feeling of pressure I was beginning to get again, and will give me time to gather the scattered pictures to-gether.

I had intended to-day to begin a view of the park across the street, painting from the window. But a violent rain is flinging stuff at the studio, and I am mist-bound. I have in mind a large painting of two butchers, one standing, one carrying an animal of some sort. Walt has been doing photos of the meat packing district and I think I can use some for study. White aprons, blood streaked—permalba run through with alezeran, beautiful. [Permalba and alerzeran are colors. Permalba is a white, and alezeran is crimson red.]

Dec 15
Pressure on again—Jane can't show in March, she hasn't enough pictures. So I can't send any new things to Minnesota—they wouldn't return in time. Obviously I don't do enough work—but how can I do more—how can I do *anything!* I am completely distracted and confused.

Dec. 19
Had a long and intense talk with the Rosenbergs [Harold Rosenberg, art critic, and May Natalie Tabak, writer] here, with innumerable martinis. It did

me a lot of good somehow, I felt like a fool with my complaints about "fame." I simply *have* to be durable, tough.

A little work on the view of Seward park, but due to Xmas preparations not much. This is the first time in years that I've had some money of my own for gifts. I'd like this view to be painted full and sturdy, like Matisse's Pont St Michel. Some sure masses should do it.

Christmas Card to Grace Hartigan

There's no holly, but there is
the glass and granite towers
and the white stone lions
and the pale violet clouds. And
the great tree of balls in
Rockefeller Plaza is public.
Christmas is green and general
like all great works of the
imagination, swelling from minute
private sentiments in the desert,
a wreath around our intimacy
like children's voices in a park.

For red there is our blood
which, like your smile, must be
protected from spilling into
generality by secret meanings,
the lipstick of life hidden
in a handbag against violations.

Christmas is the time of cold air
and loud parties and big expense,
but in our hearts flames flicker
answeringly, as on old-fashioned
trees. I would rather the house
burned down than our flames go out.

The text of this poem is taken from page 212 of *The Collected Poems of Frank O'Hara* (Berkeley and Los Angeles: University of California Press, 1995, by arrangement with Alfred A. Knopf, Inc.) edited by Donald Allen. It is used with the permission of Maureen Granville-Smith, administratrix of the estate of Frank O'Hara.

Journal for 1955

Jan. 1, 1955

I feel body weary and soul searching this first day of 1955. We had a roaring
New Year's Eve party here, much talk, liquor, dancing, I in velvet matador
pants and bare back, the Brides on the wall surveying everything. Porter
McCray [Museum of Modern Art official] brought Alfred Barr, much to my
delight and every one else's astonishment.

Taking stock a little—I sold $5,500 worth of pictures in 1954—which means
about $3,660 of my own. I have about 500.00 left of it—some new clothes, a
few things for the idea of better living, a little dental work, some paint and
canvas. And about ten pounds too much flesh from good eating and drinking. Obviously I spend too much money—I had a talk with John about getting higher prices for my work, and he got hurt, wounded, etc. What a slob
he is. Larry got 2500 for Washington, which has been taken by the Modern
Mus.

I have a feeling of confidence in some ways as never before. There are a few
people I am thankful for—Walt, Richard, Frank in spite of everything, Larry
ditto. And my new friends like Mary Clyde [artist] & the Rosenbergs.

As for resolutions. Work *harder, more, longer*. I feel something coming, and I
must not be distracted by my growing "fame," I must stay in the studio more.

I want to finish this park picture, a small thing of Xmas tree balls, a thing of
a brace of pheasants and perhaps the butcher picture. I must learn more and
more from nature and my own personality, and leave "Art" alone a bit.

We just spent a few lazy, talky days at Larry's—I posed for a drawing and read
"Turgenev: a life." I note this quote—

"There were no 'objective talents' he declared, the greatest genius was always in touch with life in general—the everlasting source of every art—
and his own personalty in particular. . . . He must, above all, avoid being
'literary.' . . . A writer . . . ought to possess a power of concentration, a sense
of direction and *a strong & abiding faith*."

So on to 1955, and to what I must do.

Jan 4.
Worked the last two afternoons, when the sun is low on the park picture.
Going slowly.

Jan 6.
Have much that is beautiful on the park picture, but I fear a lot of it is "effect"
and not true enough, not full. So now I go to ruin it.

John just called to say that Larry & Helen have been taken for the Carnegie
International. My sinking heart reminded me of Flaubert's "Even the most
wide-spread fame leaves one longing for more." So as penance for my envy
I'm going to strip one of Larry's pictures for Minnesota.

This picture is probably finished, but it has all the worse faults of impression-
ism—All light and volume, but no structure.

Jan 7
A fine morning, over coffee, reading the new Art News with Larry's long
piece on some Master drawings and Frank's on Fairfield Porter. If my art
turns out in time to be nothing, at least I'll be a footnote in reference to the
brilliance of my friends.

Jan 10
Worked & worked on Seward Park, until at last it's a little better, and I can
leave it, and attempt another version some day.

Jan 14
I don't care about inventing a "new figure". I would however like to place the
figure in a new situation, a new relationship to its surroundings.

Jan 18
I am in one of those terrible times when I feel "painted out." I alternate
between ennui and restlessness—an ennui that stupefies me, keeps me curled
in my chair for hours and hours, reading anything—movie books, detective
stories, "literature," old journals. Or the restlessness that makes me walk the
floor, staring out one window and then another, or sends me dashing into the
street to stare into people's faces or dash from one gallery to another, or pace
frantically through museums looking for what, some clue, some hint, anything in life or art that will get me out of this pit.

Jan 20

I've just been re-reading Harold Rosenberg's brilliant article on "Red coats & Coon-skinners," and he said much that echoes Turgenev. I feel that I have had too much of basing art on art—not only "copies," which I haven't done for a year or two, but keeping in mind any preconceived ideas of "composition" etc. The other side of the coin can be basing art on energy, like Pollock, but I've had all that. With me now its all a matter of finding my world, my subject material. So far the greatest clue I have to this is "costume."

Jan. 24

I went through a nervous crisis last night of such madness that I am frightened. I fear that some time an "attack" like this will send me into the pit, from which I may not be able to find my way out. It is all so hard on Walt, he has to go through it all with me.

Jan 25

I'm on a painting of a night club singer that seems to be coming much better to-day. Also am clarifying my ideas about Frank's article on "nature and new painting" for a talk at the club on Friday.

I am glad to be living in the same world with Alfred Barr.

Jan 28

This lady may be finished now, bathed in a spotlight of pink paint—what shall I call her? The Entertainer? Chanteuse?

I am nervous about the panel at the Club to-night I fear the atmosphere will be hostile, and that always brings out the worst in me.

Jan 31

I need not have worried about the club panel. It was all intelligent and witty, with no fights, and none of the *real* issues were touched.

In spite of a growing cold, I have a feeling of elation. My pictures are all here to be reviewed by Larry Campbell, and they look good to me, spread around the studio. I am especially glad to see Lady w. Fan, and Masker again.

Also River Bathers is going to Paris for a show of American ptgs at the Musée d'Art Moderne. It amuses me to think of my work crossing the ocean before I do.

Also I'm told of a feature article on the Whitney with three reproductions, one mine, Larry, & John Graham. They say that "Odalisque" shows "poetic revulsion"—how apt.

Feb 6
Drawing to-day, some tulips which Jane & Larry brought for my cold, and two artichokes. It is foolish for me to try to force myself to do quick drawings, or those with ink & brush OR pen—in spite of my intense admiration for Goya's I can only draw with charcoal or pencil, working over & over, erasing often, until the line reveals itself, the volumes begin to fall in the right place.

Feb 9th
To make a virtue out of mediocrity seems to me a most horrific kind of daring, like a beggar showing his sores for pity and profit.

Feb. 11
This is one of my "in myself" times, when even conversation is difficult and I seem to be gathering who knows what to-gether.

What must I paint—*Not* how? But what?

I think I'd like to do a full length thing of Anne Meecham [Meacham] as Aurora, in the white gown she wears, on stage with all that phony scenery.

I'd like to do something ambitious, with a lot of figures, but it hasn't come to me. Would also like to do small group studies, and things not life size.

I thought yesterday while at the Metropolitan how the inclusion of a figure, no matter how tiny, gives a landscape such an intensity of meaning.

I think I've been relying too much on the contemporary presentation of the figure as the composition, it fills the canvas, it is the space. The Masker is an exception (this year I mean)

One of the things that gives Bacon's figures their meaning is the strange environment in which he places them.

Feb. 16
Saw Escudero [famous flamenco dancer] last night his farewell. An old man, sad and rigid, trying to use wit to fill the gaps, moments when one realized what a great artist could be.

Feb. 17
Started a painting of Flamenco dancers in which none of the figures are more than a foot high. I foresee great difficulties, but I'm determined to do it.

And I have a new haircut and am beginning to diet, so all in all spring must be coming.

Al has left the gallery.

Mar 3
My show is up. Art News & the Times reviews are out, everyone compares me to one expressionist or another which is infuriating. I think much of that comes from my use of black in the contours and definitions, especially in the 2 large ptgs. I like Larry's review otherwise, it is full of life and wit.

Evidently Daniel Rich's [director of the Art Institute of Chicago] short trip to the studio last week was enough to make him decide to take Masquerade, so it will go to Chicago when my show is over. This acceptance just involves prestige, for the money has long ago been spent, as has all my money—I have $1.99 in the bank. So again I *must* sell. Ben Heller has Odalisque on approval, and the Neubergers want something but don't know what. Jimmy Merrill can't take anything until 1956—at which time he'll spend $2000, but that's a long time to live on $1.99.

～

A portion of Howard Devree's review in the *New York Times* on 3 March 1955 reads as follows: "Turning from her earlier, more abstract work, Grace Hartigan, at the de Nagy Gallery, 206 East fifty-third Street, has been moving toward a more expressionist manner, somewhat reminiscent of Beckmann, especially in large paintings of groups of figures. There is no denying the vigor and dash of her work, but since realization of faces and figures is not pushed very far, and backgrounds are flat or only suggested, the larger works

NEW PAINTINGS . . .

GRACE

H A R T I G A N

Opening: *MARCH 1* — *4:00* — *6:30 P.M.*

Closing: *APRIL 2, 1955*

TIBOR DE NAGY GALLERY

206 East 53rd Street, New York, N. Y. · PL 9·1621

Ken,
Can recommend
this show

Cover of the catalog of Hartigan's March 1955 exhibition at the Tibor de Nagy Gallery.

seem left a little hectic and up in the air. More surely designed is the 'Seward Park,' subdued in key and quite convincing. 'Chanteuse' is cleverly manipulated to achieve the atmosphere of artificiality intrinsic in the theme, a device also successful in "Grand Street Brides," which might have been inspired by a store display of costumes or an example in a streetside photographer's window. All the work is tensely personal."

~

Mar 4
Pacing the studio, working on the Flamenco Dancers, drinking beer, worrying about money, cursing expressionism.

Mar 6
Terrible fears, depression. It seems ironic that a few months ago I was complaining of "success"—now I fear nothing will happen, that I've used up my buying audience, oh what paranoia. And the cursed weather, nothing but rain. And this picture just won't go, I don't know what to do with it.

1. Grand Street Brides — *Whitney Museum* 1954 *2000.00*
2. Two Women 1954 *300.00*
   Collection Daisy Aldan
3. Lady With a Fan *Guy Weill* 1954
4. Spanish Still Life — *al Bing* 1954 *# 400.00*
5. Masquerade 1954 *– 1000.00*
   Private Collection — Col. art Institute of Chicago
6. Seward Park *Col. Ernest Peters.* 1955 */400.00*
7. Interior with Bridal Gown *Col Dr. Yellen* 1954 *for dentistry*
8. The Masker 1954 *500.00*
   Collection Vassar Art Museum
9. Peonies and Hydrangeas *+ Nelson Rockefeller)* 1954 *300.00*
   Col. ...
10. Chanteuse *Guy Weill* 1955

List of the artwork in Hartigan's March 1955 exhibition at the Tibor de Nagy
Gallery with her annotations indicating the disposition of the works. Note that
Interior with Bridal Gown went to the collection of Dr. Yellen "for dentistry"
while *Masquerade* went to the Art Institute of Chicago.

Mar. 12
Painting going impossibly bad. And still no sales, neither of us has a cent. I
can't tell how I'll pay my rent. The only bright spot has been a perceptive essay by a Vassar student [Emily Dennis] on some of my paintings in the show
there. It's encouraging to know that someone appreciates the formal qualities
of the work and doesn't think of it as emotionalism.

What has happened to joy?

Mar 13
Bless Alfred Barr, again he has given me such encouragement when I need it
so badly—he's taking Peonies & Hydrangeas for the Mod. Museum, seemed
filled with enthusiasm for the show, loves the Brides.

I am abandoning the dancers—the surface is gone, and I worked it up to "the
moment of truth"

I must try to keep some balance between my "subject," thoughts of *what* I must paint—and my "form," *how* I must paint. I go all off beam when I get too involved in either one to the exclusion of the other.

Figures in movement are not for me, at this time anyhow.

Mar 15
Yesterday and now to-day on pins and needles, waiting to hear if Mrs. Rockefeller has come to the gallery. Alfred Barr is sending her to see if she will donate P & H to the Museum, and *perhaps* buy the Brides! Also Soby is writing something on me for Sat. Review, so at last it looks as though something is happening. My rent is due to-day, I must borrow the money to pay it.

Thinking of a large painting, a "still-life" of a store window filled with crystal vases, lamps, roccoco figures, nubian slaves in china, all madnesses—Walt has taken photos for me.

Mar 18
Nelson Rockefeller is donating P & H to the Museum—sight unseen. It would be maddening if this were the only purchase out of the whole show.

Lunch and brandy and a long afternoon of talk with Helen, after these last two or three years of avoiding each other. I am as fond of her as ever, I only wish for the sake of her talent she would rebel against the tyranny of Clem's ideas.

Clouds of snow to-day. I intend to start the crystal painting.

Mar 21
This is Spring?

I have a 5 x 7 canvas tacked up, and a drawing in charcoal of the bric-a-brac on it. Now for some color washes.

Mar 22
No Ben Heller sale, no Roy Neuberger. Oh my pride. Alfred Barr, if it were not for you, where would I be, what would I think—

Mar 23

I was drunk and feeling sorry for myself last night when I wrote the above wail. And as usual, Walt had to bear it with me. My plight is nothing compared with de Kooning—he is famous, and such a great and mature artist, and he is penniless.

My last hope for the show is that the Whitney will take the Brides, and arrange for an advance on the money—Merrill will pay for it next year.

I do believe I have learned a great deal from the show—wisdom in relationship to my "place" in the art world and a great deal about my work—I must have more and more formal values in my painting, much more architecture.

Mar 25

A visit yesterday from Katherine Ordway, a collector and former Hoffman student, who wants a picture but wants the "right" one.

Borrowed $50 from Jane. Pleasant evening with Al B., looking at Van Gogh drawings and painting reprod.

This morning reading Barr on Matisse, a book that I should know by heart.

This canvas now is covered with thin washes of high color, I am now going into it with drawing, wiping down continually to preserve the surface until the moments when opacity is *necessary* and not just energy.

Mar. 28

Trying to think of a message for myself on my thirty-third birthday, but the only one that occurs to me is "Courage!"

With all the descriptions of the objects stated on the canvas, I am now opening it up with slashes and strokes of white, to refer it to the surface and loosen the contours in order that the volumes may fall right. I have some idea of hot pure high color with a pearly grey for this, if it works out.

This stage is one of the most difficult of all, and I must force myself to the canvas, to destroy all the falseness and brilliance of a good beginning. This destroying of a first "effect" to get to the deeper, truer one causes such conflict in me that I want to seek refuge in sleep, my eyes keep closing, I am almost stupefied with drowsiness.

Mar 30
Al Bing is buying "Spanish Still-life" for himself or a donation—so that makes a little difference in my financial situation. If only Katherine Ordway turns out to be as devoted to my art as he, I could have peace of mind.

Emily Dennis was here yesterday, she has such youth and enthusiasm. I let her pick out a '53 drawing. Strange how seldom I draw these days.

Bric-a-brac is coming to a crisis.

April 1
After a long soul searching the Whitney has decided to take the Brides. They will advance me half the money soon, the other half in the summer, and Merrill will pay them back on the first of the new year. So after all my fretting things have turned out well.

Still struggling with this picture, nothing sits right.

Eight intensive hours of work on this thrown off for a short time by John's phone call telling me how Dorothy Seckler hates my painting, after which I began to search this suffering, yet unborn canvas for "holes." I must learn more strength, not to take criticism so seriously.

April 4
Work, work, work. Now I find what I must do is discard all elegance, skill, "style," and become terribly simple. The spirit of Matisse and not the look. And so as a result I *must* have the courage to look clumsy.

April 11
The Gift Shop Window (Bric-a-brac) is finished. It is precariously close to being an "unresolved" painting, it has so many warring elements. I think in the final analysis, however it comes to-gether.

Now that the weather is warm I want to do some drawings from the studio fire escape, and then perhaps a painting of Marcia.

April 18
Weak, bored and irritable from a sudden virus. Terrible fears and fever dreams.

Richard hates Gift Shop Window, thinks it could have been done by anyone, etc. This may be true—or it may be that the "clumsiness" of the handling puts him off. At any rate since I rely on his judgement so much it upset me.

I think I am one of those "born to disturb the slumber of the world."

April 21
Soby's article in Sat Review is out, it is everything that I could have hoped for, a real rave. I feel now the only thing that I lack is a real collector, someone interested in my most daring work, who would buy regularly and steadily from year to year. Al Bing is fine for museum donations, but for his own taste he is only interested in my most lyrical, least characteristic paintings. And Kath Ordway is too neurotic about art to ever buy for herself, although I think she too might donate to a museum.

James Thrall Soby's article in the *Saturday Review* of 23 April 1955 carried this commentary about *Grand Street Brides:* "'It is such a relief nowadays,' a museum director said recently, 'to find a new artist working with authority in a non-abstract style.' The remark is meaningful in that the man who made it is by no means reactionary in taste, but has been a consistent defender of many of the most advanced trends in the art of our century. The remark was made while a group of us were looking at some pictures by the British painter Francis Bacon. It would have been as appropriate, I think, if the works on view had been done by two young Americans: the painter Grace (George) Hartigan and the sculptor Elbert Weinberg. Both artists seems to me extremely gifted in their separate media and directions. My guess is that larger fame will soon be theirs. Born in Newark, New Jersey, in 1922 and first trained as an artist by Isaac Lane Muse, Miss Hartigan was herself once an abstract painter. And then quite suddenly she felt impelled to paint figures in recognizable, if still far from conventional terms, and to rediscover in the process qualities of moment and human aura which she thought abstractions tended to omit or disguise. Her revelation, if one may call it that, occurred only a few years ago. It was accompanied by a thorough reappraisal of virtues in the art of the past that could help her in her new resolve. Matisse had long meant a great deal to her. But now she studied intently the old masters, especially those of scintillating flourish, as when in 1952 she made studies after Velasquez's 'Infanta Margarita' and Tiepolo's 'The Building of the Trojan Horse.' She wanted, she said, to try to penetrate the mystery of *painting*. In so doing she naturally broke with some of her former colleagues in abstraction, whose scholasticism and restraint no longer appealed to her. One might say in brief that she began to evolve a more overtly emotional kind of art, though one must keep in mind her deep mistrust of expressionism's introversion, whether tormented or musical. Her natural language was color. She learned to speak it with vivid spontaneity and a remarkable subtlety of emphasis and change. Hartigan could not, however, be satisfied for long with color for its own sake, even if brilliantly orchestrated, as in the early works of Kandinsky and Delaunay. During the past two years her instinct to create an imagery whose juxtapositions would be wry rather than fantastic has made itself felt more and more clearly. Thus far the preoccupation has reached its climax in her picture of a shop window on New York's Grand Street, where wedding gowns for the budgeted bride are on display in a strange rivalry of ugliness and hope (see illustration). The picture's virtuosity is so entrancing that one peers at it intently, inch by inch. Afterwards one becomes aware of the work's monumentality and cohesion: live beings have donned the mannequins' clothes; a quiet, tenacious drama unfolds. It is no accident that Hartigan greatly admires Picasso's 'Les Demoiselles d'Avignon' of 1907. For her, presumably, the picture is important not because it announces the beginning of cubism's esthetic, but because it proposes a bold choreography involving disparate figures, their action united by swift fusions of color and line. At any rate, Hartigan has made open reference to the 'Demoiselles' in a few of her recent paintings. Her rereading of its meaning is one more indication that masterpieces are often freshened in impact by the predilections of succeeding generations of artists. In general aim Hartigan is allied to other younger American painters, among them Larry Rivers, Elaine de Kooning, and Robert De Niro, with Willem de Kooning a respected predecessor both in technique and because his 'Woman' of 1952 was a powerful stimulus for the newer artists in their effort to move away from abstraction. The group (and the term applies only in its loosest sense) has found an eloquent champion in Frank O'Hara, whose article 'Nature and New Painting,' published in *Folder* in 1954, is a valuable document on the new movement. And at the time of Hartigan's solo exhibition at Vassar College last year, an undergraduate, Emily Dennis, wrote a perceptive thesis on the artist; I can't for the life of me understand why it hasn't been reprinted in one of the art magazines. Well, at least Hartigan's pictures can now be seen for themselves in the collections of the

Museum of Modern Art, the Art Institute of Chicago, the Whitney Museum of American Art, and Vassar College. Go have a look. The young woman is a born painter, improving all the time and already most persuasive."

~

April 22
Thanks to some perceptive remarks by Jane yesterday I was able to-day to affect some changes in the left side of G. S W. that have improved the composition enormously.

April 27
It's strange, but I simply cannot do any drawing—oh I suppose I could doodle, or describe, but that isn't enough, I think of drawing as a thing in itself, filled with a vital life of its own, real work like Matisse's great charcoal things.

So I'm back to starting a painting, small, of some wax fruit and crystal bottles.

Jay Steinberg [art patron] killed himself, horrifying.

May 2
This is a terrible time for me, I am lost and floundering—and worse of all, I can't even flounder on a canvas, it is all in me, I can barely force myself to work. I don't know what I want to paint, or how. I feel as though I am waiting, waiting. Its terrible.

Thank heaven I have the Window, at any rate it makes me feel I haven't lost all my energy. The only thing I have in mind is a large composition of nude mannequins. Why can't I paint small pictures?

May 4
I went through another of my nervous crises two nights ago, much to my humiliation Joan was with me to witness it.

To-day however I feel miraculously as though all my strength had returned, I am thinking with eagerness of the window nudes and ready to attack this small picture with a bilious green.

May 7.
Finished Wax Fruit to-day, and began with Walt to search shop windows for nude mannequins

The criticisms of the Stable show are out—Larry & I & to a lesser extent the other de N. [Tibor de Nagy] artists are singled out for the most vicious criticisms. I feel the jungle.

May 15
I am writing this in a rooming house in East Hampton, by a window overlooking a calm cool graveyard and a shingled windmill with a red window. I spent two days with the Rosenbergs, and with Walt here to-day, we return tomorrow. Then in two weeks we go to Mexico with Jane and Joe. I am leaving thoughts of the nude manneq. till the end of June.

I feel strongly that I need to get some sense of perspective in order to not be defeated by "professionalism," to find out truths that will help me devote my thoughts and energies to my work, where they belong. Already these few days here, with much talk with May and Harold, have given me a great deal of objectivity, it is my miraculous good luck that I have found them as friends at a time like this. Harold has one of the sharpest minds I've ever encountered, and May some of the most intense human understanding.

The big thing I have learned from them is that I must fight only my own battles, not Larry's or Jane's or Fairfield's or *John's*. Much of the attack, especially the "conservative" and "reactionary" talk is not directed at me at all, and it has been one of my biggest confusions. And once again I must remind myself about John, how he works on my fears and nerves, and takes and takes of my time and energy. I *must* rid myself of those people who drain me and upset me, it is sheer self-preservation that I do so.

I'm afraid that for me, as an artist, there is no "we" and may never be, there is only "I." My work has nothing in common with any other painter, I am completely alone.

May 25
The last ten days have been spent in going away preparations, and I feel busy, happy and optimistic. I've thought a lot about pace, of the necessity of the life tempo coming from oneself, and not from outside pressures. My own speed, my growth. Art cannot be seized head on, it must be stalked, it is elusive. And the only way it can be ever found is not knowing it except through occasional flashes of insight and revelation.

[Hartigan, Walter Silver, John Ashbery, Jane Freilicher, and Joe Hazen traveled to Mexico between 28 May and 15 June. The main reason for the trip was that Joe Hazen needed to obtain a divorce in Mexico so that he and Freilicher could marry.]

May 28
We left at six this morning, after a send-off breakfast with the Reed's, and now I am in a shabby motel room in Roanoke, Virginia. Everything is bucolic and green so far, with new Virginia's grass becoming touched with blue, and the air soft, it all sucks you in. We drove too long, Joe nervous, W [Walter Silver] & I windburned from the back seat, but still all jokes and good spirits.

I want to find out this trip things about not only the New York world, or about nature, but "America," how can I say it?

I thought of the "screen" in a painting, vague ideas—television or movie screen, repeating images projected smaller or larger than the personages in the painting, here they are, there they are—which is real?

May 29
Tonight in a super motel with swimming pool this side of Nashville, Tennessee. Black green forests, pines like Maine, high sweeping skies, big, big—I Love America.

May 30
Personalities are beginning to clash. Joe is driving, driving towards some imaginary paradise, with nothing but the goal in view. I am loving the now, here, to-day in Arkansas was what I've been hoping for, that huge feeling— flat rice fields, where the skies have more form than the land, one would need paint sky scapes. God how I love this country, its immensity—I feel I must interpret it for the others, I possess it. How will I understand those artists who were drawn to doing "Americana"—the trouble is they were too puny to cope with it—my country needs giants.

May 31
I picked a handful of Texas mesa flowers to-day, burnt crimson daisies and white ones, pale violet ones with yellow centers, some delicate lavender, and some spindly centered marigolds. We're all almost delirious with excitement over the newness and the anticipation of Mexico—and dead tired, and

hilarious over the Americana. This motel is like a Hollywood B glamour film—I'm half in it and half laughing at it—Giant cheeseburgers, kidney shaped pools, green flood lights.

June 2
This is the second night in Mexico. We are in Hotel Valles, a "tropical paradise" which Jane says is probably like Miami Beach. So far the pace in Mexico has been the American Tourist groove, living well, watching food and water, and for me such a flood of memories and associations—I realize how much I love this country, and how it puts me off at arm's length. Last night in Monterrey we stayed at the Gran Hotel Ancira, and Walt and I did the same things Harry & I did for the first evening in Mexico—the same buggy & horse driver, the same "residential" part of town, Sanborns, a walk in the Plaza. Our room was like a British Hotel room in Africa—ceiling fan, shutters opening on the square and mountains, high double bed, gold bath fixtures.

How difficult it is to be understood, and how ten times more difficult outside of one's own country. Americans are so absurd here, with their quickness and stiffness and pasty skins. And of all things, that which brought Mexico closest to me, with a terrible ache was the first smell of a small town, the human stink plus charcoal plus hung meat plus dry earth and funny stiff vegetation.

Now after a swim in a green pool with oleander petals floating and several Tequila cocktails, I wonder if I am being true to myself and Mexico by coming like this, skimming the surface, taking the cream with all my past knowledge and rawness.

June 4
The Hotel Montejo in Mexico City on the Reforma—this is the first morning in this little continental hotel, and I am happy in spite of the familiar traveler's bowels. We all will separate here for a week—the driving has been a terrible ordeal, and I cannot bear to see Mexico as the other three want to see it, so protected and timid. We will stay here for a few days, and then take a tourismo to Guanajuato.

Yesterday was filled with joys in spite of the others. The Hotel Valles was like a Hollywood movie, completely unreal—but then a few hours later it was market day in a purely Indian town, ours the only pale skins, where cheap threads and ribbons were on display, and we bought a peon shirt and two Creada rebozos. Then much mountains, with John and Jane studying Spanish grammar, and Walt being nagged by Joe to photograph mountain peaks, and me insisting on lunching in a *real* Mexican restaurant. We found one and had a typical comida—the others looked as though we were trying to poison them—and two of the most beautiful men sent over some tiny sharp avocados.

Then this hotel, which I think could be in Madrid or Paris, and John Hohnsbeen and Bridjet [Bridget] Tichenor met us in the lobby, and we had a late and sublime supper in Prendas with tequila raw and broiled crawfish, a mango and muddy good coffee.

Now I am looking at the thin light—we woke early, and have already had breakfast. This is the "smart" section of town, and I am eager for a day of tramping around markets, pawn shop, cathedral—with many stops at many kinds of bathrooms.

June 6
We have separated for a week—the three J's to Acapulco, Walt and I to Guanajuato. I am sitting now on a balcony overlooking a small square with green boxy trees and silver roccocco benches. This is a lovely colonial town, and our hotel is all tiles and high ceilings with pale blue whitewash. I feel peaceful and dosed with stomach medicine, Walt is a bit uneasy but going along with this immersion into the heart of Mexican life—we are the only Americans we have seen so far in town. Our room is 85 pesos a day for two with meals—a peso is 8¢ now.

We walked and walked through markets in Mexico City—hand work is becoming more and more rare and everywhere Grand Rapids type furniture and Montgomery Ward type clothing is taking over the City Mexico has a tempo almost like New York, and I am happy to be in a low paced small town for a while. Last night we had chocolate at Tina Bourfaily's house, a great 200 year old casa, and talked bullfighting with Bette Ford, an ex-model turned bull fighter—so odd. I'd like to paint her.

Now Walt is napping. I am sipping rum at $1.00 a bottle, the birds are settling in the plaza, our room has already a few fantastic toys hanging that I found in the market.

June 8

Our third day in Gunajuato. The first night we entertained every mosquito in Mexico, so we have changed rooms—a very quiet one, with our own sun terrace.

Yesterday we walked the market and found a coarse heavy made serape for 100 pesos. The breakfasts here are divine—melon, papaya, fresh pineapple all oranges and pale yellow. And spicy huevos rancheros with green or red sauce, thick black coffee. Dinner at 2 or 3 PM, many odd dishes—perhaps goat? and undecipherable sticky stewed fruits. For supper just chocolate for me and crumbly sweet cookies.

I feel completely passive here, just receiving impressions, I am no one, I leave no mark.

We are sunning on the hotel roof, all white columns and pink tiles, yellow ochre walls—the red of the geranium almost hurts. Mexico has so little high color, contrary to popular notions—everything is muted. So Walts yellow shirt screams high.

This morning we found a sympatico young taxi driver to take us around— First the catacombs, to see the mummies. People caught in a flow of lava and turned to stone, where death left nothing but horror on the faces, no peace, terror and anguish—open mouths, hands flung across the breast or eyes, even the very old were not resigned.

Then narrow dirt roads to a magnificent church—Valencia—all roccocco and gold. And a crude hammered gold necklace that I may not be able to give away, and a look at a silver mine, still being used, with old crumbling walls and new. The old and the new live so harmoniously in this country.

June 10

Back in the City again, Hotel Montejo, where the proper ladies look askance at our ragged bulging baggage, my pierced ears and rebozo and all. I must remember the Tourismo ride to Gto—the Padre and good spirited Mexican middle class business men, me the only woman—from Gto, the respectable looking pimp and his little girl, flirty brown eyes, no lipstick but blood red nails. And the silence and resentment. The green earth hills—now I know

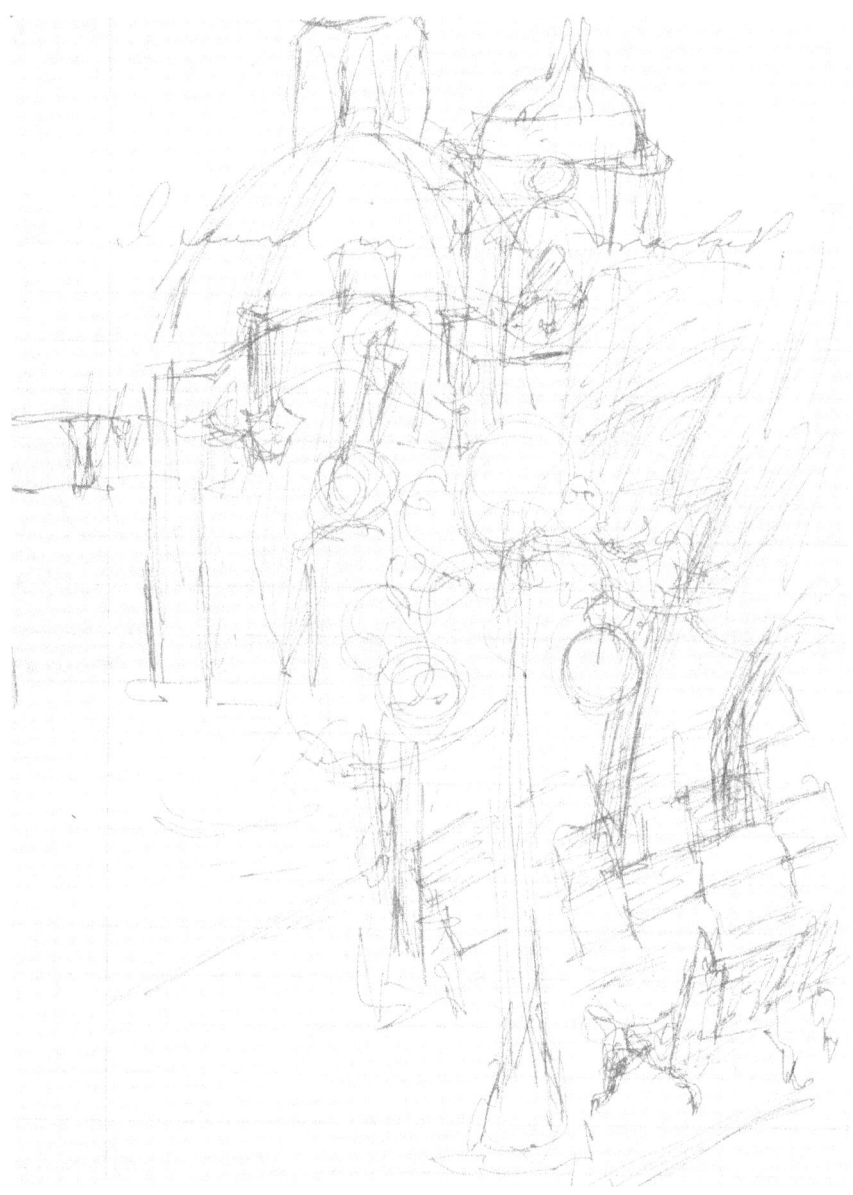

Hartigan's ink sketch positioned before her journal entry for 8 June 1955 while she was in Mexico.

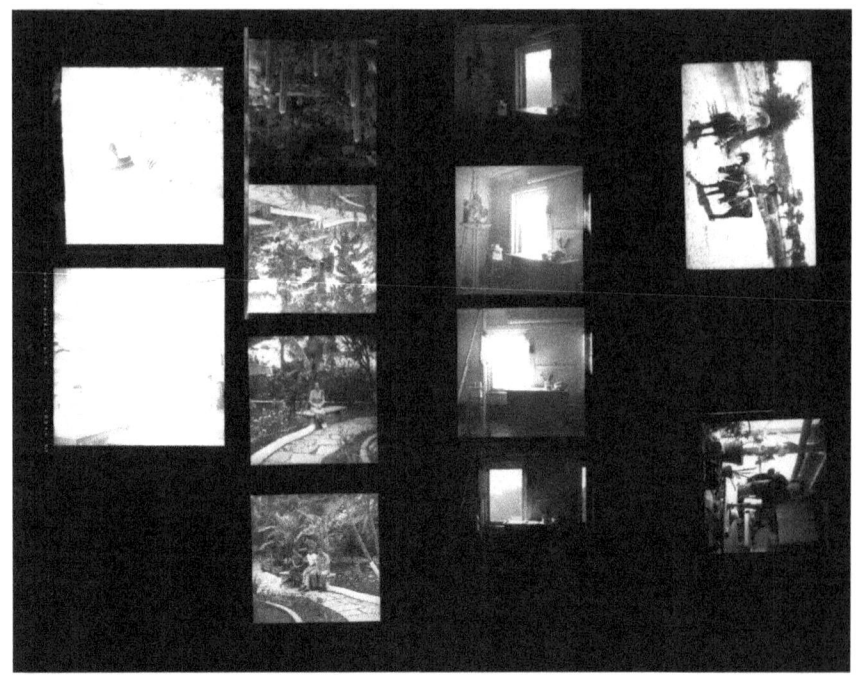

Contact sheet with images taken during Hartigan's trip to Mexico. Photographs by Walter Silver.

what terre verte is—and Indian villages with orange brown tiled roofs, cold air and high sky.

I am not glad to be back in the City, I felt happy and relaxed in Gto in spite of mosquitoes. Yesterday we rode to the old parts of town, a ruined church 400 years old, with powdering walls of blue, such silence—and the strange statues of santos turning green mold, rising out of the water, one still pink column.

Mexican cognac, and the band playing horrible music with the boys and girls walking round & round & round the Plaza under the square trimmed trees.

The afternoon toy fiesta, paper maché dolls with staring eyes, mock bulls, masks and hats with reptiles crawling up.

June 15
Back in America to-day, a long hot ride on the Central Highway, with mesas,

mountains, skies—desert after desert, one lonely strange stretch like Africa, we all have chapped lips, but it was glorious. Then a sordid morning in Juarez, Joe divorced and us looking for Cha-cha-cha records, and an incredibly fast customs inspection, and now a rum-rebozo-toy laden car.

Can it be true that the thing one admires most about one's country is it's health, neatness, efficiency, wealth?—The sleek fat horses and cattle, so different in only a few miles, and neat fences as far as one can see, and pure water. But the relief from worry over the basic things of eating without becoming ill, and sleeping well at night etc really are *freeing*—now I can think.

June 23
I'm in a fit of energy, fixing up the studio for a summer of work, and eager for work but willing to hold off for another day or two. It seems odd that the trip gave me all that I needed, in spite of the other three, their AAA guide and terrors and superficiality. But I do feel more objective and stronger about the "world" and my painting. One must be fierce.

June 25
Reading Lawrence's "Plumed Serpent"—I am amazed by his perception and intensity about Mexico—not so much the evocing of the ancient gods, parts, but the capturing of the feel, the look, the smells—superb.

Began the Display Mannequins to-day, trying to incorporate a vague idea of a "screen." As always, the beginning is intensely painful, I resist it violently and must force myself to it.

One of D. H's insights—that Mexico has soul but no spirit.

June 26
The beginnings of my paintings are always distinguished by their lack of distinction—of any quality whatsoever.

June 27
Walt's sense of self-preservation has finally asserted itself and he has left— And I am shaken with shock and the Big Fear, aloneness. And the terrible incomplete feeling of a woman without a man, without love. But it is wrong to cling out of fear and desperation, I must learn how to live with myself, it seems that I will never never have the comfort of a permanent relationship.

My throat is chocked, my stomach ill, and I'm flooded with tears—I'm going now to see if I can paint.

June 29
This thing with W. is vacillating back and forth—I seem to me such a difficult creature to love, but once loved I don't see how one could give it up, like acquiring a taste for my favorite, Rose's lime and seltzer water, a terrible taste of medicine at first, but now so pungent and refreshing that all other hot weather drinks seem insipid by comparison.

Painting each day—but such chaos!

June 30
The core of the W. problem is very Lawrencian. Concerned not with his loving not enough, but too much, thereby losing the *self* completely. So the fight is for a separate identity. On the other hand I have this fusing with another or the loss of self only in the love act—then, having loved and been loved I rush into myself with new strength, it is only love that can make me free and objective and whole.

Reading Gide's earliest Journal, odd how I like *him* so well but none of his work—this passage electrified me, I relate it to what I've been thinking of as a "screen." "In a work of art I rather like to find transposed, on the *scale* of the characters, the very subject of that work. Nothing throws a clearer light upon it or more surely establishes the proportions of the whole. Thus, in certain paintings of Memling or Quentin Metzys a small convex and dark mirror reflects the interior of the room in which the scene of the painting is taking place. Likewise in Velasquez's painting of the "Meniñas". Finally, in literature, in the play scene in Hamlet—. In "Wilhelm Meister" the scene of the puppets or the celebration at the castle. In "The Fall of the House of Usher" the story that is read to Roderick, etc."

For myself I might add the open doorways and windows in Matisse.

Another essential point he makes is that one must feel as though one works in the absolute—"One should want *only one thing* and want it constantly."

The mirror
The television & movie screen
The painting within a painting.

July 1
Now W & I have gotten to the bottom of some of our difficulties, and have decided to spend some nights apart—some here, and some at his studio, I feel a great sense of joy with my life.

I love the Essex St neighborhood, now full in summer heat—the watermelons and pineapple slices on ice, the park filled with people, all the life & smells in the street. And it was so hard combating Walt's hatred of all this, it left me no strength. I think boredom comes from the feeling that one would be happier some other place.

Now my days alone have a certain shape to them—I wake about nine, turn on the symphony and have juice, fruit and a pot of black coffee. Read a bit (still Gide's Journal), talk on the phone—to Richard, or Frank—sometimes Mike [Goldberg], or others. Then three or four, sometimes five hours on this canvas—it hasn't begun to come yet, but I keep thinking of things to do.

Then a few domestic chores for myself, a cold shower, a cold hard boiled egg and one or two rums with Rose's lime, more reading, some records. To-night I meet Frank at the Cedar for dinner, then to the late showing of "East of Eden." I feel sharp, my reading is concentrated and not "escape." I have thoughts, ideas. And the news of Tom Hess' coming article on the younger painters, profuse reproductions of "everyone," but me, does not fill me with paranoia and depression, I am interested, but not upset.

July 4
How can one work in such heat, the canvas won't stay still in front of my eyes.

I make a great mistake when I try to keep anything in a painting. I get tight and timid—it *must* always be in a state of flux till the last moment, every-thing should be potential.

July 6
Worked until eleven last night—now to-day it begins to go, a fever of heat

and work scraping, adding, rubbing, drawing—muted color, that same old "expressionist" look!

But I am powerless to prevent it, when the picture gets to this stage it begins to paint itself, my likes and dislikes have nothing to do with it, I am only a medium.

July 7
Today destroying all of yesterday.

July 8
I note with joy this passage from the second volume of Gide's Journals— certainly the answer to Larry, Jane, Fairfield and all the "new realists"—

"Paul Laurens takes advantage of the great leisure his canteen leaves him to 'go back to school' as he says, and 'to learn how to draw all over again.' Together with two comrades, he requisitions a model and sits down to work for hours at a time. I cannot rejoice with him over this. *A bad time to learn when everything is again being questioned.* Besides, did he sin through lack of technique? I believe, on the contrary, that his originality might have been better seconded by a less ready technique, and even by a little clumsiness. Virtuosity never produced anything but banality. *The only technique that is worth anything is the one that emotion itself has created and can invent again when need be.* I want to write nothing except under pressure of necessity."

Sun. July 10
Friday to Monday Walt is photographing Marca-Relli in Springs [East Hampton], and I am with myself in this steaming hot city, trying to give birth to "The Mannequins" Many times with it I have been close to a "finish" resembling the Daisy & Olga picture, but I can't do that any more, I want something I can't imagine or see, and so I go on messing and correcting.

This has been the weekend—Friday dinner & Brazilian movie with Mike [Goldberg], then till 3:00 AM talking with Kline [Franz Kline, abstract expressionist painter] in the Cedar on—of all things—the British royal family. Yesterday cleaning, buying Italian coffee and cheeses, reading Gide & I. Compton-Burnett, dinner with Richard and Floriano in that gemültlich outdoor restaurant on 79th St, a breezy walk and sit by the river, talk of our adolescent search for "beauty." It is now eleven this Sunday AM, I have read the Times, eaten melon and smoked cheese, and with dread and fear I keep pushing off the moment when I must plunge into the canvas waiting me in the next room.

I note that I am unhappy—not suicidal or hysterical, just unhappy.

July 12
A half-hour of weeping with rage and impotence, then *hurling* myself at this painting, using the brushes like clubs, the wall shaking with the blows. Now what is there is obvious—nothing but a scream. How can there be art if there are no artists?

July 13
Scraping and wiping off the entire canvas, inertia, melancholia, stupid smeary daubs.

A very good evening yester. with May and Harold [Rosenberg]. Perhaps one of the reasons I value them so highly is that they always bring out the best in me—those qualities which I feel are most sincere, most deeply felt and thought. Talked much of the two kinds of painting so prevalent to-day—"self expression" (or "action" painting) and "sensibility" (the new-realists).

July 14
An hour or two of drawing from the nude last night at Mike's [Goldberg], good work because I became involved immediately.

How stupid I can be! [This appears in the margin, and the following two sentences are lightly crossed out.] Speventa there another one of the de Kooning followers who has adopted all the mannerisms, speech, etc of the master. For instance in speaking of his own work he says—as Bill often does—it stinks! it's no good!

With de K. this is the sublime cry of the artist beating against the far reaches of his own powers—with the mediocrities it is a pretence of modesty, hoping to accumulate credit for what is after all a rather accurate summary!

"Indeed I do not insist that the tower in which I take refuge should be an ivory tower! But I am no good if I leave it. Glass tower; observatory in which I welcome every ray, every wave; fragile tower in which I feel badly sheltered;

do not want to be; vulnerable on all sides; but confident in spite of everything, and my eyes fixed on the east. My desperate waiting, despite everything, takes on the color of hope"—Gide's Journal, Vol III

July 15
How sad it is for me that painting can never have the solace of an "activity".

These last weeks of work seem to be leading nowhere, I have no conception, no life, vitality, spirit—I am not bored, but sad, alone—to-night the "color of hope" seems grey indeed.

July 16
Perhaps the only real problem in painting is that of the contour.

Could it be true that this picture is really going better to-day?

Speaking to Richard, I said I was not one of those artists who could work well while his life was in chaos. Must this always be so—? My life has been so often in turmoil, why can I not find in my art the peace, the refuge the form and order that life doesn't seem to have for me?

July 17
I think that Walt loves *me*, but cannot bear my life. Why should he—how could he when I can scarcely bear it myself.

July 19
Everything on this painting is interesting and painted with spirit, but *nothing is in the right place!*

—At last! Life is flooding me, I am filled with it—sure, excited. Work until 8:00 PM, everything right so far. I can't even read now, just scrambled eggs, four highballs, smiling in the wing chair, schmaltz music & *early* to bed—alone of course.

July 20
Another morning of work, sure and decided work. And now "The Showcase" is here or just about. It will of course be called "expressionistic". God knows I wish for a calm, classical art—perhaps in time, if I have enough time, this will come.

July 21
I'm going to let this sit and jell for a while, there may be more I must do to it, I don't know.

[Complete entries end here. The last partial entry is as follows.]
Observed from the window a wonderful creature to

[Beyond this point in the journal, there are the remnants of eighteen leaves of entries that Hartigan cut out and destroyed.]

INDEX

IN THE INTEREST OF CONCISION, "GH" is used as an abbreviation for "Grace Hartigan" throughout the index. Works by artists other than Grace Hartigan are followed by the name of the artist in parentheses; an example would be "*Les Demoiselles d'Avignon* (Picasso)." If no artist is cited, Hartigan may be assumed to be the artist. Names that appear in square brackets with a question mark (for example, "Tomlin, [Bradley Walker?]") are educated guesses based on the context of the entry. Hartigan's personal opinion of individuals was often affected by her evaluation of their art. In the entry for 9 September 1953, for example, Hartigan comments that "Jane will be returning the end of this month, but I am so embarrassed by the weakness of her painting I can't bear to see her." For this reason, the subheading "differences with GH" encompasses both personal differences and artistic differences.

Unidentified
_____, Alan, 55–56
_____, Ben, 55–56
_____, Jani, 75
_____, Johanna (model), 94, 95, 97
_____, Kate (aunt), 51, 52
_____, Marisa, 172
_____, Sandy, 55, 57, 59

A
Adam Bede (Eliot), 159
Aldan, Daisy, xxi–xxii, xxv, 86, 120, 137, 138, 139, 143, 149. *see also* Two Women
Aries, 1, 2, 5, 9
Ashbery, John
  biographical notes, xxv
  Folder and, 86
  friendship with GH, 28, 62, 78, 101
  "Heroes," 82
  Masquerade and, xxi, 144, 145
  Mexico trip, 177, 179
  Myers and, xviii
  opinion of GH's work, 35, 160
  at *Oranges* opening, 75

paintings of, by GH, 39, 43, 50, 57, 60
  Schuyler and, xxvii
Attic (de Kooning), 127
Avery, Milton, 44, 89

B
Bacon, Francis, 133, 167, 173
Baldwin, Lansing, 75
Balzac, Honoré de, 71, 97, 111, 113
Barneby, Rupert, 155
Baroque Square, 1, 2, 5, 8
Barr, Alfred
  Freilicher on, 81
  friendship with GH, 128, 163, 169, 170
  GH's opinion of, 107, 125, 151–52, 165
  Greenberg on, 128–29, 133
  O'Hara and, 53
  opinion of GH's work, 12, 63, 126, 160, 169
  Persian Jacket and, 77–78, 80, 81
  River Bathers and, 121, 126
  Rockefeller and, 170
  mentioned, 75

Barzun, Jacques. *see Berlioz and the Romantic Century* (Barzun)

Baur, John I. H., 119, 120, 121

Beckmann, [Max?], 144, 167

Beethoven, Ludwig van, 38

Berlioz, Hector, 110, 113

Berlioz and the Romantic Century (Barzun), 102, 104, 111, 113

Bing, Alexander
  financial support from, 104, 116, 117
  Masquerade donation, 149
  opinion of GH's work, 173
  relationship with GH, 98–99, 99–100, 101, 104, 171
  River Bathers and, 121, 126
  Spanish Still Life purchase, 172

Black Spring, 5

Black Still Life, 105, 125, 138

Black Widow, 20, 21

Blaine, Nell, 33, 47, 53, 75, 96, 116

The Blue G, 11, 13, 17

Blue Inscape, 11

Bocour, Leonard, 63, 116

Boileau, Nicolas, 71

Botticelli, Sandro, 35

Bouché, René, 23

Bourfaily, Tina, 179

Bowles, Jane, 119

Brach, Paul, 10, 54, 71, 86, 92, 99

Brandi, Cesare, 117

Breughel, Pieter, 31

Bridal Portrait, 129, 131–32, 138

Bridal Store Mannequins. see Grand Street Brides

Bridal Window. see Grand Street Brides

The Bride and the Owl, 130, 138, 148, 149

Briggs, Ernest, 140

Brodie, Gandy, 118

Byron, George Gordon Lord, 92, 113

C

Cage, John, 47

Campbell, Larry, 165

Carousel
  GH on, 57, 63, 64–65, 66, 73, 74
  interruptions, 42, 43
  preliminary ideas, 36, 37, 39, 55
  sketches for, 56, 59, 60, 61

Castelli, Leo, 19, 23, 53, 86, 98

Castelli, Nina, 67

Cat, 16, 17

Cézanne, Paul
  GH on, 31, 34, 62, 92, 108, 124, 134, 159
  influence on GH, xvii, 30, 32, 39, 91

Chanteuse, 165, 168, 169

Chmela, Lara, xi, 202

Chopin, Frédéric, 67, 95, 113

Christ Dead (Leslie), 36

Claflin, Agnes, 154

Clyde, Mary, 163

Coffee Pot and Cucumber, 109, 125

Coggeshall, Calvert, 24

Coloring Book of Ancient Egypt (Malina), xxii

Combs, Michele, xi, 202

The Confidence Man, 17

Conrad, Joseph, 35

Corinth, Lovis, 68

Courbet, Gustave, xx, 51, 58–59, 66, 67

The Cue, 10, 11, 13, 16, 17–18, 19, 29–30, 31

D

"Daisy & Olga" painting. *see* Two Women

Dancer (Jackson), 151

de Kooning, Elaine, 174

de Kooning, Willem
  Attic, 127
  biographical notes, xxv
  differences with GH, 37, 141

Fitzsimmons on, 74
GH's opinion of, 4, 44, 67, 73–74, 82, 171
influence on GH, xv, xvi, xvii, 36, 54
influence on other artists, xvii, 45, 98, 187
at *Oranges* opening, 75
Soby on, 174
de Nagy, Tibor, xxv, xxvi, 9, 21, 81, 85, 96
De Niro, Robert, 22, 33, 174
de Rivera, José, 30
Dead of Night (film), 61
Delacroix, Eugène
GH on, 108
influence on GH, 21, 31, 73, 77, 113
journals of, xv, 70–72, 117–118
Massacre of Scio, 80
Delaunay, Robert, 174
Les Demoiselles d'Avignon (Picasso), 36, 133, 174
Dennis, Emily, 169, 172, 174
Desire (Picasso), 26
Devree, Howard, 167
Dido, 44, 45
Display Mannequins, 183, 186
Disraeli (Maurois), 131
The Divine Sarah, xxii
Dubuffet, Jean, 155
Dürer, Albrecht, 30, 77
Dzubas, Friedel, 18, 26, 53, 62, 68

E

Egan, Charlie, 25
Eisenhower, Dwight D., 55
El Greco, 46
Eliot, George, xx, xxx
Ensor, James, 38
Escudero, Vicente, 167
Evans, Mary Selden, xi

F

Fantin-Latour, Henri, 104
Feldman, Morton, 47, 55
Ferren, John, 63
Figures in Landscape, 78
Fisdale, Bobby, 95, 101
Fisher, Gertrude, 82
Fitzsimmons, James, xvi, 63, 74, 75, 77, 81, 115, 135, 136
Flamenco Dancers, 167, 168, 169
Flaubert, Gustave, 141–42, 164
Flower Pots, 95, 97
Folder, xxi, 86–88, 90, 93, 98, 143, 144, 145, 154, Plate 5
Fondren, Hal, 78, 153
Ford, Bette, 179
Forst, Miles, 47
Four Square, 9, 11
Franceschini, Edi, 47, 51, 55–56, 101, 102, 122
Francis, Sam, xv
Frank O'Hara and the Demons, xix, xx, xxi, xxii
Frankenthaler, Helen
biographical notes, xxv
de Nagy Gallery and, xviii, 107, 132
differences with GH, 2, 27, 28, 31, 37–38, 72, 164
friendship with GH, 18, 37, 132, 170
GH's opinion of, 4, 8, 68
Greenberg and, 27, 28, 170
on her work, 12, 15–16
opinion of GH's work, 24, 26
painting of, by GH, 36
Freilicher, Jane
Corinth and, 68
differences with GH, 33, 37
friendship with GH, 28, 57, 59, 66, 73, 75, 97, 99, 101, 111, 124, 166, 171

GH's opinion of, 45, 57–58, 67, 82, 91, 95, 97

influence on GH, 36, 73, 175

Masquerade and, xxi, 144, 145

Mexico trip, 176, 177, 178, 179

as "new realist," xviii, 186

O'Hara on, 28, 118

opinion of GH's work, 35, 48, 81, 98

mentioned, 21, 25, 47, 90, 160

"funeral procession" painting, 46, 52

G

Giacometti, Alberto, 25

Gide, André, 184–85, 186, 187–88

Gift Shop Window, 172, 173, 175

Giftwares, Plate 8

Gladiola Still Life, 78, 79, 81

Goldberg, Michael, 69, 71, 86, 98, 136, 185, 186, 187

Goldwater, Robert, 63, 85

Goodman, Jerry, 57, 60, 62

Goodnough, Robert

 differences with GH, xviii, 45

 friendship with, 28, 75

 GH's opinion of, 2, 4, 14, 23, 26, 67, 127

 Greenberg on, 18, 128, 133

 on his work, 68

 influence on GH, 127

 Mitchell and, 67

 Myers and, 19, 62, 86

 opinion of GH's work, 31

 mentioned, 125

Goodrich, Lloyd, 119

Goya, Francisco

 GH on, xxi, 46, 47, 51, 59, 108, 118, 166

 influence on GH, xvii, 44, 52, 118, 120, 126

Graham, John, 166

Grand Street Brides, Plate 6

Barr and, 169, 170

 as *Bridal Store Mannequins,* 133–35, 136

 as *Bridal Window,* 131

 Devree on, 168

 named, 138

 O'Hara on, xxi

 Silver's photographs, xvi

 Soby on, 173–74

 Whitney Museum acquisition, xviii, 171, 172

 mentioned, 160, 163

Granville-Smith, Maureen, xi

Greco, El, 46

Greek Girl (originally *Seated Greek*)

 begun, 95

 GH on, 96, 98, 108, 131, 132

 Leslie's opinion of, 96, 121

 payment for, 127

 Stable show, 110, 115, 118

 Whitney Museum of Art and, 97, 124, 126, 132, 154

Greenberg, Clement

 on Barr, 128

 biographical notes, xxv

 on de Kooning, 4

 differences with GH, xviii, 28, 31, 48, 49, 107, 132–33

 Frankenthaler and, 27, 28, 170

 friendship with GH, 1, 11, 16

 GH's opinion of, 28, 63, 71, 129

 on Goodnough, 18, 128, 133

 on Jackson, 26, 28

 on Leslie, 18, 26

 Myers and, xvi, 107, 128

 on Pollock, xvi, 26, 28

 on Rivers, 18, 26

 opinion of GH's work, xvi, 26, 128

 on women painters, 18

Grillo, John, 60

Guest, Barbara, xviii, xxv, 36, 55, 62, 82

H

Hansen, Waldemar
    differences with GH, 95
    friendship with GH, xxi, 24, 26, 28, 43,
        51, 55–56, 62
    GH's painting of, 56
    on Goodman, 60
    on his work, 43, 81
    opinion of GH's work, 13, 44
Hare, David, 4
Hartigan, Arthur, 88
Hartigan, "George," xx, xxi, xxx, 28, 29, 51,
    76, 120, 121, 155, 173
Hartigan, Virginia, 72, 127
Hawthorne, Nathaniel, 67, 92
Hazen, Joe, 81, 84, 101, 176, 177, 179
Heller, Ben, 141, 167, 170
The Hero, 12–14, 16, 17, 18, 19, 31
"Heroes" (Ashbery), 82
Hess, Tom, 119, 127, 185
Hinton, Mary Beth, xi, 202
Hohnsbeen, John, 179
Holliday, Betty, 72, 73
Hollywood Interior, xxii
Hopper, Edward, 45, 95
The Horseman, 17, 18, 19, 42
The House, 23, 24
The Hunt, 39, 47, 57, 82
Hydrangeas, 125

I

Iceland, 17
The Impressario, 47–48, 51, 57, 61, 75, 79, 98,
    108
Infanta, 50–51
Ingres, Jean-Auguste-Dominique, 59
Interior with Bridal Gown, 169

J

Jachens, Bob, xvi, 6, 74, 89, 123, 128, 140
Jachens, Jeff
    appendicitis, 123, 124, 126, 128
    grandfather's death, 89
    parents' separation, xvi, 6–7
    portrait of, by GH, 44
    vacations with, 12, 39, 146
    worry over, xvi, 59, 111, 157
Jackson, Harry
    on artists, 107
    biographical notes, xxvi
    on de Nagy artists, xviii
    differences with GH, 26, 37
    GH's opinion of, 4, 8, 28, 45, 53, 100, 106,
        108, 151
    Greenberg on, 26, 28
    marriage to GH, xvi, 92–93, 178
    opinion of GH's work, 10
James, Henry, 3
Jarrell, Randall, 30
Jim, Marian, 117, 128, 130
Joyce, James, 46

K

Kahn, Wolfe, 47, 60
Kandinsky, Wassily, 68, 174
Kaprow, Allan, 47–48, 49, 60
King Is Dead, 1, 8
King of the Hill, xxx, 1, 54
Klee, Paul, 47
Kline, Franz, 140, 186
The Knight, Death, and the Devil, 30, 32,
    34–35, 47, 55, 57, 77, 160
Koch, Kenneth, xviii, xxvi, 47, 86
Kresch, Al, 47, 81

L

La Moy, William, xiv, 202

Lady with Fan, 158, 159, 160, 165, 169

Lang, V. R., 119

Lansner, _____, 150, 154

"last respects" painting, 52

Lawrence, D. H., 183, 184

Lemons, 9, 13

Lenya, Lotte, 143

Leslie, Alfred

  biographical notes, xxvi

  differences with GH, xviii, 45, 54, 157

  friendship with GH, xvi, 2, 3, 21, 28, 37,
    56–57, 62, 94, 95, 99, 115, 121

  GH's opinion of him, 60, 62

  GH's opinion of his work, 4, 8, 9, 17, 19,
    23, 24–25, 36, 37, 45, 67, 73, 98, 102,
    140

  Greenberg on, 18, 26

  O'Hara and, 53

  on his work, 15, 25, 33, 68

  moves out, 11

  Myers and, 10, 62

  opinion of GH's work, 21, 52–54, 57, 60,
    84, 96–97

  painting of, by GH, 66, 67

  relationship with GH, 72

  Rivers on, 122

Leslie, Esta, 37, 52, 66, 67, 68, 94, 97

M

Machiz, Herbert, xviii, 71, 75, 79, 82, 98, 101,
  103, 119

Maharaja #2, 44, 47

Malina, Judith, xxii, 108

Malraux, André, 77

Manet, Édouard, 46, 51, 52, 59, 66, 96, 108,
  117, 118

Manhattan, xxii

Marca-Relli, Conrad, 186

Maritain, Jacques, 132

The Masker, xxii, 50, 149, 150, 151, 165, 166,
  169

Masquerade, xxi–xxii, 50, 144–47, 149, 150,
  152, 158, 167, 169, Plate 7

The Massacre

  Bridal Store Mannequins and, 136

  creation, 21–24

  GH on, 25, 29, 30, 35, 55, 69, 78

  Greenberg on, 26

Massacre of Scio (Delacroix), 80

Matador, 104, 105, 109–10, 115, 116, 117, 120,
  125, 132

Matisse, Henri

  Bathers and, 39, 80, 81

  death of, 157

  GH on, 30, 33, 42, 82, 91, 108, 127, 184

  influence on GH, xvii, 17, 23, 85, 89, 129,
    161, 172, 173

  influence on Jackson, 106

  The Masker and, 151

  Nude with Reboso and, 142

Matisse, His Art and His Public (Barr), 84,
  85, 129, 171

Matta, [Roberto?], 4

Mattison, Robert, xi

Maurois, André, 97, 100–101, 131

McCaffrey, Joseph, xiv, 202

McCray, Porter, 163

Meecham [Meacham], Anne, 166

Merrill, Jimmy, 78, 82, 167, 171, 172

Mexico, 82–83, 89

Mid-August, 11

The Mill on the Floss (Eliot), 159

Miller, Dorothy, 63, 78, 83, 97, 126, 160

Miller, Richard

  Aldan and, xxi

  Brandi and, 117

Folder and, 86–87, 94, 143

friendship with GH, 100, 101, 110, 111, 127, 142, 154, 163, 185, 186, 188

opinion of GH's work, 131, 148, 173

Pernas and, 149

Still Life with Blue Wall purchase, 109

Vecchi and, xxi–xxii, xxvii, 87

Miró, Joan, 5, 119

Mitchell, Joan, xxvi, 22, 25, 67, 71, 85, 91, 94

Monacco, Don, 51, 55

Months and Moons, 1, 19, 36

Moore, Herman, 119, 160

Motherwell, Robert, xv, 49

Muller, Jan, 60

Munch, Edvard, 56

Murillo, Bartolomé, 46

Muse, Isaac Lane, xvi, 35, 89, 173

Myers, John Bernard

    Barr and, 63, 80, 126

    biographical notes, xxvi–xxvii

    on Byron, 92

    differences with GH, xvii–xviii, 10, 32, 67, 86, 103, 124, 127, 140–41, 163

    Frankenthaler and, 107, 132

    friendship with GH, 4, 9, 21, 62, 99, 101, 110, 111, 153

    GH's opinion of, 50, 71, 92, 140, 176

    Goodnough and, 19, 62, 86

    Greenberg and, xvi, 107, 128

    Hansen and, xxi, 13

    kite-flying party, 5–6

    Leslie and, 10, 62

    Merrill and, 78

    opinion of GH's work, 17, 35, 46, 47, 57, 79, 96, 98, 120, 160

Oranges and, 75

    paintings of, by GH, 46, 47, 109 (see also *The Impressario*)

    Paris show, 19

poets and, xviii

on Rivers, 14

sale of GH's work, 54, 60, 78, 82, 83, 84, 85, 121, 126, 149, 155

shows, 62, 81, 109

Tibor de Nagy quarrel, 85

Whitney Museum and, 97

mentioned, 2, 12, 15, 25, 63, 81, 94, 137, 157, 164, 172

N

Nana (grandmother), 10

"Nature and New Painting" (O'Hara), xix, xxi, 165, 174

Negri, Pola, 142, 143

Neuberger, Roy, 167, 170

Newman, Barnett, xv, 18, 23, 30, 45

Nude with Blue Stole, 146

Nude with Reboso, 142

O

Ocean Bathers. see Sea Bathers

Odalisque, 160, 166, 167

O'Hara, Frank

    on art/artists, 101, 148

    biographical notes, xxvii

    "Christmas Card to Grace Hartigan," 161

    differences with GH, 111, 150, 157

    essay on GH, 55, 56

    Fisdale and, 95, 101

    Folder and, 86, 143

    "For Grace, after a Party," 112–13

    Frank O'Hara and the Demons, xix, xx, xxi, xxii

    on Freilicher, 28, 118

    friendship with GH, xv, 28, 39, 40, 43, 66, 99, 101, 118, 163

    GH's opinion of his work, 40, 55, 56, 118

    influence on GH, xviii–xix

Leslie and, 53
loans to, 129, 130, 138
on Machiz, 103
The Masker and, 149, 150
Masquerade and, 144, 145, 149
Myers and, xviii
"Nature and New Painting," xix, 165, 174
opinion of GH's work, 35, 47, 48, 79, 98,
    135, 160
Oranges opening, 75
paintings of, by GH, xix, 37, 39, 44, 47,
    55, 56, 57, 66, 95 (see also *Frank
    O'Hara and the Demons*)
"Poem for a Painter," 25–26
on Porter, 164
"Portrait of Grace," 40–41
review of GH's work, 115, 116
Rivers and, xxi, 28, 43, 62, 84, 85, 111, 118,
    150
Soby on, 174
Schuyler and, xxvii
"Second Ave," 81
self-image, xx
shot by robber, 129
on *Washington Crossing the Delaware*,
    xxi
"Why I am Not a Painter," 69–70
mentioned, 27, 63, 68, 78, 82, 88, 91, 94,
    111, 119, 147, 153, 185
Oranges: 12 Pastorals, Plate 2, Plate 3
Barr on, 78
GH on, 56, 61, 68, 69, 73
O'Hara on, 70
opening, 72, 75
mentioned, xix, xx, 57, 60, 66, 86
Oranges #1: Black Crows, 56, Plate 2
Ordway, Katherine, 171, 172, 173
Osborn, Peggy, 9–10, 121

P

Paris, 1920, 17, 18, 19, 156
Pasilis, Felix, 69, 118
Pasternak, Boris, 98
Pastorale, 105
Pease, Roland, 62, 75
Peonies and Baby's Breath, 143, 146
Peonies and Hydrangeas, 169, 170
Pernas, Frances, 149
Persian Jacket, Plate 1
Barr on, 77–78, 80, 81
GH on, xv, 55, 108, 116, 131, 154
Grand Street Brides and, 136
Leslie on, 60
The Masquer and, 154
Museum of Modern Art acquisition, 82,
    83, 85
payment for, 92
shown, 57, 76, 105, 153–54
significance of, xxvi
sketch, 53
Persian Robe, 87, 89, Plate 5
Petroff, Olga, xxii, 118, 120, 137, 138, 139. *see
    also* Two Women
Pfeiffer, Alice Randel, xi
Picasso, Pablo, 16, 26, 52, 82, 91, 105, 142,
    174. *see also* Les Demoiselles
    d'Avignon *(Picasso)*
Pitzele, Mel, 109, 110
The Plumed Serpent (Lawrence), 183
Poindexter, George, 82, 85–86, 92, 113
Pollock, Jackson
    differences with GH, 26, 32, 45
    Frankenthaler and, 68
    friendship with GH, xvi, 1, 18
    GH on, xv, xvii, 2, 8, 18, 118, 165
    Greenberg on, xvi, 26, 28
    mentioned, 151
    on nature, xix

Parsons Gallery and, 23

Porter, Fairfield
    criticism of, 47
    friendship with, 73, 147
    GH's opinion of, 45, 67, 118
    as "new realist," xviii, 186
    O'Hara on, 164
    opinion of GH's work, 47, 48
    mentioned, 176
Porter, Lawrence, 147
Portrait of A, 11, 13
Portrait of W, 23, 24, 26, 30, 31
Poussin, Nicolas, 35, 78
Preston, Stuart, xvii, xxx, 28, 121
Price, Winston, xxii
Proust, Marcel, 97
Pumpkin's World, 17

Q

Quennel, Peter, 92
Quimby, Sean, xi

R

Racine, Jean, 71
Rappacini's Daughter, 67, 68, 72
Red Bowl, 85, 86, 95, 125
Red Sun, 19
Reed, John, 14, 128, 129, 177
Rembrandt, 31, 44, 46
Remet, Sylvia, 84, 85, 115
Renoir, Pierre-Auguste, 36, 108
Rich, Daniel, 167
Rilke, Rainer Maria, 36, 38, 79, 92, 95
Ripley, Dwight, 23, 155
Ritter, John, 9
River Bathers, Plate 4
    in *Arts Digest,* 157
    Barr and, 126
    Fitzsimmons on, 135

Freilicher on, 81
GH on, 78–79, 80, 127, 131, 151, 152
Greenberg on, 128
Leslie on, 84, 96
Matisse influence, 80, 81
at Musée d'Art Moderne, 166
Museum of Modern Art and, 121, 125,
    126, 138
payment for, 127
Silver on, 80
Rivers on, 84
Whitney Museum and, 97, 124
mentioned, 83, 86, 91, 107
Rivers, Augusta, 79, 122
Rivers, Larry
    biographical notes, xxvii
    differences with GH, 33, 37, 62, 140–41
    friendship with GH, 21, 28, 59, 66, 73, 85,
        99, 109, 111, 118, 153, 163, 164
    GH on, 49, 57, 69, 86, 107, 109, 137
    GH's opinion of his work, 14, 25, 45,
        62–63, 67, 68, 74, 94, 106, 115, 137
    Greenberg on, 18, 26
    heroin use, 96
    on his work, 122
    influence on GH, 22, 36, 48, 133
    The Knight, Death, and the Devil and, 35
    on Manet, 118
    as "new realist," xviii, 186
    O'Hara and, xxi, 28, 43, 62, 84, 85, 111,
        118, 150
    opinion of GH's work, 35, 43, 84, 96, 98,
        129, 131
    Oranges opening, 75
    review of GH's show, 167
    Soby on, 174
    Stable show, 62, 115, 176
    Steinberg purchase, 127, 140–41

Washington Crossing the Delaware, xviii,
  xxi, 107–8, 163
  mentioned, 47, 75, 81, 95, 119, 135, 160,
    166
Riviera, xxii
Rockefeller, Nelson, 170
Roethe, Theodore, 67
Rogers, Gaby, 82
Rose, Leatrice, 33
Rosenberg, Harold, 160, 163, 165, 176, 187
Rosset, Barnet Lee, xxvii
Roszak, [Theodore?], 4
Rothko, Mark, xv, 4, 5, 23, 45, 151
Rough, Ain't It, 39
Row of Flower Pots, 105
Rubens, Peter Paul, 2, 31, 34, 35, 38, 72, 77,
    138
Ryan, Ann, 98

S
Salute series, ii
Sand, George, xx, xxx, 100–101, 113
Schapiro, Meyer, xvi
Schapiro, Mimi, 94
Schuyler, James
  biographical notes, xxvii
  "Dorabella," xxi
  Folder and, 86
  friendship with GH, 62, 111
  on GH's work, 35
  Myers and, xviii
  quoted, 42, 50
Scriabin, Alexander, 126
Sea Bathers (alternate title: *Ocean Bathers*),
    xx, 89, 91–92, 94, 109, 126–27
Seated Greek Girl. see Greek Girl
Seckler, Dorothy, 172
Secuda Esa Bruja, xvi, 36
Self-Portrait as a Matador, 122, 123

Self-Portrait with Jack-o-lanterns, 101
Seurat, Georges-Pierre, 30, 31
Seward Park, 161, 164, 168, 169
The Showcase, 188
Silver, George, xi
Silver, Walter
  closeness to GH, 43, 111, 152
  at Coney Island, 59
  difficulties with GH, 97, 99, 165, 184, 185,
    188
  financial support of GH, 28, 42, 61, 86,
    92, 124, 128, 129, 130
  GH's opinion of his work, 114
  Grand Street Brides photographs, 131, 134
  Hansen and, 51
  Lady with Fan photographs, 159
  leaves GH, 101, 183–84
  The Masker photographs, 150
  Matador and, 115, 116
  meat-packing-district photographs, 160
  Mexico trip, 177–80
  opinion of GH's work, 23, 24, 39, 66, 80,
    98, 131
  paintings of, by GH, 66, 67, 68, 104, 109,
    137, 149
  relationship with GH, xvi, 12, 13, 14, 19,
    66, 77, 117, 163, 185, 187–88
  reunion with GH, 101
  Rough, Ain't It sale, 39
  sculpture show, 113
  support of GH, 62, 67, 159, 171
  Two Women photographs, 138, 139
  mentioned, 21, 36, 60, 60–61, 70, 84, 140,
    141, 153, 156, 175, 176, 186
Silver Nutmeg, 1
Simon, D., 121, 122, 129, 130
The Sitters, 46, 47
Six O'Clock, 44, 45–46
Six Square, 1, 2–3, 5, 8

Slimbach, Robert, 202
Soby, James Thrall, 63, 120, 121, 170, 173–75
Soulages, Pierre, 140
Southampton Fields, 155
Spanish Still Life, 159, 169, 172
Spaventa, George, 187
St. Serapion, 34, 35, 57, 59, 60, 61, 63
*Standing Figure (Self-Portrait with
       Hydrangeas),* 119, 125, 160
Steinberg, Jay, 126–27, 130, 138, 140, 141, 175
Stendhal, 114, 115
Stevens, Rex, xi
Stevenson, Adlai, 54, 55
Still Life, 63
Still Life in Primary Colors, 87
Still Life with Beets and Peppers, 97, 98
Still Life with Blue Wall, 109, 125
Stone, Bob, 96, 110, 111, 117, 118
Studio Interior, 115, 125
Studio Landscape, 16, 17, 23
Sutherland, [Graham?], 74

T
Tabak, May Natalie, 160, 176, 187
Terrible Angel, 37
Thalo, 8, 9, 10–11
Thorin, Suzanne, xi
Tichenor, Bridjet [Bridget], 179
Tiepolo, Giovanni Battista, 33, 174
Tintoretto, 31
Titian, 31, 33, 59
Tomlin, [Bradley Walker?], 74, 81
Tracking the Marvelous (Myers), 5–6
Tribute Money, 35, 138
Trojan Horse (Hartigan), 33, 34, 84, 85
Trojan Horse (Tiepolo), 33
Turgenev, Ivan, 163, 165

Twarkov, Jack, 37–38
Two Women ("Daisy & Olga" painting),
       138–39, 142, 160, 169, 186

V
Vanderbilt, Gloria, 85
Vecchi, Floriano, xxii, xxvii, 87, 110, 111, 143,
       154, 186
Velasquez, Diego
       GH on, xxi, 44, 46, 108, 184
       influence on GH, xvii, 50–51, 117, 174
Venetian Self-Portrait, 47, 57, 63, 82
Vermeer, Johannes, 119
Vollard, [Ambroise?], 110
Vuillard, Édouard, 119

W
Warhol, Andy, xxvii, 110
Washington Crossing the Delaware (Rivers),
       xviii, xxi, 107–8, 163
Wax Fruit, 175
Weaver, Bill, 86
Weinberg, Elbert, 173
Weinstein, Arnold, 160
West, Penny, 21
White, 9, 11
Williams, William Carlos, xv, xviii, 40
Wilson, Angus, 144
With Red, 9
Woman, 19, 20, 21, 22, 24, 26
Woolf, Virginia, 152–53

Z
Zola, Émile, 144
Zurburán, Francisco de, xvii, 34, 44, 46, 51,
       52, 159

Colophon

This volume was edited and annotated by William T. La Moy and Joseph P. McCaffrey. William La Moy designed it entirely in Adobe Minion Pro, an Open Type font developed by Robert Slimbach within the traditions of the classical typefaces of the late Renaissance. Mary Beth Hinton and Lara Chmela skillfully assisted with the transcription of the text, and Michele Combs prepared the splendid index.

We deeply regret that Grace Hartigan did not see the completed state of this book, but she returned the final permissions forms required by Syracuse University Press and thus had the full assurance that it was, indeed, in production. The Special Collections Research Center at Syracuse University Library is proud to serve as the repository for the papers of Grace Hartigan.

www.ingramcontent.com/pod-product-compliance
Lightning Source LLC
Chambersburg PA
CBHW060830170526
45158CB00001B/129